In Her Bathrobe She Blogged...

Robin Amber Kilgore

For Gumma and Gang-Gang,
You have set an example that is hard to beat. I hope to be mature
enough to follow it one day.

Mary Ann and Theodore F. Nowak
Still this close and cool after all these years.

And for my mother, Penny Nowak Buenger,
Thank you for teaching me to stand strong, to be independent
and to speak my mind.

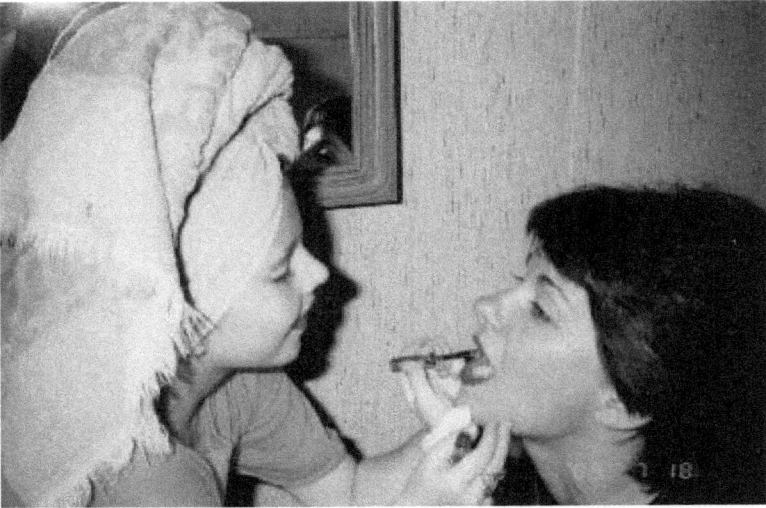

A little insight to part of my future...Damn, those were some red lips.

The Way It All Started

Somewhere in the Spring of 2005 during a typical, stressful day of work as a corporate paralegal, a job I didn't realize would eat my soul, an attorney named Steve Morrissey asked me to create some files for a new case The Firm had just accepted. While sorting through the documents that had arrived that morning, Steve handed me some papers that were print-outs from some Internet website. Trying to be as professional as possible, I asked how he would like them to be classified. He said, "These are print-outs of the client's blogs. It would be great if you would print them out daily and keep them in a subject file." Blogs? I had no idea what he was talking about. I hadn't ever worked with Steve as I had just recently transferred from the Houston office to the Los Angeles office and wasn't sure how he would react when I admitted that I wasn't already two steps ahead of him with the process. I bit the bullet and asked, "What's a blog?" He looked up from his computer with a bit of a quizzical smirk on his face and asked with an amused tone in his voice, "You don't know what a blog is?"

It was at that moment that I exploded. That was the final straw. I hated my stressful job. I worked for an amazing firm of genius Super Lawyers. I was so emotionally exhausted from never feeling quite up to par with their quirky requests and intelligence. Office politics had destroyed a part of my rationale. No day was complete without a few moments of some sort of staff meltdown, a "hot document" photocopying frenzy way past quitting time or a mad rush to have something delivered to someone somewhere by yesterday. I hadn't had a real vacation in years. I got up, went to work, went home, fell into bed and got up to do it again the next day. Sometimes, the "went home" portion didn't happen. That was it. I snapped. I reached into my pocket and pulled out a cigarette lighter. Without so much as word, just a simple roll of the thumb, I ignited a flame and proceeded to set everything on Steve's desk ablaze. Crucial documents were gone in seconds. The look on Steve's face was priceless. Utter disbelief. He actually didn't move from his chair until the flames were so high that he couldn't see me standing there tossing more and more of the documents into the bonfire that was building on his desk.

"No, Steve, I don't know what a fucking 'blog' is. Perhaps you should find a paralegal who does," I expelled. I turned on my high heels and walked out like a diva, slow, sultry and in control of myself for the first time in way too long. A mad flurry of people were rushing past me in what seemed like a frantic slow motion to try to put the fire out. They were shouting things. I couldn't hear them. Their mouths were moving, their faces making wickedly animated expressions, but all I heard was the powerful beat of "Eye of the Tiger," my internal theme song, booming in my soul. I picked up my purse and walked out. I had never felt so free.

Ok, No Really...

Perhaps most of what you just read was slightly embellished. There was some "fun with hyperbole" thrown in just to hook you and make you wonder if I was recounting my life from the confines of federal women's correctional facility. The truth? I was a very stressed out corporate paralegal for an amazing firm of Super Lawyers who had just transferred from Houston to Los Angeles, and I really didn't know what a blog was in the Spring of 2005. My true response to Steve's question, "You don't know what a blog is?" sounded like, "Steve, I use a computer to check email, word process, manage documents and for online purchases in between the aforementioned. What is a blog?" I liked working with Steve. He is a laidback, genuinely appreciative, nice person who is not on my list of people to set on fire.

He shortly explained that a blog was a web forum where people posted thoughts on whatever they wanted in order for people to leave comments about them and essentially create dialogue about different topics. My only thought at the time was, "Who in hell has time for that?" Little did I know that a short time later, I would figure out the answer to my own question.

After not being able to stand one more grueling, cellulite, flat-ass-causing moment of cross town morning and evening LA traffic, I made a huge decision to quit my job, cash in my 401k, take out a loan and pursue a dream of working my way into the world of cosmetics by going to a school for make-up artistry. I had stumbled upon the school while out for a walk in my neighborhood one afternoon as I was playing hookie from work. It was like finding water in the desert, a place where I could stop and take refuge and hydrate the dry portions of my soul with brushes, paint, latex and glitter, among other things. I had found an inlet to the mysterious and intriguing world of Hollywood's film and television industry. Make-up had always been a guilty pleasure since the first day my grandmother handed me a sample tube of Avon lipstick at age five.

It was so freeing to toss on jeans, my smock and tennis shoes and walk to school with my make-up kit for three months. I didn't have a care in the world for the first time in so long. I had never really slowed down after high school or college. I threw myself into working without a break. So when our make-up instructor assigned our class the task of drawing fifty pairs of perfectly shaped classic eyebrows with single hair strokes by hand, I couldn't have been happier. I was surrounded by the most unique individuals, most of whom were artists, designers, recent high school grads or people who recoiled at the thought of a typical "nine-to-five." Creativity surged through them. I ate it up and worked diligently on shedding my corporate skin. I had basically just enrolled in art therapy. I enjoyed the projects, the lectures, learning about a zillion products and meeting people who had been on movie sets and who had worked with some of the most famous people in the biz for decades.

Then, it ended. And just like post college graduation, I found myself trying to figure out how I was going to make it financially. My new life status category was "starving artist." I found myself with more free time than I could have ever dreamed of. I was in heaven. And then I fell into a sort of hell. Money was not steady, jobs paid little and the torrid politics of a much filthier industry were right back in my face. Not quite finding what I thought I was going to, I refused to go back to work at the firm from which I ran screaming and was determined to prolong my sabbatical from the mainstream as long as possible.

In between projects and my new found ability to travel about the country on a whim after cashing unemployment checks, I was somehow suckered into creating a profile on MySpace. "Everyone" was doing it. A friend wanted me to look at some photos she had taken, and there was a crush on a guy that iced the cake. Before I knew it, I was spending ridiculous amounts of time looking up old friends, talking to potential new ones and praying for a digital camera so I could post the story of my everyday life in photographic glory. It wasn't until I was home for the Christmas holidays that I answered the question of, "Who in the hell has time for that?" I was up late at my parents house, trying to find the last person in my "extended network" while stewing about some things that were on my mind. I noticed the area of the MySpace page where I could "Post a Blog." Curiosity as to whether or not anyone would read what I wrote got the best of me, and I began to blog.

It turned out that people were actually taking the time to read my thoughts. They commented. They encouraged me to write more. I found myself looking at the world in a whole new way. Each day I sought out things to write about. It was as fulfilling for me to post a new blog as it was to spend a day on a set doing a face of make-up. I was in a delusional heaven. None of the things that made me ultimately happy (living in my bathrobe, writing and entertaining people or altering people's looks on movie sets) were generating substantial bread for the table or the pocket. How many Hollywood tales begin this way? Countless. The last category I ever want my life to fall into was trite. (How gross.) Yet, I never would have imagined how dynamic and challenging 2006 was going to be. So sit back and enjoy this purge of drivel, passions, rants, loves, hates and whatnots that emerged while I was in my first true phase of throwing all caution to the wind. Go on. Read. You've already opened the book!

Saturday December 24, 2005
Well Isn't That Just Special?

I wish I had a dollar for every person I know this year who is having kids or getting engaged. I seriously think I'd be able to buy at least a new pair of shoes. Ok. Fine. Perhaps I could buy a decent six pack of beer, but whatever...

Steph, my hair stylist in LA, says she's not surprised to hear that all of the people I grew up with are getting married, as "Texas is a breeder state where people who don't move away get married and pregnant really young." I'll be damned if she isn't right.

I'm happy that others are happy, but I'm still a little grossed out...

Sue me...

As you were.

Sunday January 15, 2006
Peeping Tom

Each time I sign onto my MySpace, I notice that the number of times my profile has been viewed has gone up sometimes as many as fifty views, yet I might not have a single new comment or message.

How can that be possible? The laws of statistics say that at least one out of five should leave a trace that they were there. (I think...I got a "C" in statistics in college.)

My real concern with the issue at hand isn't the need for comments, but the idea that so many people are basically peeking into my life without letting me know. Perhaps they are simply left with nothing to say. I can't tell whether I'm boring or just another outlet for someone's viewing pleasure.

The number of views is the silent reminder that there are people watching my friends and me at any time. Sure, we've put ourselves out there for the viewing, but it's still unsettling to think that there might be those onlookers in the darkness of cyberspace, keeping up with our every move...

Maybe I should concern myself with my privacy settings. Hmmm...

As you were.

Monday January 16, 2006
Potty Pics

I love the amount of people who take self portraits of themselves in their bathrooms for posting on MySpace.

It never fails...I see one almost everyday. Some of my closest friends have them.

But I must ask: Why? Can you not wait until someone else can take a picture of you? Does your self-portrait have to be into a mirror? Are you doing it because you want to really work on those "sexy smirks" that you can only do in the privacy of a bathroom?

1

Or is your mom on the other side of the door asking, "What's taking so long?"

Why can't you work on your self-portraits in front of objects like cars, snow covered trees, pretty flowers, blank walls or something that lets us know a little about yourself?

The bathroom shots just let us know if you keep a clean john or not and lend the imagination notions of the "purr" of the overhead exhaust fan, the smell of tidy bowl or worse, and the cold chill of tile. Is that how you want yourself represented?

If you say so...

As you were.

Tuesday January 17, 2006
Holy Moley!

I have a fair complexion and am not in any way a tanning goddess. As a child, I used to look nice and golden in the summer, but as an adult I have tried my best to keep up the milky look. I did spend one summer in a tanning bed, but I probably wound up a shade darker and was left with a longhorn across my ass. That's another story for another day.

Back in the direction of my point. A few days ago I was getting out of the shower and noticed a mole on my back. Normally it looks like a light tan mole, but it now carried a little espresso-colored monkey on its back! It was slightly dry and a bit scab-like. Freaked out, I got on the Internet and looked up skin cancer. I didn't see anything that looked like my mole and its guest, so I was calmed. I decided to go see my dermatologist anyway.

This morning I got up thinking that Dr. Lewis would look at it and refer me to someone if needed. Upon arrival I was ushered into the examination room. He looked at it, told me to lie down and asked his assistant to set up for a removal for a biopsy. What??? Startled, I asked about the referral idea and he said, "I don't want you to wait any longer. How long have you known about this on your back? When you come back for your follow up, be prepared for a full body exam. You are too young to die from skin cancer."

In less than two minutes he was stitching me up. I didn't have time to think about what he was doing much less even take my shirt off, phone my mother or a friend or say a rosary. I hadn't even had a glass of water or breakfast yet. The next thing I knew I was standing at the front desk, a little shaken, deciding on which credit card to put this $200 procedure and fumbling with the words "pathology report."

I'm sure I'm fine and the mole removal is the end of all of this, but it struck me as one of those tiny milestones in life where I'm kindly reminded of my own mortality. I'm a pretty healthy person, yet it's the silent killers that plague me like a monster under the bed. Heart disease. Cancer. Losing fashion sense. I spent a good portion of the rest of the day thinking about the way I eat and the exercise I don't get much of. I'm twenty-six. I'm not getting any younger and my body is giving me little signals: lines around my eyes, joints that snap, crackle, pop like no cereal you ever heard, a heart rate that speeds up in the middle of the night for no reason and body parts that, well, just don't look like they used to.

I'm a very happy person and feel awesome about the way my life is going (even though I'm broker than broke these days), yet I can't help but get a little thrown by this little mole.

And with that I bid you all the same. Have your skin looked at by a doctor, eat veg-atables and salmon, take a long walk everyday and stretch, drink green tea and sleep at least seven hours a night and love your neighbor or something.

::sigh:: Oh hell, who am I kidding? I ate an enormous piece of cake as I was typing this...

As you were.

Tuesday January 24, 2006
Kandoo Poop!

I was shopping at Target today and saw two products that made me laugh out loud.

The first: Toddler ass wipes called Kandoo's. They came in three scents: jungle citrus, some crazy berry scent and original. (Perhaps that one just smells like new toddler). The packaging was bright and fun. It was complete with a cartoon frog actually wip-ing his little frog ass with a little wipe. How smart-instructional marketing. Are kids dumb? If anything, by the time they are wiping their own ass, they at least know where it goes. Wipe away your poo with a Kandoo! You Kandoo it! I'm going to go work for their company...

The second: The Poop Bag. Yep. It's one of those dispensers that holds little trash bags used for picking up after your animal craps in restricted areas. (Shouldn't all areas be that way? I mean, really. When your Great Dane unloads a steamer on the sidewalk where kids are playing and people are riding their bikes, you really should clean it up!!!)

Is our society getting so fast paced that we have to show our children how to wipe their asses with a cartoon on a moist towelette wrapper? Are we so overloaded that we have to use the word POOP on packaging because we don't know what size bag is best for pooch fecal waste? Damn. If that's the case I can't wait to see toilet paper, tampon and condom packaging in the future! Come to think of it, Charmin already has commercials with that butt-wiping bear...

As you were.

Tuesday January 31, 2006
Holy Moley 2!!

Today I went to the dermatologist to have my stitches removed from my biopsy experi-ence. The results came back "abnormal but clear." I thought that was pretty telling of my life, actually. So I assumed we were done and could move on.

But NOOOOO. As I was lying there under the infamous paper gown, the good doc-tor began to tell me that I have tiny pre-cancerous spots on my nose and back. He then proceeded to attack me with LIQUID NITROGEN. What? I saw my face this

3

morning, and there was nothing there, or so I thought. The way he got me to cave was by telling me that it might only take three weeks before they go from pre-cancer to things that we have to CUT off of my face. Well in that case, please burn away. Only now, I look like I have small cigarette burns on my face. I can't wait to go to some job interviews with this.

I told him that he was an S&M freak, and he kissed me on the forehead and told me that would be $85. I think we are in love. His name is Dr. Eric Lewis. I found him through one of my make-up school instructors. You can find him in Beverly Hills. 310-289-9700.

Floss, wear sunscreen, stretch, drink plenty of water, eat right and call your mother more often. Actually, if you will just call your mother more often, she will remind you to do the rest.

As you were.

Saturday February 4, 2006
What Happens in Vegas…Takes You To New Jersey?

Let's start this off on a positive note. I don't have any STD's! Hoooray!

Now, let's get scrappy.

Last June, I got a phone call from a long lost friend who had no idea I was living in LA. She was calling to catch up and tell me of her engagement. (Yes, just like everyone else I know.) Once she realized where I am currently living she got excited and asked me to join her bachelorette party in Vegas for the weekend.

Thrilled, I called in sick to work and drove as fast as I could through the desert. It was my first trip to Vegas. It was all that I expected for the most part: extravagant casinos, flashing lights, dinging bells, lots of tourists, overpriced everything, a million degrees in the desert…booze…hookers…douche-bag-looking dudes...your typical dream summer weekend getaway. I only knew the bride-to-be, so I spent a good deal of time solo, site seeing and trying to stay out of dumb, girl drama.

After seeing the famous Chippendale's show, (something I found particularly homo-sexual), we went to Club Rio and began to dance. Again, as I was an outsider, I found myself solo here and there. This actually worked to my advantage (so I thought at the time) as I was approached by an incredibly attractive young man. And by young I mean so young that I made him show me his ID. He was most certainly a TDH (tall, dark and handsome) and only a few months younger than me. He asked why I was sitting alone, and I pointed to the gaggle of chickies getting on each other's nerves about fifty feet away from me. *The "Stay Single" shirt I was wearing was probably not a bachelorette party fave...

I asked him to join me and in a loud Vegas nightclub, we sat and talked for a couple of hours. We learned a lot about each other. I was the runaway Texan paralegal who ended up in California and was headed to make-up school. He was the steady New Jersey Fed-Ex Delivery Man who was in Vegas to baby-sit his uncle, a recovering alcoholic participating in a gambling tournament. I playfully named him Johnny Vegas. Though

4

he was gorgeous, he was nothing but a mess as he recently came out of a very serious seven year relationship. (He was supposed to be married, the girl cheated on him, got pregnant by the other dude, had an abortion, lied about it and then he dumped her when he found out.) Total small town New Jersey story. Gross. He was a bit of a wreck still. It was written all over his face as were the words "Stay Single" across my chest. So we made plans to go shopping the next day. And we did. At the end of our shopping excursion, (which we did drunk...I somehow bought four pounds of dark chocolate M&M's for about $1,000,000.00!) we exchanged contact info and kept in touch here and there. NO, WE DIDN'T SLEEP TOGETHER!!! NOTHING HAPPENED, HOPE-FUL GUTTERBRAINS!

Around Christmas time in 2005, I got the wild hair to invite him out for a visit to Los Angeles. He said he didn't have the time as the holiday season is the busiest time for Fed-Ex and invited me to New Jersey for New Year's. We had been becoming better and better friends via the phone, and it seemed like a great idea to spend New Year's 2006 with the HOT Fed-Ex Man. How suburban housewifey of me...ha ha ha.

So...fast forward through a really great time...and I mean a really great time. Aside from his mother coming across as a total flippin' Oedipus case, looking me dead in the face after feeding me a lovely meal and saying, "If you think you are going to take my baby from me you can forget it," Johnny Vegas and I had a fantastic, glorious, romantic, festive time. Two weeks after I got home, he called me with something he just couldn't wait to tell me. I had a surprise for him as well. I had booked a special trip to see him for his birthday the following month! His friends said that he would love it!

His big news was that I had given him an STD. What the fuck? Wow, when you know enough to send the very best, FTD!!! FTD!! NOT STD!!! MORON!!

He actually wasn't sure if he had anything or not. He was still waiting on his results.

I've been through some pretty heavy conversations in my life, but never this one. He tried not to just flat out accuse me of being a whore, but with his Portuguese mother's, "You met her in Vegas? She lives in Hollywood?" looming in his small town mind, I was reduced to less than Hollywood trash.

I flew into a militant, frantic fit of setting appointments with doctors and freaking out about being completely misunderstood. I'm the honors student, the overachiever, the former nanny of many children...who found herself sitting in a clinic somewhere in the San Fernando Valley waiting for her turn to pee in a cup and have her gums scraped to see if she had AIDS or any other STD. While sitting in the waiting room I began an STD awareness t-shirt slogan campaign on the back of a Spanish magazine: "This is the face of an STD. I'm not afraid to tell you. Why was my partner? Spread aware-ness, not disease."

What a fun day! Oh my fucking God! 2006 is starting out to be the best year ever! ::eye roll::

$500 later, and just before I started calling non-profit organizations to start my plight, I got my results and I was clean as a whistle. When I called Johnny Vegas to tell him the good news, he didn't seem as thrilled as I had hoped. He actually felt very guilty for making me feel bad and causing me to question myself. It turned out that he didn't have anything either-just a urinary tract infection (so I am led to believe…).

Driving home after talking to him on the phone, I realized that I was glad he made me question myself a bit. Though he was many wonderful things, prepared to engage in any real relationship with a woman outside of his extremely close-to-home comfort zone, he was not. Part of him hoped I was the dirty culprit. It's easy to rid your life of people who are problematic, right? He wasn't in any way prepared to have a good, strong, independent woman in his life.

The "Stay Single" shirt is the t-shirt of choice again.

Christ, most people go to Vegas and come straight home with this kind of crisis. Not me. Oh no, my friends…I like to drag this shit out and take it all the way to the East Coast six months later.

Scratch another life lesson off the list. Next!

**He should not have said a word to me until he was sure he had an STD.

**For the record, he should have offered to pay for at least half of my doctor bill.

**I should have gone to Planned Parenthood as I am unemployed and have no insurance.

**I should send his mother the bill and my test results. What an unhappy bitch, that woman…

As you were.

Wednesday February 8, 2006
When the Queen Calls, Answer The Phone!

Oh man, once again I am reminded that LA is just one of those places where opportunity is EVERYWHERE.

Last night I was crawling into bed after a shower around 12:30 am and saw that I had a missed call. I listened to the message of a very excited and hard-to-understand gay man. He said a few key words that let me know he was looking for me, and it was something to do with make-up.

Thinking like a person who has set working hours, I stupidly decided to call back at a more appropriate hour. It turns out that the person calling was the concierge at a posh, exclusive Beverly Hills boutique hotel. A woman I did make-up for months ago had referred me to him. (I was so touched. I called and suckled her breast already.)

Hello! Turn on "Access Hollywood," Los Angelinos. It's Grammy Night. The concierge was looking for someone to do make-up on someone attending the Grammy's. Damn it. And he had already found someone to do it. Damn it, twice! Of course, I said I would come follow-up and toss his salad if he would keep me in his records for future engagements and such emergencies.

I couldn't help but ask, "Who, pray tell, would I have been working with?"

"Oh honey, I wish I could tell you, but our clients ask us to preserve their privacy." (Understandable, I thought until he said) "But I can tell you it's one of the presenters."

Grrr...What ticks me off about this more than anything is that one of my dear make-up artist mentors told me not too long ago, "Oh I keep the phone in the bathroom with me when I shower. You never know when a good call is going to come in." I knew better.

Ok, floss your teeth, wear sunscreen, stretch, eat right and ANSWER THE FUCKING PHONE!!!

As you were.

Monday February 20, 2006
I'm Melting...I'm Melting...

I'm not going to lie; it hit me like a ton of bricks this Valentine's Day that I have been actively dating for over TEN years! I might be truly interested in someone and vise versa, but by definition, I'm single. I was pretty upset, yet I think I was cured of ever getting too worked up over it on Saturday night.

I had flown out to New Jersey to see Johnny Vegas for his birthday, a surprise trip previously planned before the STD scare. *It was a trip that was once an offering of affection that was now turned into a chance to smooth things over and put some closure on a sad situation.* Anyhow, a group of people had gathered at a Jersey lounge and were enjoying some drinks, music and polite fellowship. Johnny Vegas was celebrating his twenty-sixth birthday. I heard a voice behind me say, "Oh, twenty-six sucks. It's just an awful age." Johnny Vegas introduced me to a gal who was the girlfriend of one of the guys working at the lounge. She was introduced by her first name and his last name, jokingly giving the implication that they were going to get hitched. She began a Jewish princess monologue that surely was taken out of "Sex and the City." It began with the words, "I don't think I'm ever going to get him to marry me. I'm almost twenty-seven years old." It went on to end with, "By the time he's ready to impregnate me, my eggs are going to be dried up."

Her nasally voice was bad enough, but her words were awful. I can't imagine saying those things out loud to a bunch of strangers. Then again, I don't feel like she does either. Her focus is not my focus. Is this what happens when women's clocks start to audibly tick? I knew her words were poison when I looked over at Johnny Vegas and saw him literally crouched down near the floor, holding his ears, saying, "Eww...Noooo!!!"

It was one of the most unattractive displays of female expression I've ever witnessed. Did she want to be in a solid relationship with someone who loved her and wanted to create a life with her, or did she just want to produce offspring? She used the word impregnate for God's sake. (Sounds like she's on her way to being treated like a Thanksgiving turkey, if you catch my drift.)

I wished I was able to say "Beetlejuice, Beetlejuice, Beetlejuice" so a huge sandworm would have come through the floor and snatched her away, never to melt the ears of nice young men again. Isn't there something you can give women like this to put their hormones on "Hey Bitch, Be Patient" mode? I was told by my neighbor that around the age of twenty-six or so, women begin wanting to "nest." I'm not aware of the official definition, but if it's anything like what I saw, I know I haven't hit it yet. And when I do, I hope someone reminds me of this poor girl. Just look at me, hold your hands over your ears and say, "I'm melting...I'm melting," and I will fuck off instantly.

As you were.

Tuesday February 28, 2006
Sounds Good

I have a cold. I hate having a cold. It's not the end of the world, but it feels like it in waves off and on throughout the day.

I made a trip out to the mailbox to (well, duh) check the mail, and I was happy to find the forty-five second walk audibly pleasant.

The door opened, and I was hit by the sound of my neighbors speaking what I assume was Hindi and laughing instead of screaming at each other like they normally do. Interesting.

As I opened the hallway door, the sound of my jeans swishing along the carpet was interrupted by another neighbor's bird chirping away. Nice.

As I journeyed on, two musical sounds compounded, instantly drawing a smile across my face. One neighbor practicing his clarinet met the sound of the nearby church's chiming bells. La la la...

Clinking keys hit the mailbox as I opened it to find it bill free! Who-hoo! Whew.

The grumbling elevator labored open, allowing a happy couple to spill out, chattering away. Sweet.

As I passed the chirping bird and opened the door on the return trip back into my apartment I could hear my cell phone ringing. I love that!

No screaming, no ghetto bird hovering above Hollywood in pursuit of criminals, no sirens, no screeching breaks...just a peaceful walk to get the mail.

I'm a pretty simple girl at the core. Time to stretch out on the couch and relax! What a day. :)

As you were.

Wednesday March 1, 2006
Ashes, Ashes, We All Fall Down...

Today is Ash Wednesday, the beginning of The Lenten Season for the believers out there. I could ramble about its meaning and significance in the Catholic faith, but what is hitting me most deeply is where my heart goes on a day like today. Houston.

I think about The Chapel of St. Basil at the University of St. Thomas and the church I attended, St. Anne's.

Part I: I was baptized and confirmed at The Chapel of St. Basil during my junior year of college. I can still remember my first mass, who went with me, and how I cried to be in the presence of such community, routine, peace, love and hope. The Chapel offers the most elegant presentation for Catholics, combining outstanding elements of historical artifacts in a breathtakingly peaceful, modern setting. I spent most Sunday evenings going to the 9:00 pm mass where the younger crowd gathered. I used to see it as great way to start the week instead of end it. My baptism and confirmation was a beautiful event. The memory I hold of the initial ingestion of the body and blood of Christ still sends the same shivers down my spine. My favorite part of that Easter Vigil was, in fact, the enormous neon Jesus an alter boy created that glowed brighter and brighter as we all sang, "Christ has died, Christ has risen, Christ will come again..." The damn thing illuminated the whole chapel! UST is a liberal arts university...

Part II: After I moved a step away from campus, I began attending mass at St. Anne's in the River Oaks community. What a gorgeous church. What a huge congregation. I never really got to know many of the people who gathered there, yet there was always the same energizing sense of faith, hope, love, etc. I have great respect for Father Robbins. I'll never forget the first thing he said at the membership meeting I attended. He said, "Welcome to St. Anne's where we open our doors to all walks of life. If that is not comfortable for you I'm sure you can find a home at a Church down the street." I always imagined that I might get married in that church, but as my life has taken so many new turns, I have no idea or care to know where such events might happen.

Part III: Despite it all, I'm a terrible Catholic. The list of wrong-doing is far too long to go into. But we have these obligatory Holy Days to try to get back in the swing of righting our religious wrongs. The Lenten Season is perfect. We're about to go into this very solemn, dark phase where the churches are less luminous and we are leading up to the betrayal of Christ where he will die! It's the part of the year where we make sacrifices/additions to our faith that help remind us why Christ died for us. (What a guy!) Every year, I seem to fall off Catholic Truck, then I go get some ash smeared on my forehead and I'm back on board. This year will be no different. There is a Catholic Church literally on the next street from me, so close I can hear the children playing in the school yard at recess.

Part IV: I have to go to a new church. Our Mother of Good Counsel...sounds pretty good actually. My mother isn't here to counsel me in person, so I will take my happy ass to Our Mother of Good Counsel and have her set me straight!

To those who I cannot hug at mass in person I send to you in spirit:

May peace be with you.

As you were.

Thursday March 2, 2006
I'm In Love

My new laptop arrived today. She's beautiful. I named her Hope. 'Nuff said.

As you were.

Sunday March 5, 2006
Stunning, Not Startling

I was shopping at the Ralph's on Hollywood Boulevard, and I saw something disturbing.

I saw the concrete reason for not getting a boob job. Standing in front of me in the check out line was a woman whose hands were rather crinkly and dotted with age spots. Hands don't lie. She had to be in her sixties at least. I noticed that her face obviously had some work. Lips plumped with something, forehead line free, and she had a really deep fake tan. I was shocked by that alone, yet brought to my knees when I noticed that this woman (wearing a slightly unzipped tracksuit) had implants. Imagine trying to hide two grapefruit under a piece of used speckled orange(ish) tissue paper. It just doesn't look right at all. The other work that she had done was not nearly as disturbing as implants. I wondered how long she had them and by what method they were implanted. She was super thin so I have a hard time believing that they put them under the muscle, as she has no mass of that sort. Maybe they were just held on by magnets? What do her grandchildren think when they crawl up in her lap and their heads "thud" against Nana's rock hard mammaries? Wait, what am I thinking? Women like her don't have grandchildren, and if they happen to, they certainly don't cuddle them.

Anyhow, my point is that I just can't do it. I've thought about balancing out my figure with some boobs, but why? They wouldn't get me anywhere. Sure, you can disagree, but the places they would get me, I really don't want to go.

When I'm stiff on the slab I don't want the coffin prep squad to be speculating about what a freak I was. I want them to treat my body with kindness and imagine me as a stunning little old lady. My small, beautiful breasts will just have to do.

Besides, have you seen my ass? Smokin'!

As you were.

Sunday March 5, 2006
The Perfect Couple

Tonight I uncovered the recipe for the perfect couple.
She has no arms. (Women have more lower-body strength.)
He has no legs. (Men have more upper-body strength.)
Strap them together and they can finally experience walking, crawling and waving.
Now that's teamwork.

As you were.

Thursday March 9, 2006
Feel the Burn…Five More…Four…Three…

I am one lucky little girl. I wear a size 3.5 kid's athletic shoe. Today I went to a sporting goods store and found a pair of cute pink and grey New Balance shoes for $30. A similar New Balance shoe in a woman's size 5 was $75! Now that's savings!

I'd never felt so confident doing my Carmen Electra "Fit to Strip" DVD as I did today in a pair of kids shoes...

As you were.

Tuesday March 14, 2006
Leggo My Oreo

Nabisco has it right; twist open an Oreo, and unlock the magic.

Hand me a package of Oreos and glass of milk, and leave me alone. I love Oreos. Oreos are amazing. I try to eat pretty healthy, but I can PUT AWAY a pound of Oreos in no time. There is something about the feel of that crisp cookie blending with the cream in the middle in my mouth after it's been dipped in milk...

It always starts off the same. First, I eat a couple while preparing my plate and glass of milk. Then I dip some until I can't reach the milk in the glass with the cookie any-more. I drink the rest of the milk and proceed to twist the cookies apart. Fresh Oreos will separate with all of the cream on one side. I eat the half with the cream on it first and then the clean crispy cookie second. On late night trips to the bathroom I might actually skip into the kitchen to indulge in a cookie. And trust me I've had Oreos for breakfast more times than I can count. I had a few with my eggs this morning, well, while my eggs were cooking that is.

Let's talk flavor. There are the originals. There are the Double Stuffs...and then the Heaven's parted and God sent the Mint Cream Oreo and The Chocolate Cream Oreo. Oh my God! What is it about this little cookie sandwich that holds such power over people? They are sooooo unhealthy. It's lard we've been scraping off the sides of those cookies!!! Would you eat a spoonful of Crisco? There must be something subliminal in the jingle.

Oh Oh, who's that girl with the Oreo Cookie? She looks sweet and harmless, but try take to her Oreo. She'll hunt you down and drain your blood. You'll die alone begging for your mother. It's hard to see the demon inside...O.R.E.O...Nabisco...Ding.

Unlock the magic. You mean SATAN? (insert the voice of Kyle's mother from South Park) I get it. Those crispy cookies hold the EVIL inside, and when you twist one open a little Satan slips out into the world. But if the only evil that is caused is that we eat more Oreos, I'm cool with it.

Damn, I hope this blog doesn't get into the hands of some group of crazy thumpin' Bible Belters. Oreos would be banned from vending machines, grocery stores and school lunches everywhere. An entire civil war could start only to leave our country in ruins. Generations from now children would be digging through the rubble we left behind and would find a package of Oreos. The wild kid in the bunch would say, "Oh come on guys, let's twist open just one..." The second the cookie separated from the cream, like a genie out of a lamp, Satan would come blustering out in a cloud of sweet smelling smoke to steal their souls and start his cookie brainwashing all over again!!!!!

Yes, unlock the magic; the black magic!

11

Should I really be blogging about Satan during Lent? This is why I don't give up sweets for Lent.

Whew...

As you were.

Thursday March 16, 2006
Purse Pooches

I'm seriously disturbed by people who carry dogs (animals) into places of business. Why? Why do you need to carry a small live creature with you at all times? Are you lonely? Why not take up text messaging or useless airtime on your cell like everyone else? Oh...you do that, too.

I was at the Century City Westfield Mall waiting in line for some Greek(ish) food when out of the corner of my eye I saw something moving at about waist level on the woman a little behind me. Then I heard a bark. I'll be damned; that woman had a dog hanging out of her purse. The poor little thing was on a teeny-tiny strap that was attached like a keychain to the bag. It was a very expensive Todd's bag, surely one with a matching wallet inside. She paid no attention to it whatsoever. It just flitted around, yapping. Wasn't she afraid that it was going to make a break for it and hang itself? Hell, I would have.

My friend Tracy called not too long ago so furious I thought she was going melt the phone with her hot rage. She works at Blockbuster Video. A customer had come in with a dog. She mentioned to the woman that they really don't allow pets in the store. The woman, ignoring the dog as it ran about (no doubt trying to free itself from its life in Hell), began to personally insult Tracy instead of taking the dog outside. After the woman finally gathered her animal into her purse, her movies and what was left of her dignity, she took off with her nose in the air. Another customer came to Tracy, already fuming, and said, "I didn't want to say anything while she was in here, but her dog peed on a box of candy." Yep...that little bitch peed on a huge shipment of candy. Tracy is still red in the face over this. Since when did Blockbuster become Gymboree for dogs?

If I had a dog, brought it to your house, walked into your kitchen and let it lick the fruit in your fruit bowl, you might have a problem with it, right? So why in the fuck would you bring your damn dog to the grocery store with you? There I was pushing my cart into Von's and I saw a woman with no teacup poodle mind you, but a watermelon sized dog, dangling over the produce trying to paw at it. Fucking gross, just fucking gross. I wanted to walk over, piss on her leg and say, "Oh, I'm sorry, you looked like a tree. This is the dog park and all."

I can't believe in a town that is now starting to ban smoking in public areas, people are allowed to carry animals into places where food is served. I hope these people never plan on having children. Those little dogs must come with the purses. Aren't you afraid they are going to shit inside your purse? Hello! Animals carry all kinds of germs and fecal waste on their paws, and there it is getting all in your bag. And I bet you're the type of person who sucks on your pen or blots your lipstick with random paper floating in your bag. Fucking gross.

If you're not going to pay attention to it, why does it have to be alive? Just carry a stuffed animal. Oh, but wait, that might make you look like an insecure child who needs a security blanket in public. I may have just answered my own question.

As you were.

Friday March 17, 2006
4, 2.5 and .5

Many of my friends know that I have been a nanny on the side for years. For the most part, I have worked with families that have children who are ranging from ages nine to eighteen. My areas of influence included issues like: homework, setting trust boundaries, peer pressure and basically everything that teenagers go through. As a young adult, I got to be a role model, a big sister, a buffer and a confidant. My job was both heartwarming and gut-wrenching all at the same time. Over the years I have accumulated truly impressive references, making myself quite marketable in the childcare department, which is amusing to me as I honestly don't know if I will ever birth a child.

While trying to find a "regular job" here in LA, I've been stepping up to the challenge and pleasure once again. This go round is on the opposite end of the spectrum. I've been working with children ages four, two-and-a-half and six months. Luckily, the parents are stellar and are doing a wonderful job with the formative years. I have no experience in this area and find myself just staring blankly at the six month old as she screams for what seems like no apparent reason again and again. I'm having serious discussions with the two-and-a-half year-old as to why we don't crawl inside the fridge to play while I try to come up with solid reasons that satisfy a four year-old's questions as to why she can't draw on the walls of HER room.

Mealtime: Prepare the meal. Get this kids involved so they understand the importance of hard work for reward. Have them help set the table. Feed the baby while I feed myself. Look out! The baby spits her food all over the place. Try to engage the children in fun, yet responsible conversation about school, games they have played that day and people they talked to, etc. Encourage good table manners and praise them for taking their plates to the sink. Prepare bottle for baby's bedtime feeding. Time frame: One hour. Whew.

Bathtime/Bedtime: Immediately following mealtime, head to the bathtub. Put the older children in the tub first. Let the baby play on the floor within eye shot. Fight the hair washing fight. Take one child out, brush hair and teeth; send the child to the bedroom for quiet play. Put the baby in the bath in the safety seat. Bathe. Take the second older child out of the tub; teeth and hair...quiet play. Take baby out of the tub. Dry, dress and sit down to feed the nighttime bottle. Put the baby to bed. Quiet reading time with the older kids. No more than two books! Lights out. Time frame: One hour.

That's only two hours out of a very loooong day of child-rearing, minus all of the interruptions and hang-ups throughout both routines. I cannot imagine being a stay-at-home parent. I would lose my mind. Adults may suck a lot at times, but I can tell an adult to fuck off when they are out of line and walk away. Yeah, can't do that with kiddos. I need to deal with people who can be at least somewhat rationalized with.

I was really good with the older kids. I felt like I made a difference with them. Yet, as I look down at my shirt to see what look like slug tracks running across it, which is actually snot that the six month old smeared on me with her face, I wonder: am I making a difference or just getting them by? I suppose I work on homework and peer pressure issues, etc. with them, only it's on a much younger level. God, it's hard.

I dare any of you to do it.

As you were.

Saturday March 18, 2006
Prelude To An LA Sunday

There is fun and entertainment to be found in my current town every day of the week, but I love Sundays in Los Angeles the most.

When I consider entertaining visitors or go to bed on a Saturday night and imagine the activities for the next day, I picture the following:

Wake up (usually a good sign when this happens).

Put on some sneakers and take a walk through the neighborhood behind me and up into Griffith Park. The weather is so great here; I probably won't even break a sweat.
Yet there is no fooling, it's quite a hike!

With an appetite all worked up, it's time for Roscoe's Chicken and Waffles! I like the one on Pico and Le Brea. The typical wait-time is about an hour, but trust me, it's worth it. It's a Soul Food treat. *If you've never been order the #13; it's a waffle and a succulent breast. Get a glass of orange juice. It's fresh squeezed by hand every morning. Be prepared for butter, grease and fried love on a plate. $15 (including tip) and you're full for hours and hours.

Waddle to the car and head to Melrose to stroll off the meal by window shopping and looking for a sale or two. There are tons of fun stores with some great bargains if you know where to look! (There's an Aldo Outlet store where often times shoes are buy one get one half off!)

Time for some culture. Zip over (if that's possible) to the 405 and head for The Getty Museum. $7 gets your whole car load in. Park under the mountain and ride the tram up the side of the hill to the museum which houses an amazing, diverse collection. The building itself is a work of art. It's huge. Take in the views for a bit. You can see all the way from Griffith Park to Catalina Island from the top.

Seeing the coast from The Getty makes the sand seem mighty inviting. It's time to head to Venice for the Sunday Venice Beach Drum Circle. You've never seen a drum circle until you've been a part of this ritual. A crowd gathers in the hundreds creating beats that can be heard half a mile away. It looks impressive from the outside, but step inside the circle and the beats will take over your body! Dancing and letting go is highly encouraged. As the sun begins to set over the Pacific Ocean, the circle turns and sets the sun. It's the most magical/spiritual feeling to be a part of a group like that. It makes up for not going to Mass in my book. (You might have to pay between $5-10 for parking; the beach is FREE!)

With renewed vigor and serenity, it's time to head to the house for some D&D, dinner and downtime. Stop by Trader Joe's on the way home and pick up some of the most amazing organic and cheap food and you're out! *Seriously, $50 takes care of almost two weeks worth of my groceries. Head home, eat, relax, watch "Desperate House-wives" and "Grey's Anatomy."

The weekend isn't over yet! Around midnight head out to Deep. Deep is one of the best after hours dance spots ever. My dear friend, Tako, brought me to Deep when I had just moved here and I fell in love with the atmosphere. DJ Marcus Wyatt spins until 4:00 am. If you've never been on an LA dance floor, you've never danced. I've never seen so many different people in one room who are there for the beats. It's not about being seen or looking at what shoes someone is wearing; it's about really losing yourself in the music.*It moves locations occasionally so when you're on Melrose, stop by Fatbeats and pick up some flyers so you know where to find it. $20 and it's worth it!

Overall, this is an entire day of relatively cheap entertainment. When the night is over, you feel like you have truly lived. You will have climbed into the hills, eaten well, met God at the edge of the continent, been cultured and gotten a great workout all in one day for less than $100. One trip to a trendy night club in LA could cost that, and how much fun are you really having at those places anyhow?

I like living here. I always laugh when people think that this town is a concrete jungle. Green space and natural wonder are everywhere.

As you were.

Sunday March 19, 2006
You Know, Because It's Lent...

Ok, I've said it before, I'm not the best Catholic in the world and probably will never enter into the running, but every now and then I have to pause and look at a fellow Catholic and say, "Hey, what the hell are you trying to do? Who are you trying to im-press? Who are you trying to fool?"

I was at Trader Joe's the other day. As I was heading down the isle with pasta noodles and such, I heard a woman talking to one of the stockers. Quite audibly she told him, "But I'm looking for pasta that isn't made with eggs. It's Lent, and I need pasta that isn't made with eggs." He walked away and came back in a second and showed her some package. She read the back and said, "No. See this ingredient. It's an egg by-product. I can't have this. It's Lent, and we've given up all meat."

**Oh-she was a large woman and was taking up most of the small isle, so I had to wait for the stock guy to scoot so I could squeeze in. I could care less about what's in my pasta. I was actually looking for the pesto basil flavored ones. (So good with a little olive oil and shrimp...and a glass of vino)

I stepped in, focusing on the shelf and she turned to me and said, "Do you see the color of these noodles? How can noodles be this color and not have eggs in them? I'm look-ing for eggless pasta, you know, because it's Lent."

I just smiled and said, "Sounds like it would have been easier to give up pasta for Lent."

The look on her face was priceless. She was puzzled and insulted. The Lenten Season isn't just about meat. It's about sacrifice for someone who sacrificed for us so that we may be more able to help others in need. And there's that whole section of the scripture that tells us to give halms with the left hand so that the right hand doesn't know what the left hand is doing (OR SOMETHING LIKE THAT - I DON'T KNOW, FUCK OFF!). Point being, don't be showing off your sudden acts of sacrifice, like it's really something. Sacrifice quietly in honor of what has been done for you.

She totally reminded me of Charlotte on "Sex and the City" when she decided to become Jewish to be able to marry her second husband. She went on this Trani-Jew Frenzy, and when he wasn't completely in tune with it she yelled at him, "But I'm giving up Christ for you!"

I could absolutely see that woman with her thick hand around the stocker's neck, tossing that poor kid around yelling, "I need that eggless pasta you advertised!" And when the police are taking her statement and ask why she attacked the young man, she would say, "You know, because it's Lent."

Oy Vey.

As you were.

Sunday March 19, 2006
Pass Me a Joint, Would Ya?

Growing up I was always a pretty physically flexible person, and with minimal warm-up or stretching I could throw myself down into the splits with ease. The one thing that would always make people cringe, though, was the sound of my hip joints popping as I slid down onto the floor.

Next, my neck. In intermediate school I remember developing the ability to crack my neck several times a day. And then the back. From a standing position, I can twist from the waist and pop, top to bottom. If I'm lying down, all I have to do is throw one hip and leg over to the other side, and I have given myself a chiropractic adjustment for free.

It's starting to get a little scary as I get older, though. Everything is starting to pop, multiple times a day. I could never sneak up on anyone. First thing in the morning, my feet hit the floor and my steppers sound like popping bubble wrap. I shuffle to the bathroom, and while sitting for the first glorious morning wee, I turn each leg out and let the hip joints release. Ahh. Then I go lie back down and do the back. Wow. It's like a spine made of Rice Krispies doused in milk...Snap, Krackle, Pop! As I reach over for the laptop and begin to type, creak, creak, go the wrists and fingers; better pop them. My neck gets stiff while returning emails. With a quick turn of the head in both directions, there is the beautiful release of pressure made possible by the sound of thunder between my head and shoulders. When I get up and decide to actually stretch, look out. My ankles make a dull sound that resembles the thud of stone being slammed into someone's head. I hate it when my knees pop. It just sounds like potential surgery.

16

Alien movies have nothing on the ripping sound my sternum makes as I try to touch my hands together behind my back. I'm waiting for the day when the little critters inside my chest come busting through!

Sometimes, the explosions in my joints happen in social settings involuntarily. I'll be sitting there talking with my elbow on the table and will lean the wrong (or right) way and whoops, there goes my shoulder. The look on the faces around me makes me wonder if I have some sort of problem. My roommate, Michelle M., cringes when she hears my back crack. Sometimes I wonder if I'm just going to break off into all 206 pieces. (Isn't that how many bones we have in our bodies? Tune in 6th grade biology. Mrs. Ewing where are you???)

I kinda' remind myself of one of those wooden donkeys you get at flea markets or in Mexico. You know, the ones that you push the button on the bottom and they fall limp. I have this funny image in my mind of someone putting their thumb in my butt where I fall to the ground like a Mexican wooden donkey with only my skin to act as a sack to hold my bones together. Good thing those donkeys pop back into place when you release your thumb. **And for the record, if anyone tries to stick their thumb or anything else in my butt, you aren't getting it back and it will more than likely be the last time you ever do that to me or anyone else again.

Anyhow, my favorite joint issue is my jaw. My jaw has cracked for as long as I can remember. So far, it isn't too bad and only aches when I'm beyond stressed out, but it makes some noise all the time. It becomes much louder during extreme amounts of activity like biting into and chewing apples, chewing gum or oh yes, you guessed it, making out. There's no better way of getting out of giving head than to say, "Oh yeah that cracking sound? I have TMJ. It doesn't hurt much, but it does tend to lock up sometimes when I'm using my mouth a lot." Perks to poppin'...

When I'm seventy and an arthritic mess, I hope I can read this and still think it's amusing. I wonder if I drank more water if it would help lubricate my joints...

As you were.

Monday March 20, 2006
Uptown Girl

In a town where you can make more money on unemployment than working most "regular jobs" after taxes, I am once again amused by the inner workings of this Pacific beast called Los Angeles.

Somehow, I managed to mess up my unemployment claim form this week and was asked to call the office. Yeah, that number is 1-800-B-ON-HOLD. The call volume can actually get so high that the system kicks you out by saying, "Our employees, computers and general interest in your concerns are too slow and low to be able to take any more callers. Call back later. Goodbye." And then it hangs up on you after you've played the "Press one for a poke in the eye; press two to set yourself on fire..." game.

I actually set my alarm to get up early to start calling ahead of time not to get kicked out of the system but just be put on eternal hold. The best part about that is the "estimated wait time" where a pre-recorded voice helps you count down the minutes to getting through to someone. In between the, "I'm sorry, all of our representatives are still busy," that cheesy elevator music plays, you know the crap that is usually old Top 40's hits played with synthesized muzacical instruments. This morning I was shocked to hear that my eternal hold song was Billy Joel's "Uptown Girl." What the fuck? No one on unemployment wants to hear that song! If you're a man, you feel insecure about yourself. If you're a woman who's "never had to stoop" to unemployment, you feel insecure about yourself. If you are from another race besides the "white-bred world" you feel insecure about yourself. I could go on.

Where's the motivational speaker? Where are the pre-recorded resume tips? Isn't this where, like, I don't know...Celine Dion's shit music belongs? Her show in Vegas is called "A New Day" after all. (And no I have never seen the show, but you can't miss her entire wing and souvenir mini-mall at Caesar's Palace...)

And when I got passed the muzak, I got Nina, a woman who sounded ancient and spoke in broken English. We had a pleasant yet labored conversation which was full of very long, dramatic silences, followed by me saying, "Hello. Nina?" As if she were reading it off a post-it, squinting from fifty feet away, she would then respond, "Oh...Please hanged on, whilt my computer process you infomation."

I'm just going to digress now and go take a lap...

As you were.

Tuesday March 21, 2006
Forward Ho!

Someone I don't know sent me the link to the quiz: "Why don't you have a boyfriend?"

Deciding that it was surely my grandmother posing as some young dude on MySpace, trying to send me hints, I took the quiz after reporting the message as spam mail.

My results: I'm too forward. "No doubt you've got game. But maybe too much for some guys. Maybe it's that some guys like a challenge and don't know what to do with you. You get bored easily with guys."

Yep. For once an internet quiz is almost entirely correct. I wouldn't say that I'm TOO forward. Being forward and honestly having my cards on the table is not a flaw; it's The Holy Grail. WAKE UP, XY'ers!

However, it is true. Every time a new guy gets interested, he walks around doe-eyed for a while telling me I'm amazing. But then there's a tragic turn where he starts realizing that he isn't quite as comfortable with who he is or feels that he doesn't measure up to me. (Which is so LAME. I'm not perfect. I'm just really honest, open and able to balance things.) Before you know it, I'm bored and tired of meeting another guy who "isn't ready for a girl like me," and he wanders off into the sunset only to meet and marry the next Pollyanna wrapped around a Cosmopolitan who has helplessly batted her eyes at him. *I could start a business as a Relationship Fluffer. I will be the plant.

Women would show me the men they want; I'd date them for a month or so. When I scare them off, we'll set it up so that they run into my clients and fall in love. Awww.

I could never be that girl. Entrapment isn't my game. That girl either flips and becomes an obsessed bitch or is so whiney he cheats on her. How do I know this? I get The Phone Call. I get the call that says, "You know, I really should have given us a better shot." ARG! You must be kidding. Once you are married you have no face and become androgynous to me.

Am I ready to get married: NO. (I've got my own shit to work on still.)

Do I talk to men about getting married as if they are the one: OH, FUCK, NO.

Do I pressure them: WHY BOTHER? They have their mothers for that.

Do I want to meet a guy I can consider marriage material: SURE, WHY NOT? I've had my fill of "Nowhere Near Mr. Rights." A "Mr. Hmmm...Maybe" would be nice.

I've come close to "Mr. Hmmm...Maybe," but once again, he ran scared when he realized that I'm really this normal and understanding and fun all in one.

I know I'm not the only girl who feels this way.

Oh, Yawn.

As you were.

Tuesday March 21, 2006
Happy Birthday Benito Juarez

My mother mentioned to me that it was the first day of Spring. I went to check my calendar as that is usually one of those noted dates and instead of the first day of Spring, today, March 21st, is noted as Benito Juarez' Birthday (M). Who the hell is Benito Juarez, and why do we care? Well, according to a Google search:

"March 21st is a National Holiday in Mexico to commemorate the birthday of Benito Juarez, who rose from humble origins to occupy the Presidency of the Republic on several occasions during the turbulent second half of the 19th century.

One of the reasons Benito Juarez is seen as representing Mexico is because his indigenous roots and seminary education seem to reflect the national mixture of races and cultures. Indeed, Juarez did much to overcome the prejudice against indigenous heritage, so prevalent in the 19th Century. He was fiercely anti-clerical, believing that the excessive power of the Catholic Church was one of the main obstacles to the development of the country. He led the nation in a struggle against neocolonialism and French intervention, earning the title of "Benemrito de las Amricas", or deserving of the Americas' praise."

George Bush, take note, one day you too might have a day where we commemorate you, too.

I hope not.

Ok, there you have it in case you needed a reason to have a beer and a piece of cake.

As you were.

Wednesday March 22, 2006
Thank You, O.J. Simpson, For Starting LA's Favorite Sport

There is an underground sport in Los Angeles that tax payers endorse, fear, and live for: The Car Chase. We love The Car Chase. Our law enforcement teams are extensively trained both on the land and in the air for such an event. When a chase occurs, our news crews abandon all other news stories to give full, live coverage of the chase.

As I walked in the door this early evening from an invigorating walk in the hills behind my apartment, I was instantly glued to the television. The battle was on between Torrance and Los Angeles police and a white man driving a green Toyota Highlander. The pursuit had been going on for two-and-a-half hours! Wow. Our driver was good, weaving in and out of traffic on surface streets at speeds varying from 60-100 miles per hour.

Diligently and with ease, the ground enforcement trailed him while ghetto birds kept track of him from above. He took some amazing turns, made it through some packed intersections, and jumped medians to speed the wrong way down busy LA streets. A pit maneuver didn't even stop him. I became torn with whether I wanted him to get away or not when I saw him defeat gridlock traffic on the 405 at 5:00 pm without hitting a single car! He was a Chase God! Naturally, I wanted the chase to end so that he didn't harm anyone, but he really was giving them a run for their money.

Finally, half-an-hour later, in an attempt to make a wild u-turn across a large median, he hit some loose gravel, spun out a bit and ran into a tree. The cops were still on him and just when I thought my adrenaline was at its peak, oh yes, he took off on foot!! Oh hell, yeah, we had a runner. The news team was hilarious. Very calmly one anchor said, "Oh. There he goes on foot. Oh. He's got on those baggy pants. He could have a weapon hidden in there. Those officers really need to look out for those baggy pants." Uhhh...those baggy pants were the downfall of our driver, as they kept causing him resistance, sliding down his body, showing off his ass. Yay!! Skin shots!!! Who-hoo. An officer closed in on him. He ran around the buildings. He wasn't done yet. He threw a few punches and was taken to the ground, biting and kicking as eight officers held him down. Yes, eight officers.

I couldn't help but cheer.

My favorite part of the whole chase was the news footage of him being walked to the police car. He was wearing a white American Pride t-shirt that said, "Free Spirit" with a bald eagle on it. "Well, you were," I thought.

Tonight I will play "Freebird" in his honor.

As you were.

✳ Wednesday March 22, 2006
Deadly Health Code Violation

A mortuary in LA somewhere that has been in business for, like, twenty years is being closed down. The news reported it has been charged with health code violations.

What?

Ummm...Who's complaining? That's what I want to know!

Do health code violations translate into dignity violations?

Does necrophilia translate to a health code violation? Are dead bodies refusing to go in the ground due to injustices performed on them?

Perhaps they are refusing the mixture of fluids that are used to flush the body during the embalming process. "I'm not going to rest in peace until you send one more gin and tonic through me." (That would be my protest.)

Did some snooty uppity-up have hidden cameras planted on the bodies of their relatives and see the party that goes on at the mortuary during the night? It's like *Weekend at Bernie's,* I'm sure. (::eye roll::)

Maybe they were selling internal organs to local taquerias as animal parts and got busted when someone figured out that those weren't cow sesos or tripas.

Are they trying to revive the dead?

Are they doing tacky make-up jobs on purpose? You know, like a tire track across the face?

What could you really do to a corpse that is a health code violation?

I'm sure if this becomes my personal problem, I won't be able to care.

As you were.

✳ Thursday March 23, 2006
Narcoleptic Nuggets

This afternoon I was chillin' (translation=babysitting) with a couple of lil' people and during lunchtime I discovered a new sedative: Trader Joe's Chicken Drumettes. (Yes, as you can see by my blogs Trader Joe's comes up a lot. It's a rad organic grocery store. Cities without them are really missing out. Austin, Texas needs one badly!)

Anyhow, for lunch, the kitchen was serving a fantastic array of foodie goodness: Chicken drumettes, fresh steamed green beans, sliced strawberries and choice of milk or fizzy juice (there's a secret recipe for fizzy juice, sorry, can't share).

The older lil' person and I were discussing mermaids and what they do for a living. The phone rang, and during the call I continued to help feed the younger lil' person. The older one got kinda quiet, and I could only be happy about that. When the call ended, I came around the corner and found the older lil' person face down in his plate on the table, sound asleep. Naptime directly follows lunchtime, but usually doesn't overlap. I woke him enough to wipe the ketchup off his forehead and tell him to head upstairs to his bed. He toddled off, and I continued with the younger lil' person. I noticed that he only ate the Chicken Drumettes.

When she was done we headed upstairs. Passing through the living room, I saw the older lil' person zonked out on the couch. He didn't even make it upstairs. I looked at the younger lil' person who was yawing and rubbing her eyes. She was fading fast! I got her to bed and came back downstairs to tidy up the kitchen. As I stood there, I realized that I was also feeling drowsy and needed to lie down. We all wound up taking really long naps!!!

Two things come to mind: I love getting paid to sleep, and instead of slipping hyper lil' people children's cold medicine I'm going to just feed them Trader Joe's Chicken Drumettes! No medicine chest is complete without them!

*Please note: Shut up! Chill out! Put the phone down. Stop calling CPS. I have never given a child cold medicine unless he/she needed it, though it couldn't hurt them. I know. I've taken cold medicine to knock myself out and have risen like a new person.

As you were.

Friday March 23, 2006
Juggernauts

While going through some job postings, I ran across an ad for an "industry juggernaut" in need of a personal assistant.

I had never heard of that term so I looked it up. It is defined as "an overwhelming force that crushes or seems to crush everything in it's path."

I wonder how many calls they really got. I can't imagine wanting to work for someone who is described like that. God knows the personal assistant would be taking serious hits in the line of fire. Why didn't they use words to romance you into the office like: elite industry leader?

I guess they were trying to be nice. Would you answer the ad that says, "Hi. Wanna work for a great big asshole? He'll treat you like crap, keep you attached to a black-berry 24/7, smack your ass, cause heart attacks and strokes, and nothing you do is ever good enough. Call now!" Probably not...

God, I'm tempted to call the Surgeon General and see if we can get that man a warn-ing label...You know, one of those that says, "Over exposure to this entity might cause health concerns ranging from heart problems to anal leakage."

Oh, honey, no.

As you were.

Friday March 23, 2006
Do I LOOK Bisexual?

What is it about my profile that attracts so many requests for bisexual/bi-curious activity? It's a slow day when I don't get five or six requests for girl-on-girl lovin'. The dumb guy requests consisting of: "Hi. You're really hot. Wanna chat?" don't even bother me anymore because of the volume of dumber girls sending me long detailed emails about their fantasies. And might I say, there is nothing romantic about being cut with a knife while having sex. This is America...Hello!!!

I am not bisexual. (So I French kissed a girl once, but it wasn't a kiss for pleasure; it was a defense mechanism in a bar.) I'm not bi-curious. I have girl parts, and I take care of my own. I don't want to do anything with yours or watch you do anything with anyone else's.

I actually responded to one girl, simply asking her to leave me alone as she had emailed me more than eight times in two days. She responded back that I was "clothed minded." Yes, you read that correctly, "clothed minded." She was from Kentucky. Perhaps she had a tongue ring or a lisp and was sounding out words as she typed. That would make her from the "Bluegrath Thate" I presume...and that she likes to eat puthy. Ok...I'll stop.

::shaking head:: I don't see the allure of begging for sexual favors on the net. How in the world do they know whether or not I'm who I say I am, or if I'm some sixty-five year-old retired gym coach with a sagging sack who gets off on watching naked little kids eat Jell-O out of each other's asses?

I just report them as spam mail. I don't know what that does, but it makes me feel better.

So, if you see anything on my site that might warrant a bisexual urge in someone, please, let me know and I'll take care of it.

My message to those requesting attention: truly flattered, but really, please fuck off...

As you were.

Saturday March 25, 2006
In Her Bathrobe She Blogged...

Many have asked what compels me to write about the things I do.

I'll lay it out straight. I'm convinced that it's my blogging uniform. You see, most of the time I find myself lounging about the house with the world on my mind. I tend to wear a fluffy, make-up stained, pink bathrobe. Who needs to get dressed if they don't have to? Not too long ago, I added a pair of black sunglasses after a glass of wine. I joked with myself about having quite a pimp life right now, perched upon my thirty year-old curvy, golden velour sofa typing away.

The blogs just took off. I don't know what it is...the dark glasses just help me focus. Maybe it's my own personal form of medicating my undiagnosed adult ADHD or life dyslexia. Whatever the case, if you want to imagine me typing away, that's what I look like while doing it.

I think I'm going to save the world with blogging. It could happen. People would stop freaking out over nothing and start thinking about the little things in life. Little kids everywhere would be trying to wear tiny bathrobes and sunglasses. Four letter words would emphatically fly out of their mouths over inconsequential injustices and well, basically everything. I could start my own line of "Beanwear...for the Blogger in you!" bathrobes and sunglasses. (*Bean is the nickname given to me by children for whom I used to nanny in college.)

Now, if I could just get some hot house guy to make me lunch so I wouldn't have to stop, that would be great.

**If I could add a song to type this blog to it would be, "The Future's So Bright I Gotta Wear Shades" by Timbuck 3.

Life inside my head is really fuckin' RAD.

As you were.

Sunday March 26, 2006
Say It In Green

I'm a really practical person and have a hard time accepting flowers as a gift on special occasions from people who are very close to me. Flowers worth giving are fucking expensive! I would much rather have an item that I can use or a contribution to my student loan payments. If you said, "Here's $50. Take this off the light bill," I would faint with delight. Better yet, if you donated money to a charity in my name I would suck your toes! *Which reminds me - Jeff Yaworski gave me $20 and a funny card he made on his computer when we were in High School. Good man...good man. I still have the card, too...But I never sucked his toes.

The people you would expect to really understand this about me would be family, right? Nope. Not mine. (As of late, I believe they have finally gotten the message, but I think that's only because they think I'm starving, sitting on an egg crate in an alley in LA. So not true...yet.)

My grandmother, Gumma, is the prime example. She used to send me care packages to the dorms. Care packages are supposed to be filled with fun stuff like candy, gum, girly shit like hair products and nail polish, homemade cookies, magazines or a pair of socks with $20 in each toe. Gumma missed that memo. I loved getting her packages because I loved showing dorm residents the silly stuff she'd send. Sometimes she would even send stuff to my friends in the dorms. On Nick Moorehead's birthday she sent him a bag of kumquats. He looked at me and said, "These are called, what?" Some of her most unique sends were:

Cowprint pot holders: I don't even know if there were stoves in the dorms. I don't cook and I HATE that crafty kitchen shit. You know, the country garbage you see at craft shows that have ducks and apples and crap on them...::shudder::

Calcium Enriched Chocolate Chews: They give you the squirts. Yeah, I learned the hard way. I was in my early twenties. Was my calcium intake really an issue?

Stickers: How old am I? Am I supposed to be worrying about osteoporosis or trading scratch 'n' sniff stickers with dorm mates? Make-up your mind!!!

My mother is not much better. She has given me (with LOTS OF LOVE) so many things I cannot use. I wind up giving a lot of it away. It's awful, I know, but it's true. Her most recent display of useless item love expression was my final case and point to her. She worries about being on a "fixed income" as she is now retired and often says things like, "I wish I could send you money, but I just can't afford it." However, she called recently and asked, "Have you gotten anything from me in the mail lately?" I said no, and she became furious. Turns out, she sent me a package over a week prior and was assured that it would arrive within the next few days. UPS is a crap shipping service. I prefer FedEx or U.S. Postal Service Express Mail. When the package arrived it was addressed to me and some other person. The box was destroyed, and it had gone to several different addresses. They actually charged her credit card for all of the different shipping which turned out to be a grand total of $54.83. When I opened the package I found a $5.00 pair of enormous fuzzy house shoes. She spent almost $60.00 sending me something I won't use or keep. Yet she can't send me any money. *She has recently purchased a plane ticket to bring me home for a week, so in my eyes she has fully redeemed herself.

Work with me, people!!!

As you were.

Sunday March 26, 2006
All That Junk, All That Junk...

Dressed in the most nondescript, blah, baggy paint-stained workout clothes, I ventured out for one of my great Hollywood Hills Hikes. The sun was out. The temperature was moderate. The breeze was light.

I was covered from head to toe as I usually am, determined to defeat skin cancer. I was standing at a busy intersection that leads to the hills. On one corner (where I was waiting for the light to change) is a gas station, and on the other side is a place to eat. Across the way is the start of the residential neighborhood. Cars were all lined up at the light, and people were pumping gas. In the distance behind me I heard, "All that junk... Look at all that junk..." I really didn't think anything of it because people yell crap all the time on the streets of LA. I would only perk up to things like "Oh my God, he's got a gun," or "Fucking bitch, give me your purse," or "Like, Oh My God, is that Alex Trebeck?" Anyhow, then I heard, "Girl you know you got all that junk. Yo one fine, feline. Damn. Whoooo..."

When it didn't stop, I turned and looked over my shoulder. There was this ghetto dude in some POS motherfuckin' car with a kid in the passenger seat pumping gas. I was honestly still uncertain that he was talking to me. So I turned around. Again: "Girl, you know I'm talkin' ta ya. Awww damn. Owwww. Girl. I gotta have ya." He was being so loud that cars waiting at the light were rolling down their windows to figure out what and why he was yelling at me. I looked over my shoulder again, and a man pumping gas into his motorcycle gave me that, "Are you ok? Do you want me to do something body language." I shook my head at him and shrugged then looked over at my suitor and waved and nodded so that he would get his approval and acknowledgement. This only fueled his fiery passion for me. "See...that's right...that's right...You know where to get it. Right here, baby. Right here."

Just when I was about to unleash my fury of "Listen here you under educated piece of ghetto ass mother fuckin' shit talkin' no good useless crossed eyed must be confused if you think you're gonna stand there and talk like that to me, asshole," on him, I looked at the kid in the car. He was looking out the window, staring into the distance, with the saddest look on his face. You could tell he was so ashamed of what he was connected to. I just kept my mouth shut and walked away when the light changed. I actually felt a sense of embarrassment, and it takes A LOT to get me to that point. I felt it for myself because that was entirely too much attention drawn to me at an intersection looking like I did, but mainly for that child who has to endure God knows what else from a man like him.

What a freak. And he was at the right gas station for freaks. He was at the Bayless Chevron where Charles Manson and his family went to wash the blood off their hands and dump their clothes after killing the LaBiancas. Where's Charles Manson when you need him, you know?

As you were.

Sunday March 26, 2006
Raped With Plastic

My ass is still bleeding. It had been bleeding for a while, and I didn't know why until I started paying attention to the new series that Oprah has on called her "Debt Diet."

I have some debt. It comes from three places: My car, my student loans and one credit card. The car and the student loans will get paid off in time at fixed rates...pretty standard types of debt that we incur to make our lives better. The credit card is the dangerous one, as it accrues interest monthly. I keep that in mind and usually keep a very low balance on it. In the last year, I had some unexpected purchases and a couple splurges that have left me with a decent balance.

I saw an episode of "The Oprah Winfrey Show," in which Oprah had financial experts working to help families reduce their debt. One of their pieces of advice was to look at the interest rate that you are being charged and see if the credit card company isn't willing to lower it. I looked at my card. The rate was 18.54%! That's pretty high, considering that I've never even had a late payment. So I called and told them I had gotten an offer from another credit card company that was willing to give me 0% finance charges. I was lying, and they couldn't prove it and didn't want to lose my business, so they were willing to lower it to 13.9%. That was a start!

The part where I realized I was being raped, no, gang-raped by the company, was in the "credit protector fee." Somehow I got sucked into purchasing this monthly monitoring service which I was led to believe was a fixed charge every month. NOPE. The cost is

26

based on the balance of your card! Fuckers!!! Each month I was seeing a higher and higher "monthly protector fee" on my statement, which was driving up the balance as well as the finance charge, hence the gang-rape.

When I called to cancel this amazing monitoring system that does nothing, they tried to convince me to keep it in case I suddenly lost my job. (Joke's on them...I already don't have a job!) They said I could freeze my credit card for up to two years with this service and not have to worry about it gaining interest or making payments for two years. I asked if I could make any payments on it while it was frozen. They said no. I said, "Fuck off." Wouldn't you want the option of using a credit card in case of an emergency during those two years? Umm...No thank you.

With two, five minute phone calls I just saved myself about $60 a month in useless credit card fees.

Jesus, people, don't let what happened to me happen to you or your family. Stand up for what is fair and just. Put nasty creditors in their place!

As you were.

Monday March 27, 2006
Who's Going to Make the Cookies?

I was informed that a woman I used to work with died yesterday. Holly Bodger had worked for The Firm I left in Houston for YEARS!

I'm writing about her not because I'm so personally heartbroken to lose her, but because she deserves to be written about. Holly was this Middle-Aged-Mother-Hub-bardesque, quirky character in our office who made her living as the floating night legal secretary. Holly had zero concept of time, but she was the kind of soul that would never tell you no, and she would work until midnight if she had to, ultimately presenting you with perfect work. The Firm likes those qualities in people. So they kept her, and she stayed.

Holly had the gift of high intelligence and was incredibly pleasant. She loved to go on road trips. I remember when she got her PT Cruiser and took a 2,000 mile journey through the colonial states. She was so tickled about her adventure. During the time I knew her, she was also able to buy herself a house. She was so excited, and I'm still kicking myself for not going to her housewarming. She had a tea in honor of the day she cut the ribbon.

She loved her family and her cats so much. I used to tell her that when I died I wanted to come back as one of her cats. Imagine how she spoiled them. Just look at how she spoiled us! Most of her vacations were spent traveling with her family. She leaves behind her parents, a sister and a nephew that simply adore her. Holly told me many neat stories of her childhood in which her family would have themed dinners.

The one I remember hearing about was a Russian feast where they talked about Russian history, music, etc. while such music played in the background and they learned Russian words. What a fun way to grow up.

It's no wonder Holly's true gift in this world was entertaining and nurturing with food! She could really cook and loved to bake. Each year around the Holidays the cookie trays started coming in covered with the most delightful hand decorated treats. She also made about seven different types of dough that she would sell in the office in case you wanted to impress you friends with your "own" homemade goodies.

When my friend Nichole and I were discussing her passing today, she reminded me of times when Holly came through when others didn't. Nichole had thyroid cancer and during her recovery it was Holly who made sure her refrigerator was stocked.

Another former co-worker and I laughed about how Holly was so misunderstood. The Firm wasn't made for people like Holly. When he answered the phone the first words out of my mouth were, "Don, who's going to make the cookies?" He said the holidays were screwed from here on out, as many people we know have been serving her treats for years!

During the dark days at The Firm when I was working nearly seventy hours a week, napping in conference rooms, changing clothes and washing my face in the bathroom before people starting arriving back at work, Holly and I would visit about life and how she always wanted more and to make a difference. We agreed that we didn't want to die at our desks. She encouraged me to get out into the world and really live. Memories like these make me proud that I took a risk, and left my comfort zone and tried out a new part of the country.

One morning when I arrived at work there was a tiny lady bug made out of small stones on my desk. Holly had come around and put one on each of the legal assistant's desks. "It's good luck if a lady bug lands on you, you know?" she said when I figured out it was her. My lucky lady bug has been on my desk ever since. I think I'm going to glue it to my forehead.

It was the extra touch she added to life that made her so special. The late nights, the hand decorated cookies and the extra attention to detail. So here's to my friend, Holly, who was anything but cookie cutter. She brought softness to stressful times and thankfully did not pass away at her desk, but on one of her vacation adventures.

Thank you, Holly, for giving me a little of your luck and inspiration and allowing me to be at peace with my views of the world.

As you were.

Monday March 27, 2006
Bless Me!

Wow! I just sneezed four times with such force that I broke a sweat, won't have to do sit-ups for a month, farted so hard that I almost blew a hole in my pants and instantly had to whiz.

The human body is such an amazing creation.

***Oh, I'm sorry, I swear I just tooted a little. It just made a teeny *squeak*. You guys know what a prude I am, and how I believe that women should never do icky things...

Really, they should just be quiet, barefoot, pregnant and in the kitchen...

Oh wait...Now I just threw up a little. ::eye roll::

Pull my finger...

As you were.

Monday March 27, 2006
American Airlines, Would You Go Bankrupt Already?

In February I flew American Airlines and will never do so again if I can avoid it. I was shocked and disappointed with all of the terrible service and communication break-downs.

::Deep breath in::

Fasten your seatbelts. It's going to be a bumpy ride.

Departing to New Jersey:

I get to the Burbank Airport extra early on my departure date. As I approach the check in counter, the attendant informs me that my flight to New Jersey has been cancelled due to icy conditions...in Texas (I had a layover in Dallas). Right there, I was a little amused. Snow was falling in Jersey, but ice was stopping planes in Texas...Go figure. The man tells me, "We'll be happy to put you on the first flight tomorrow." No. I had to leave that day. I asked about other flights during the day, other airlines... "We'll be happy to put you on the first flight in the morning." I'm not dumb. Icy conditions aren't just going to go away by the morning of the next day. Morning time is when the ice is the worst. Duh. I ask about flights leaving out of LAX. The counter agent tap-pity taps on his keyboard and says, "We'll be happy to book you on the first flight out tomorrow morning." I just stood there. "Look again, would you? I have a pair of Fuck Me shoes in this bag that must be worn tonight in New Jersey." The man smiled and said, "What do you know, there's a direct flight leaving from LAX at 8:00 am."

I was in Burbank. Burbank to LAX takes about twenty-five plus minutes with no traf-fic. That's about an $80 cab ride due to current gas prices. I asked them to pay for the cab. They wouldn't do it! Assholes!! Oh, fuck it. At least I was able to get out of LA.

I get in a very long line to go through security, and I'm the nearly the last one on the plane. There are a few people behind me. I hear the flight attendant say, "Ma'am, if your bag is too heavy for you to lift, you're going to have to check it. I'm not going to put it up there for you." I turn and look. The woman she's speaking to is obviously very pregnant. A man already seated quickly got up, staring at the flight attendant and said, "Here let me do her job for her." What a bitch.

Whatever. I prepare to fall asleep and just as I'm dozing off and feeling the plane start to back up, it stops and the captain comes on and says, "Due to the fact that our airline sucks, I'm drunk and my nuts itch, you're all going to have to change planes. But don't worry, your seating assignments are going to stay the same." Oh Jesus. You must be kidding. So, like cattle we get off the plane and head to the new terminal and go through the boarding charade again. This takes another hour! ::ahhh::

29

And now on another plane, the flight attendant comes on and says, "This is a non-stop flight headed to Newark, NJ. Estimated flight time is about four-and-a-half hours. There is no meal or snack provided. One of our gourmet snack packs may be purchased for $4. It includes cheese crackers, a fruit bar, something that will give you herpes and a meat stick." I heard a passenger yell out, "What the fuck is a meat stick?" Gross.

I never thought I would be so happy to actually be in New Jersey.

Returning to Los Angeles:

I get a phone call on the eve of my return from Travelocity.com. My morning return flight had been cancelled. Let me guess...Ice in Dallas...yep. I was in the car and couldn't really figure out when was best to get a ride to the airport, so I asked if I could call them back. "Yes, that's fine," said the lady. Later I called and rescheduled my return flight and was given a confirmation number: A479B1...I should have known that actually meant: "Guess what? We're going to fuck you around some more."

I get to the airport and try to do the self check-in, avoiding the American Airlines people as much as possible. It won't work. It keeps saying that I'm not scheduled to fly. Arg. I stand in a line of two people and still have to wait twenty-five minutes to talk to someone. I have officially missed my flight. I get to the counter agent and she says, "You were supposed to leave yesterday." "No, I was supposed to leave twenty-five minutes ago," and I gave her my confirmation number. She looked at her screen, made two phone calls and said, "You need to talk to another agent who has authorization to override the mistake you made in scheduling." Ummm, I didn't make a mistake!!! So I talked to another agent, watched her make several phone calls and tap on her keyboard. "Well, look at that, we have a flight for you," she said, as if she just suddenly realized she worked at an airport. "Oh my God, really?" I said, acknowledging that she just realized that she works in an airport.

So...another hour goes by. We board the plane. I pass out sitting next to a man who smells really sweet, yet sour like Chinese food. When I wake up, he's reading the book I brought on the plane. He just smiles and gives it back to me as we land. Whatever. Layover in Dallas, another hour. I'm worn out. Back on another plane. Who am I? A man who looks like he might be a serial killer on the lamb (you know, average white guy, shifty eyes, slightly nasty hair, deeply inhales with his eyes closed as you squeeze by him to get to your seat) is my flight buddy, and just as the plane starts to taxi down the runway, I hear the cough of a small child. The cough becomes a hack, then a retch. Gross. A two year-old not six feet away from me is tossing her guts up. Oh, the smell of the toddler stomach virus. Creepo next to me GRINS!! All of the other people around just kinda' look at each other and hunker down, covering their noses. The flight attendants don't do a thing!!! The poor parents were doing everything they could to keep the mess contained. The dad got up to go to the bathroom and was told to SIT DOWN! When the drink cart came by, they asked for a towel and the flight attendant said, "I'm sorry we don't have towels. You could use the baby blanket you carried on," in this cranky, flat Jersey tone.

Damn. I wonder what they would have done had someone had a medical emergency that required serious attention. "Ehh, let's let them sit a while, see if they turn blue... Wouldn't want to react too quickly. I might break a nail and what if they live? A broken nail for nothing? No way."

What happened to just getting on a plane and taking a little trip? Huh???

I never thought I would be so happy to be in LA.

American Airlines, I detest you. Take your meat stick and shove it. I thought about complaining to the company, but you realize that they would just want to give me a free flight. I don't want to fly with them ever again. So I decided to blog them as dogs. You know what they say, "Have a good experience, you tell a friend-have a bad experience, you tell EVERYBODY!!"

::Exhale, exhausted::

As you were.

Tuesday March 28, 2006
Today in Crash City

I know a lot of you were stunned when Liongate's film, *Crash*, won best picture at this year's Academy Awards. I, however, (probably like a lot of Los Angelinos) felt quite connected to the film and could truly relate to the "Crash Mentality" of LA. There's so much friction in a city as big, young and chaotic as LA. You have so many natives, foreign immigrants and transplants trying to live the American Dream right here in this basin by the sea. People's agitation with the pursuit of happiness leads to using race as a crutch for their own insecurities. All of the friction builds and builds and before you know it, desensitized and frustrated, we crash into each other, seeing only colored bodies, not human persons, forgetting others rights and plights.

While driving south from my neighborhood on a surface street, I got stuck in the typical late afternoon traffic congestion. We all know that traffic makes people do crazy things but, wow, I wasn't expecting what I was a witness to today. Just above Koreatown, about ten minutes from my hood, I was trapped at an intersection by cops who swooped in from the left and the right. I couldn't see much in front of me, as I was behind a big furniture truck. When the truck pulled as far to the side as it could, I saw a SWAT Team vehicle headed north to the scene. The cops were manning their vehicles with their guns drawn, encircling a car filled with Hispanics with shaved heads. Some looked angry some looked scared. (I wonder how I looked.) The cops got on their radio and broadcast: "Driver: Slowly exit the vehicle. If you are armed, dispose of your weapons."

About this moment, I started to snap to it that I might be in the line of fire at any moment now. There was nowhere for me to go. So I just sat there like everyone else. I looked at other cars and some people were staring with interested and concerned expressions. My favorite was the woman next to me in the Mercedes on the phone, using the pause in traffic flow to file her fingernails. There were young kids who had just gotten out of school with their backpacks still on their backs, standing watching, with eyes all lit up like they were at the circus. I was trying to decide if I would fit in the floorboard under the steering wheel or not.

When the SWAT Team moved in, the street beat cops went to move some of their cars. It wasn't to clear the road for traffic; it was to make room to lay all of the guys in the

31

cars out on the street one by one, facedown for search and seizure tactics. Great. Good Lord. Stuck there, I watched the faces of these young men as they each took their spot, spread eagle on the ground. The first one looked blank and vacant. He just slowly got on his stomach and put his face to the ground. The second and third looked pissed, like they didn't deserve this. With swift, jerky movements they reluctantly got on the ground. One actually tried to stare one of the SWAT guys down as he went to his knees. The last one broke my heart. He got out of the car with his hands clasped behind his head, "Please don't shoot me," he begged. He was shaking and tears were falling from his eyes.

God knows what these kids did or were thought to have done, but in a matter of five minutes our paths crossed and they became an immediate part of my world. I could feel so much emotion building in my chest. I wasn't scared or worried about myself. I was worried about the whole situation-so many people in one spot, with their separate lives and agendas forced into each other in an obtuse way. The tension was amazing. I couldn't help but think about the families of these kids with their faces on the ground, the families of the men armed with guns, the families of the people sitting in their cars, the families of the children walking home from school and my own, who I could hear yelling all the way from Houston, "Robin Amber, be careful! Get out of the way. Why do you live there?" I couldn't help but cry.

There we were, crashing into each other, and no one seemed to notice. When the kids were in custody, one of the cops yelled at the furniture truck driver, "Hey, can you move that thing? We gotta' get traffic moving." I thought, "You idiot. It's not his fault we're stuck here."

And just like that, we were slowly on our way again, only to gripe later about being delayed, forgetting the raw emotion a group of people just shared in an intersection.

How do we live so disconnected? How can we not be more concerned about people and how all of our actions truly affect one another? Is it because we are moving too fast? It's hard to breathe when we move too fast. If we don't slow down and learn to catch our breath, these crash scenes are just going to get worse and worse...and no one will notice.

Carefully I say:

As you were.

Tuesday March 28, 2006
Tickle Me Emo

For a while now I've been hearing the term "Emo" to describe a section of the population. I've never been exactly sure who within the population is actually considered to be "Emo." To protect my bee's knees status in this world, I have been careful to keep "Emo" out of my vocabulary for fear of using the term incorrectly.

Future famous filmmaker friend, Jack Tomas (now of Brooklyn) sent out a joke he heard from his brother-in-law:

"It would be great if grass was like an Emo kid."

"Why?"

"Because then the grass would cut itself."

Hmmm....Ok...so Emo kids are cutters? Yikes. Most people who mutilate themselves were molested as children and have serious control issues. I hear kids saying that they are proud to be Emo. I'm getting too old for this shit...

So I emailed Jack and asked him for a definition of "Emo." While waiting for his response I just Googled "Emo" and good Lord; websites galore.

I went to the link that simply said, "What the heck *is* emo anyway?" :click: And I unleashed the mother load. Here's an entire site on how to be Emo. I got my definition and a WHOLE LOT MORE!!! So straight from www.fourfa.com, here's a little gift from me to you:

"This site is intended to be a basic FAQ and primer on emo - short for "emotional." emo is a broad title that covers a lot of different styles of emotionally-charged punk rock. This site is intended to introduce the reader to all the common styles, describe them musically, and give ideas about the essential records of all those styles. You will be an expert in emo, in the broad sense, after reading this website."

According to this website, the whole emo movement is based on music, not just greasy black hair and boys who wear girls' jeans and make-up. I looked at the bands the webmaster lists and there is not one band that I have ever remotely heard of. Hmmm... And I'm sure that these fourteen year-olds I see at the mall walking around all mopey with their super-skinny gaunt figures, barely filling out their size 0 jeans haven't heard of them either. I bet they are just teenagers who in "our day" would have been punk, grunge or goth. Perhaps Maude...I don't know.

My favorite part of this website lists the fashion tips. I mean, really. You can't fuck up the image or the emo leader will smile at you and ruin your life. You'll notice that I have stopped capitalizing the word emo because, well, it's more powerful that way, don't you think?

Overall, I'm quite amused by the whole image. I like the idea of calling it what it is. It's a wake up call to parents. It's the perfect teen image. "Hello, Mom and Dad. I'm so totally emo, ok?" I mean, weren't we all emo in our teens? Hell, I'm emo at least once a month still! The joke Jack's brother-in-law made is closer to true than you realize. emo kids are being open about being emo. Embrace and look out for the emo in your life. In fact, I think we should start an adoption program for emo's kinda' like Big Brother/Big Sisters, you know, take an emo under a wing and make a difference in their lives. Get them some sun, perhaps some protein, or a foundation shade that doesn't completely wash them out. Speaking of washing...teach them to wash their hair...

**These thoughts were meant to bring awareness to the emo style, and not meant to offend or push any emo into rage, depression, extreme bouts of solitude or a suicidal state. So chill the fuck out and eat something, you wispy little freaks!

:)

As you were.

Ugh...

I am still in recovery mode from that "had a nightmare, just woke-up with pillow creases in my face" haze.

Two things ensure a wild night of dreaming for me: sleeping on my back and eating anything with garlic in it before bed. Sleeping on my back is the strangest, most uncomfortable feeling. It's been that way my whole life. I only feel "heavy enough" to fall asleep if I'm at least on my side or on my stomach. When I was younger, my biological father told me the feeling I got when I was on my back was my spirit trying to have an OBE (out of body experience). Wow. I was seven. He was on cocaine. Moving on. The garlic, well, who wouldn't get a little rumbly after eating yummy garlic treats before bed?

Last night after trying a new garlic-tomato-basil sauce on some rigatoni, I seemed to have combined the two.

The dream sequence started out with the typical maddening scene of watching the boy I like make out with my friends on a bed of lettuce, followed by me, with a voice like Jodie Foster in *Silence of the Lambs*, trying to figure out a way to stop it by breathlessly running through a downtown (somewhere), looking for clues in different upscale hair salons. I turned into an alley only to find myself in what looked like the Venice Beach area, cautiously approaching some tough punks with chains staring at me menacingly. Like Julia Sugarbaker from "Designing Women," I sauntered right past them with my head held high only to realize that I was walking into a parking garage with a disco ball and a floor with fire pits. Dancers in chain metal garments and highly imaginative made-up faces were doing this slow creepy interpretive dance crap to no music around me. As they closed in I could feel their breathing, inhaling and exhaling on my face. Then I could hear the sound of a plastic grocery sack crinkling and swishing in a light breeze. It made me feel uncomfortable. Suddenly it was dark and I was alone. My head was spinning and the sound of the plastic sack was still in my head. I couldn't tell where I was, but I knew I was lying down. My eyes were only partially open, but I could see the sack in someone's gloved hands. I feared for my life. Someone was going try to suffocate me with the sack. I was getting really hot, and my mouth was dry. I was at the point where I couldn't tell if I was asleep or really awake. My breath was shallow, and I was about to start screaming. I was beginning to really panic. Then ::snap::. I was now really awake, feeling like there were weights on my body. I was sweating bullets under the bedcovers. Like I was in a pool of syrup, I slowly rolled over onto my side from my back, still feeling creeped out, and went back to sleep.

Anybody want to interpret this? *Note: I always dream in Technicolor!

I woke up later and realized that I had been asleep for almost twelve hours. Not only am I exhausted and want to go back to sleep, I can still taste garlic in my mouth, despite brushing and flossing.

Fuck, what a waste of twelve great hours of sleep that I will never get back. I feel like a two year-old who has just woken up from a nap to find that he/she has piddled in the bed. I'm grumpy, cold, discouraged about getting out of bed and I kinda' want my mommy. She might scold me, though, so fuck it. I'll just lie here while I dry out and whimper a little...

::whiney::...Ehhh...

As you were.

Wednesday March 29, 2006
Blooming Broccoli

So I was on the phone talking to one of my best friends in the world, Eric Co, while making an omelette. We've known each other since we were like four or five. My ingredients were simple: two brown organic eggs, baby broccoli and cheddar cheese. Eric and I were discussing how down-to-Earth his girlfriend is and how bummed he and I both are for missing each other in Houston by a week, etc., when I notice that there were little yellow flowers on some of the broccoli. What the hell? I knew that the broccoli was a little over a week old, therefore a little limp, but I didn't know that it would bloom. And what do you know, it blooms yellow flowers? I mentioned this to Eric, and he said that he had heard of that before, but he wasn't sure from whom. I said I guess that's why they call them broccoli florets, and he said he wasn't sure what a broccoli floret was followed by an immediate conversation subject change request, as we had talked about broccoli long enough. I agreed, and cut all of the little flowers off the stems and only put the good broccoli into my pan. We continued on, discussing our travel plans for the year. He's going to Spain with his girlfriend, and I'm going to Maui to see my friend Denise. I noticed I didn't have quite enough broccoli in my omelette and decided to throw caution to the wind and tossed in the flowers. I smelled them first and they just smelled like, well, baby broccoli. Anyhow, Eric kept saying really nice things about his girlfriend. I can't believe I haven't met her! Eric and I keep swearing that we will go see each other at some point, but he lives in DC and I live in LA...(Funny how we both moved to cities that are referred to by their initials...) Alas, we just have a meal together on the phone from time to time. I swear that omelette tasted like springtime...

I love my dear friend.

I learned something new about broccoli.

I'm going to Maui at the end of the month.

What a great life.

As you were.

Friday March 31, 2006
3121 Funk/0330 Stroke

It was Thursday, mid afternoon, and Prince's new "3121" album was shedding new funk beats and sultry salsa sounds into my living room as I danced. In case you didn't know, when I don't feel like touching the treadmill and no one is around, my living room is transformed into my own private dance studio...Debbie Allen, eat your heart out...

"Black Sweat" was blasting. The beat had me by the soul. My eyes were closed. My body was moving on Earth, but I was dancing somewhere else. Then the phone rang. It was my mother. She was calling from her cell phone. That doesn't happen often. Hmmm...Decided to take that one.

Mother's vocal tone was serious. I knew something was wrong. Her words melted into the music, "Granddaddy has had a stroke." What? He's about to be seventy-nine next month. He can't be having a stroke now. "Is he ok?" I asked. She began to ramble about MRI's and speech therapy. I waited for my "Yes, he's fine," and then put the rest of what she had to say on slow processing. What rotten timing. Grandma's seventy-sixth birthday is Sunday. He can't be in the hospital on her birthday. Good thing I'm going to be home for a visit next week.

After our conversation, "Fury" was rockin' my ears... "no fury like a woman scorned." I found myself alone in my dance studio with no immediate access to a family member-in need for the first time since I left Houston. My feet were moving me back and forth as images of my grandfather faded in and out of my mind: the flat top hair cut and thick, black caterpillar eyebrows, the smell of his aftershave, the way he whistles in the house, the pile of Chapstick Brand lip balm in his trinket drawer, his coveralls that he's been wearing for decades, the dollhouse he built me for Christmas in 1986, his stern look, his gentle nature, his funny expressions... "Gadzoooks" and "E-gadz," his AMAZING love and dedication to my grandmother, his incredible generosity in funding my private university education and the dream of him giving me away my wedding one day. I looked like something out of *Flashdance*...dancing my ass off and crying my eyes out. You can laugh. I started to. I reminded myself of that of "Saved By the Bell" when Jessie Spano got addicted to caffeine pills and A.C. Slater (I think) finds her all "cracked out" and she pants frantically, "I...just...can't...stop...dancing..." Lord...

"Get on the Boat" came on and Prince was telling it like it is, and it dawned on me that is just how my grandfather is...I began to dance with a purpose. Grandpa always says, "And this too shall pass. Ride the tide," in the hard times. If you've ever wondered where I get my rational/practical nature, it was a priceless gift from Theodore F. Nowak.

I always wonder what will happen to the living grandparent when one of them actually does pass away. They are a total package. I called my grandmother a little later, and she was just getting home from the hospital. She was in pretty good spirits, though she sounded a little frazzled. "Are you going to spend the night with Grandpa in the hospital?" I asked. "Oh no. I want him to just get a good night's rest. I'm going to have a glass of wine and take a bubble bath." I paused. "Funny, that's what I was considering doing," I laughed. "The apple doesn't fall far from the tree, my dear," she added. We laughed about how good ol' Ted had perfect timing to take attention away from her birthday. "Last year he bought me a Mustang and this year he gives me a stroke, well gave himself a stroke. Maybe I gave him a stroke," she joked. You read that correctly. My almost seventy-six year-old grandmother drives that 2006 V8 mean machine; the headrests are embroidered with the word "Venom" and she drives with a lead foot, I tell you. My image of her having to pack her bags and move in with my parents tomorrow got pushed back a bit.

When we hung up, I put on "Beautiful, Loved and Blessed." I danced my way into the kitchen and settled for chocolate chip cookie dough and milk, thinking about how lucky I am to have a set of grandparents like Ted and Mary Ann Nowak.

Who would have ever thought that a Prince album would be a part of helping me through a situation as tough as my grandfather having a stroke. Hell, most of Prince's music would GIVE my grandfather a stroke... "Little Nicky," "Pussy Control"...I mean, come on!!!

As you were.

Friday March 31, 2006
Fun At The Supermarket Checkout

Last night I walked over to Albertson's to pick up a few items:

Tampons

Hair Color (Fuck off. I'm poor. I've been doing touch ups at home in between hair-cuts. There, now you know.)

Cookie Dough

Milk

Peanut Butter-filled Hershey's Kisses

Razor blades

Tylenol PM

When I got to the check out counter and put my items on the belt, the checker looked at them, looked at me and with that "don't gaze directly into the monster's eyes" shaky grin and said, "How are you this evening? Did you find everything ok?"

I said yes and completed my transaction.

I'm sure he was thinking, "Oh Christ, here comes one of those crack-headed wannabe actors with PMS, thinking that today is the perfect day for stuffing her face with sweets, only to wind up hating herself afterwards and coloring her hair. When she hates that, she'll try to end it all by overdosing on sleeping pills and then finally by attempting to slit her wrists. Why do I have to work the late shift???"

In case that's what he was thinking, when he asked, "Paper or plastic?" I responded in a maudlin tone, exhaling heavily, methodically nodding my head, "Plastic...I think a plastic bag would do the trick."

I'm a bit bizarre even during the most normal events. I like to keep things spiced-up a tad, you know...just for shits and giggles.

As you were.

Friday March 31, 2006
Betasitting

I am completely amused by my roommate, Michelle M., and her boyfriend. Together they have purchased a fish. Our apartment doesn't allow dogs and frankly neither my roommate or I want to have any animals in the house. But I think this is one of the ways thirty year-olds do that nesting thing I hear about so often. So in our apartment, in a very nice tank, swims a red Beta Fish named Jauncino.

My roommate travels for work quite frequently, and I am put on pet care duty. It's a fish, so no worries. I can feed and walk a fish. I've been taking care of live humans for years. I think I can handle a fish.

However, I am constantly cracking up because of my roommate's emotional investment in this fish. He is to be given eight pellets of food, twice a day. The pellets are not to be thrown into the water. They must be ever so gently set on top of the water so that they don't drop to the bottom. His light must be turned off and on at the appropriate times in the morning and the evening. His water has to be changed constantly (even though betas are swamp lovers and prefer a little green muck to lounge in). I mentioned this to her and she verbally assaulted me, telling me, "When Jauncino's tank is not clean he just hangs around in the reeds and does nothing, but when it's clean, he swims around. He can't see when it's dirty." My favorite of all her overprotective acts are her phone calls. She calls to check on the fish. I'm not sure if she is really calling because, you know, she is like lactating from being too far away from her baby, or if she's just not sure if I'm competent enough to remember his feeding schedule.

I've told her already that if that fish goes belly up on my clock, it will be replaced with one that looks just like him and I will not tell her if he has died. So far, we are in the clear. We are still on Jauncino I.

My question: Why in the hell isn't this fish going to stay with Daddy when she's out of town? It's the start of the classic guppy, I mean yuppie relationship. Mom and Dad are both too busy to raise kids so they hire a nanny. I think they should go to couples pet-raising therapy.

As you were.

Saturday April 1, 2006
3 Lemon Drop Martinis

I hate being intoxicated enough to hear my heart scream at me, yet sober enough to know that my emotions are alcohol induced. ::sigh::

As you were.

Sunday April 2, 2006
Frolic in the Rain

Next to Pantages Theatre on Hollywood Boulevard sits one of my favorite bars in Los Angeles, The Frolic Room. This is the first place I took a gulp from a gin and tonic in celebration of my first night as an official Los Angelino after driving twenty-two straight hours from Houston with my friend, Tako.

The Frolic Room is truly no wider than the inside of a Boeing 737, so dark you could accidentally kiss your sister and brimming with hardest-drinking drunkards I've ever met. The bartenders, Ruben and Joel, have worked there for decades. I wouldn't say that they make stiff drinks, no, more like FUCKING SOLID DRINKS-drinks that make your face contort and your teeth grit. They are also two of my most favorite guys in this whole damn town. The bar offers the kind of atmosphere where, rest assured, you will want to make love to the jukebox, laugh your ass off, meet the most off color, unique characters and stumble out without leaving too much of your wallet behind. I've never had a bad time there. It's always interesting, to say the least...

Saturday night was no exception. Despite the chilly rain, around 9:15 pm Kim and Tra-cy picked me up and we headed over to the bar for "a drink." We walked in and Ruben said, "Hey Rovin!" above the blaring music. We ventured in deeper and waited to place our orders. An overpowering, heavy, foul, oily, musky, super funky stink-stank floated our way. There was a little man just past us who looked like he hadn't had a bath in a month trying to dance with some woman. Dear God, paint thinner couldn't have cut that stench. And just like shit, I knew for whatever cosmic reason, we would attract that pesky fly. As we sat to enjoy our first round and catch up, sure enough, here came French. That's what he was called. I wonder why... I'm not going to lie, I wasn't very nice. When he got within two feet of us and began to dance like a little circus monkey, I just began to say, "NO. NO. NO," with my hands up like they teach at self-defense classes. He tottered off to the bar, but I kept shooting the "stank eye" at the back of his head for good measure.

Within minutes we had another buddy knocking at our door, hoping to chit the chat with us. We'll call him Slick Rick. He started out with pleasantries, just typical crap-talk which quickly turned to giving us his insight into our individual personalities. He only pegged me correctly: "You da one who-wa get down...get down...don't take no shit. I can tell, girl."

Was it my "Fuck Y'all, I'm from Texas" shirt that gave it away, or my blank yet pensive expression on my sweet face? In efforts to relax and not take things so seriously, I inhaled my first drink...I think I may have actually eaten the glass. Drink number two began to flow and we were still dealing with Slick. "Now you girls know I ain't tryin' to get wit nun-uh-ya. My mother, she dead and she tode me ta treat womens like queens." Uh-huh, then get your hands off my friend, fuck face. Suddenly there was an extra round of drinks in front of us, compliments of Slick. Fuck. "This one here is muh girl, see. I like you. You sweet. You what all men want," he tells my friend Tracy as he puts an arm around her. She looked horrified. It wasn't until he planted a huge wet kiss near the corner of her mouth that her backbone arrived and she told him to get lost. He turned to me and tried to argue that he didn't kiss her. A huge string of nasty words flew out of my mouth like bats from a cave at midnight and he left. I missed him for about...oh, wait, no I didn't.

I was really feeling my drinks, thank God, when "my biggest fan" arrived. There is this short coke dealer who hangs out at the bar and has approached me on several occasions by saying things like, "I'm sorry I didn't call you when you gave me your number last time you were here," and when I tell him to eat shit, he says, "You gave me your number. You're name begins with a 'C,' right?" Then he'll tell me things like, "I love your print work," trying to get me to be flattered that he's trying to make me believe that he believes I'm a model. "I'm your biggest fan." What a tool. Ruben LOVES to make me aware of "my biggest fan's" arrivals. I hear him say with his heavy Spanish accent, "Oh Rovin, gee-yess whooze heyar?"

And just as I was getting to know my third drink and trying avoid all eye contact with "my biggest fan," it hits us, like an atomic bomb...a mushroom cloud of ass gas knocked us into the wall. French had let loose a blast of his ultimate internal funkiest stink-stank funk, nearly annihilating the entire bar. People were crumbling at the knees. Their hair was falling out. Some were simply melting into pools of lumpy liquid matter. Before the gas ignited a spark, we dove for our tabs, kissed Ruben and Joel in their gas masks goodbye and were out the door. The rain felt wonderful as it landed on my skin, washing away the funky filmy layer I had just acquired.

The girls were oddly hungry so we stopped at House of Pies. While they ate, I tried to recover from the dizzying experience. I got home, slightly tanked and was fast asleep by 12:45 am. Our adventure had only lasted about three hours, but I felt like I had been out all night. Ahhh, a night at The Frolic Room.

Betcha' can't wait to visit. (My mom loved the place! She got to see a midget dressed like a gargoyle and was hit on by two older women! When she said, "Oh no, I am here with her" -pointing to me- "she's my daughter," the women said: "Wow. That's even better!")

As you were.

Sunday April 2, 2006
What Time IS It??

I hate having to change the clocks for the beginning and ending of Daylight Saving Time.

Right now my laptop says 5:57 am; MySpace says 6:15 am, and my clocks say 4:57 am.

Every year I screw this up somehow. Today is my grandmother's birthday. I have been an hour late to her birthday lunches more times than I can remember.

I hate having the conversation with people trying to explain why it is that we "spring" forward and "fall" back to help them remember which way we go at which time of the year.

There are parts of the country that do not change at all. They aren't lucky. They are just as inconvenienced as we are if not more-having to keep up with how many hours ahead or behind the other states are.

I heard on the news that they are going to change the day we switch over next year. What on Earth for? Just to fuck with our body clocks some more? Jesus. I sleep at the wrong times as is. I don't need any help.

If I had a vote that counted on this issue, I would like to stay in Daylight Saving Time so that we have sunset late in the day. Nothing is worse than driving home from work in the dark after you drove to work in the dark. People need their playtime in the evening to feel like they have utilized their day. Americans would be more active and less obese. There would be less depression and more productivity. Companies would produce more, sell more and earn more. New economic models would emerge!! The budget would be balanced and Rodney King's dream would be realized!!!

Well hell, there you go. I just solved all the world's problems in a blog.

Somebody crank up *The Sound of Music* and pass a fuckin' bill...

As you were.

Sunday April 2, 2006
Ross Realities and Super Power Dreams

Ross. You know you love Ross. It's the discount department store where "irregular," notable name brand clothing, accessories and housewares go to die a horrible death in an unorganized, overstuffed outlet market.

I was attempting to cruise through my local Ross in hopes of finding an inexpensive, durable and most importantly, fashionable laptop tote as I will be traveling with Hope and need to keep her protected.

"I must have come at a bad time," I thought as I began to have trouble maneuvering through the crowd. It was one of "those crowds" where you had a group of women with backsides the size of eighteen wheeler trucks and loud mouths to match, standing in the middle of all of the isles, trying on clothing in front of everyone while quacking at the top of their lungs in a foreign language while their children ran about knocking into people and breaking things. Oh yes, it was that time of day at my Ross.

Simple smiles and "excuse me's" do no good. You have to actually nudge these women out of the way or kick one of their children in the shin. I held my own and kept my cool, but after about the sixth bump n' nudge, I was about to go nuts and start scream-ing, "Imigra!" (Kidding...touchy subject these days...I know...I know...just seeing if you're paying attention.)

The thought of having the power of invisibility with a dematerialization option came to mind. How fantastic would it be if at any moment you could just ::snap:: disappear! You could crawl around where people shouldn't and get through tight spaces by dema-terializing and just go straight through the wall.

Having such powers would provide endless possibilities. Just think of all the places you could go and things you could see. Feel like taking a free trip? ::snap:: Suddenly you're on a plane headed to Australia and no one knows. Want to know what your neighbors are really up to? ::snap:: You've caught them red handed having threesomes with your kids' teacher. Want to know what goes on inside the Vatican? ::snap:: Now the secrets of the city are revealed. Want to know how much money your spouse is re-ally spending at the strip club? ::snap:: There you are enjoying free lap dances.

Just as I was seeing myself backstage at an Aerosmith concert in Steven Tyler's dressing room, I bumped into yet another quacking, truck-ass woman, did the nudge and stumbled upon the purses. After playing offense through whole store, I saw her. Hanging on a rack was Hope's very own pink laptop tote. Not only did she match my luggage, but she was a $14.99 super bargain. For a brief moment I thought I had actually achieved dematerialization right there in the store...::sigh:: but then ::snap:: Back to reality. I had to make it to the cash register...

Arg.

As you were.

Thursday April 13, 2006
6 Weird Things...

My cousin, Megan, "MySpace Tagged" me, and I'm supposed to list six odd things about me. I find this difficult as there are far too many to list. Narrowing them down to just six is like asking me to sacrifice my least favorite internal organs.

Ummm...

1) I have a special way of organizing the fridge. If you don't put things where I think they belong, I will just reorganize them until you get the hint. The same goes for the dishwasher. The odd part, however, I will leave clothing on the floor of my room or at the foot of my bed and just sleep under it forever.

2) My right, upper, inner eyelid has been peeling lately. Gross, I know. I saw the "Good Morning America" reports about blinding eye viruses, and I just haven't felt like paying to go to the doctor. A handicapped sticker might get me better parking spaces, though. I'd rather buy a plane ticket to Maui.

3) When served nearly frozen foil-wrapped butter at a restaurant, I will casually place it (still wrapped) under my thigh for a second to speed up the softening process. If I'm wearing something really nice, I head for the crease of the elbow. No one has ever noticed. Pigs.

4) I love falling asleep just as day is breaking. There is something so peaceful about curling up in bed with that barely blue-gray light coming through the window. I imagine myself as an infant for some reason at this time of the morning.

5) I have been cussing like a sailor since I could talk. The theory of "ignore her and she will stop," failed in a miserable way. My mother kept a journal about me from my toddler days. An entry I saw recently said, "Robin looked under the couch today for something she dropped. When her glasses got in her way, she said 'If I didn't have to wear these shit-god fuckin' damn glasses I could get under here,' she also asks for cold beer often." What a gem. No wonder my best friend, Alba, tells people that I was raised by truckers.

6) I still occasionally host make-believe talk shows into the mirror while getting ready for the day. If you are lucky enough to be in the audience you get prizes. I gave out some really cool t-shirts the other day. One lucky viewer got a trip to Paris.

These are just the tip of the iceberg.

As you were.

Thursday April 13, 2006
Multi-Colored Mullet

My mother...Oh my mother...Where do I start with this woman? I could expel the most amazing stories about her all day long.

She is one of the most original women on Earth. She is rather Bohemian...wears shoes only if she has to, only started wearing clothing inside after her hysterectomy due to a scar she isn't comfortable with, drinks gin like it's Gatorade, gets so whipped up talking that her lips seems to disappear...she's a hell of an educator, a great wife and a zany mother.

She's never been afraid to try things: a Zen alarm clock, shoes that light up, but her biggest splurge: frequent changes in hair cut and color. There was the black pixie she wore most of my life that became the deep auburn, sweet long bob as I got older, then my personal favorite, the spiky eggplant and black messy look. She called it her "concert hair," and kept it during a year of serious concert-going. Elton John, Paul McCartney and The Rolling Stones all came through Houston during the same year, and she was there rockin' her hip do.

Sadly, every high must lead to a low. I never knew she would fall so hard, but she did. I looked at my mother when she picked me up from the airport the other day and almost fainted. Not only did she have tri-colored hair (tawny red on top, yellow and dark brown vertical strips down the back of the neck), but I swear to God she was an inch of hair away from having a full-blown mullet. I waited until we got to the house before asking what in the hell was happening on her head, but fear not, I made no bones about it. My concern came out like this, "Mother, we are very accepting people, but are you trying to look like a butch lesbian? Would you like me to get you some flannel shirts and some Birkenstocks?" There was a weak rebuttal offering some crapola about "Bonnie (her hair stylist) trying something new," and I asked if she had upset Bonnie.

I went to dinner and when I returned the mullet was gone and her hair was in a more flattering, trendy cut and a nice shade of red brown. ::To God Be the Glory::

Just puttin' out fires all over the country; what can I say?

As you were.

Thursday April 13, 2006
Pussy Galore

As I continue to remain single and continue to age, the haunting thought of growing into my twilight years to live alone with cats each named for different ex-boyfriends becomes more and more vibrant. The image of me sitting in my mauve moo-moo stroking them on the front porch keeps moving more and more forward in my mind.

Over the past year my step dad has perpetuated my fear. Now living his dream of being retired from the police force of Houston, he tinkers with his motor homes, motorcycles and well, anything with a motor. He helps friends build things, works out three times a week and generally tries to keep my mother from clogging the garbage disposal. (You'd be surprised how often that happens!)

The Chief, as my mother calls him, has discovered a past time that scares the hell out of me. He has spent the last year taming stray cats. Once upon a time, he was a little rough around the edges and might have been known to shoot cats but that hasn't been officially confirmed or denied. His collection of felines started out with one pregnant cat. Once the kittens were born, someone put out food and they never left the back patio. His skills as an undercover cop were resurrected, as he spent about a week on a cat-trapping steakout in which he lured the cats into a cage and took them to be spayed and neutered. He built them little beds. Each got a food bowl and were given a name: Mama Zelda, Socks, Whitey, Trip, and a whole slew of others. He teaches and trains them with cat toys slowly, making them worship him. There is a routine of visiting with them that occurs at least three times a day. To hear him talk to them is like listening to a father doting on his children. I came in the other night, and he was asleep in his chair with a cat on his chest. What the fuck?

I find it sweet, but disturbing. He has a million hobbies and my mother, yet the cats have still managed to get into the picture. God, am I going to wind up with a zillion cats? It's like a bad Twilight Zone episode. One day I'm going to head home and find my pops covered in fur with a tail and lapping milk out of a bowl, nibbling on cat nip...

I know one thing is for sure; this all goes to show that nothing has more power over a straight male than a little pussy...

As you were.

Leon "The Cat Wrangler" Buenger taking a night off from
The Cat Farm to celebrate my 25th birthday. He's awesome!

44

Friday April 14, 2006
Joblessness is Next to Godliness

While at home in Houston, I was able to catch a performance of a band that is dear to my heart: Rx Medicine Show. I went to high school with one of the band members and to college with two of the others. Seeing them perform their hearts out, made this huge proud grin stretch across my face.

Craig (also known as The Reverend to the band) and I had a conversation that truly boggled my mind and made me realize that my current job situation is no worse than anyone else's.

When I met Craig in 1998 at Guinan Hall at the University of St. Thomas, I was more than concerned about his presence in our dormitory. Frankly, he kinda' resembled an ex-convict: older, shaggy hair, lanky look, dressed pretty plainly, very reserved. Oh! What an ass I felt like when I found out that he hadn't left prison but rather a monastery, hence the less than metrosexual appearance.

Oops. I guess that's where the saying "you can't judge a book by its cover" came in a few minutes too late. You grow into perfection people!! Moving on...

Being a former monk has opened Craig up to many interesting situations. The first that comes to mind is move-in day at Guinan Hall...As Craig was a little older than traditional students, his roommate was older as well. Craig, the former monk met Thomas, the very openly gay porn store sales person. Walking into their room was hilarious. Craig's side was clutter free, extremely minimalistic, orderly and a simple crucifix hung over his bed. Thomas' side looked like a circus in comparison! Some drag queen threw up Broadway musical and risque novelty paraphernalia all over the place. If you stood exactly in the middle you found absolute serenity between two extremes. It didn't take long before they reached common ground and became really great friends, though people did whisper about them in the dining hall...

The notable situation that boggled my mind happened to Craig just before I saw him the other night. Craig had applied for a job in a small parish in Deer Park, Texas, to be, as he says, "a lowly youth minister." Craig has excellent credentials and the Highest of references. The former president of our university is now an archbishop somewhere in Rome and has always offered letters of recommendation to dormitory Residential Advisors which Craig became shortly after moving into the dorms. To his surprise, he didn't even get an interview! What the fuck?

If a former monk with blessings straight from the Pope's Palace in The Fucking Vatican can't get an interview in a small Texas town, what the hell kind of hope do I have for myself anywhere???

Happy Good Fuckin' Friday.

Go see the Rx Medicine Show. They will give you just the dose of healing that you might not even know you need.

As you were.

45

Friday April, 14, 2006
Bathroom Improv

My parents live across the street from the high school I attended. Since, oh, probably 1997, my now former theatre teacher has been sneaking off campus in between classes to have a smoke and a diet coke on our back patio. If my parents ever sold the house, he would be crushed. They would have to actually explain to the buyers that he is a part of the deal.

My mother was leaving the house the other day, and said that he would probably stop by again after second period (around 11:00 am). I love how my mother, a retired English teacher, still tells time in class periods and plans things according to semesters.

Mid-afternoon or so my bowels kicked in, and I was sitting on the pot producing a beautiful number two when I heard the doorbell. "Shit." (Ha ha...I chuckled here as well.) I couldn't just jump up and get the door, but I figured it was him and he would just have a smoke and I would catch him before he left.

Then, something I never would have expected occurred. The bathroom window where I was hard at work was open. I heard footsteps in the grass behind the bushes up against the house coming closer to the window. They stopped. The windowsill was above my head and I was frozen, fearing that he might be looking in. Slowly, I turned my head and looked upward. No face in the window...whew! Like a panther coming up over a rock, I methodically rose and peered out and down at the ground below. To my horror, my theatre teacher was crouched down, casually taking a whiz in my mother's azalea bushes.

I couldn't do anything! I didn't want to scare or embarrass him, but God, it would have been funny had I leaned out and said in a low throaty voice, "Had you waited another five minutes you could have done that inside like a civilized man." He probably would have, well, shit.

Instead, I just slid down the wall and sat there on the bathroom floor and waited. He taught us a lot of improvisational theatre, but I don't recall ever working through a scene like this one. I heard his footsteps fade away and looked out to see him leaving the yard. Couldn't he have just waited until he got back to the school to go to the bathroom? Dear God, does he pee in the bushes everyday?

I've always been impressed with how those bushes bloom. Now I know why. I guess he's a part of the built-in amenities like the dishwasher, the solar screens or the automatic garage door.

As you were.

Friday April 14, 2006
Kamikazed at Karaoke

I can't sing. I do not sing in public. I shouldn't sing in public. Actually, due to city ordinance, any melodic attempts that leave my mouth must happen in the shower or on lone late night drives. (With mutual consent, occasionally, a second person may be present for such activities.)

With that in mind...

I went to see some of my most fabulous friends at Guava Lamp-a gay bar. My friend Toddicus hosts karaoke on Wednesdays and Sundays. The show is a lurid array of R-rated, audience-interactive salty humor in between remarkable renditions of eighties ballads, and oddly enough, country music. (Thanks to *Brokeback Mountain*, "Cowboy Chic" is soooo IN.)

During the show, Toddicus yelled out to me, "Bean, get up here and tell everyone about my balls." Trying not to fall over laughing I headed for the stage, thinking I would tell everyone about how I truly believe that if Toddicus had been on the Titanic, fewer people would have drowned because he has the biggest balls of any man I've ever known. Damn, them some big ol' balls...Lord. If he's wearing just baggy enough pants, he can stand with his legs apart and sway his hips back and forth, and I swear to God you can see his balls bouncing back and forth through his jeans! I learned about his ginormous nuts back in college when a bunch of us somehow wound up skinny dipping in an apartment complex pool. I thought Toddicus had some flesh-colored floatie down there. They really are simply fuckin' baffling.

Anyhow, I get to the stage, prepared to tell a room full of gay men something they probably already know about Toddicus, and instead, he grabs me and says, "Bean, you've been Kamikazed. While Robin sings this next song, all kamikaze shots are $1.50." What the fuck?

The music to Patsy Cline's "Crazy" came on and I just stood there, shaking my head. "Sing, Bean," he said. My best friend in the whole world, my Main Gay, Josh, and his friend, Sean, stormed the stage and began to sing, trying to get me to sing. Truthfully, I have sung that song at every shower concert I have hosted since I was nine, yet I couldn't remember a single word of the damn thing. I looked out into a sea of glittering queens and metros and managed to croon out a few verses. What a horrible experience. I never want to sing on a stage again. I love to make people laugh, but this is not the way I was hoping to accomplish bringing smiles to people's faces.

Back to the showers for me...

As you were.

Sunday April 16, 2006
Raving About The Lord

In an effort to purchase an accordion file to better organize my bills for next years tax-time adventure, I stupidly went to Target around 8:30 pm last night. Why stupid, you ask? My single, childless dumb ass forgot that it was the night before Easter Morning. I was nearly run over by frantic breeders doing last-minute shopping as they pillaged the store for whatever might be left over in order to entertain their homegrown materialistic children on one of the Holy Days in the Christian Faith.

Somehow, knowing I was going to hang out with some friends for Easter, I became a little intoxicated by their frenzy and got a wild hair up my ass to bake these adorable little star-shaped mini-cakes out of "funfetti" batter. I must have been high, because I also decided that it was a grand idea to buy food coloring and make icing in different pastel shades. It didn't stop there. While driving home, I made a second stop at Albertson's and bought shredded coconut to color, jelly beans and glitter candles. While walking towards the check out I saw a hot pink cake. Upon close examination, I realized it was an Easter Bunny! She hopped right in my cart.

While mixing and coloring and taste testing, I started to wonder what in the hell I was going to do with all of these damn mini-star cakes. Just then I heard my next door neighbor unlocking his door. I flung open the kitchen door and told him that I had been domesticated and he had better get in my kitchen to experience the glory. He did. He said he was on his way to listen to some DJ's spin somewhere south east of USC and asked if I wanted to go. "Fuck yeah, dude. Help me ice the little fuckers and we'll get out of here."

My useless Betty Crocker-ass loves a little rave.

We drove into the hood. I love these kinds of underground shows. You have to call a number late into the evening on the day of the event to find out where the DJs are going to be set up.

After walking through the door and getting full-on frisked by a nice lady, we were given our armbands and proceeded inward. My ears were flooded with heavy beats and electronic sounds mixed with, oddly enough, rock music, then brass, then piano music. "Oh this is going to be good." I couldn't help but be absorbed instantly. We scanned the room and made our way through the diverse crowd. I let myself realize that I was older than every girl in the room for only a minute. The crowd was pumped, everyone expressing the beats in their own way. I maneuvered my way closer and closer to the speakers. Absorbing the beats, I felt one of my most favorite feelings in the world: the breeze that is created by the thump of the speaker.

Dancing, lost in the music, feeling the beats and breeze...EXHILARATION...You can't help but KNOW yourself right then...KNOW you are alive...KNOW you have a purpose...KNOW that there is a higher driving power that has given you life.

I got home around 4:00 am with my knees aching a tad, sweaty, smelling like the fog machine and weed. I slept the deepest sleep ever and woke up wondering if the children who found chocolate bunnies, Peeps and sidewalk chalk in a basket with plastic grass in their living rooms got the same sense of God that I got this Easter.

*An aside: While at Target, I saw that they only had two packages of Peeps left. They were this ugly, deep orange color. I asked someone if they still had any other colors besides, "these ugly orange fuckers." With her face all screwed up she said, "No, those are the last ones. And those are red, by the way." I squinted and thought, "Nope...Orange, deep orange, but those are certainly orange." I looked at the package which said, "Made exclusively for Target." I walked back over to her, "I see why you have been led to believe that these are supposed to be Target Red, but they are not and that's why they are still here on Easter Eve," I said as I held them up against her red Target work shirt so she could see the difference. She just looked at me like I was crazy, but I am, so the look on her face was fine with me.

Oh, and I got my accordion file also. I know some of you are anal and wondering.

As you were.

Sunday April 23, 2006
Sneaky Wes Craven

I live by a few personal rules that I try not to break, one of which is that I never watch scary movies alone or right before bed. Until a little over a year ago, I was a single female living alone. I felt no need to feed the animals in my subconscious that would most certainly make me crazy if I allowed too much suspense and terror creep in. Hell, I have my own living demons to deal with. There's no need to conjure up some extra ones that exist only in my mind. However, I have a roommate now and I feel that if I'm going to be a part of "The Industry" in Los Angeles, I need to be a little more brave in the movie-watching department.

For a reason that probably relates to special effects make-up or a comment someone made somewhere, I ordered Wes Craven's *The People Under the Stairs* from Netflix. I had been putting off watching it, as I was concerned that it would scare the shit out of me. Before watching it tonight I even tried to get one of my friends to come watch it with me. I didn't tell her that I would probably sit in her lap for most of it. Rather, I told her that I would make her some delicious Abuelita hot chocolate to drink. She declined. *Note to self: Next time offer a meal.

Determined to watch this movie, I took a nap from 8:00 pm to 1:00 am to ensure that if I was scared to death, I could at least stay awake long enough to see the sun come up, walk around outside, maybe go to a local diner and get some breakfast before going to bed.

I wound up making myself my own mug of Abuelita hot chocolate and prepared to sit alone on the couch, holding my breath with a blanket over my head. I pushed play, and what I saw surprised me.

Wes Craven didn't make a scary movie; he made a social satire about culture in Los Angeles. I wound up laughing more than anything. It was great. The whole movie is about how rich white people keep coming into the ghetto, tearing down the current housing, kicking the people out and constructing big business buildings instead. To get the message across, he suggested the notion that these white people are incestuous freaks that hide and oppress other freaks under the stairs. When they misbehave, the hidden freaks are beaten by the oppressive freaks who wear full leather bondage gear. Their prize keep is Alice, who "behaves just enough" to manage not to have to live under the stairs. Fed up with being run out of town, a couple of the tenants of one of the freako's next demo projects decide to burglarize their home. They get trapped, and two of the three die horrible deaths in this house of terror. The other, a thirteen year-old boy nicknamed Fool, befriends Alice, steals some of their gold and manages to escape. He realizes that he has to go back to save her and the future of Los Angeles by sticking it to the man. While he's doing that, the community of people who have been kicked out of their homes storm the front yard of the house. Fool saves the day by blowing the house to bits while Alice kills her crazy mother and frees the people under the stairs. Money that was stashed in one of the rooms in the house showers the poor people standing on the lawn. The creatures under the stairs join the dancing people on the lawn while early nineties hip hop music fades in and the credits begin to roll.

What? What a riot! I could go on all day about the metaphors in this movie, but you should just go rent it for yourself. Are all horror films like this? Have I been missing out?

The best part is that I'm pretty sure the house used for filming still exists and is on one of those overpriced Hollywood Homes Tours, unless some rich white people came in and tore it down to build a nicer one.

*And for the record, I'm still awake in order to squash the image of that dirty hand coming through the vent in the wall. Social Satire or not, some visuals cause me to be a complete weenie.

As you were.

Sunday April 23, 2006
Fortune Cookie Faith

I've eaten countless fortune cookies in my life. For a long time the fortunes in the cookies had little effect on me, as they were usually trite clichés like, "A penny saved, is a penny earned," or "You will live a long and prosperous life."

A few years ago, I started eating at this Vietnamese restaurant in Houston called Mai's. I fell in love with the place in college when I discovered my appreciation for spring rolls and tofu. They are open almost all night, serve fast, cheap food and, to my surprise, fortune cookies that double as guidance for my life. They are usually so dead on to what is going on in my life, that I began saving them about two years ago.

The first one I not only saved, but taped to my forehead and wore around the office which I was shackled to at the time. It said, "You deserve a good time after a hard days work." I hadn't seen the outside of the office during daylight hours in months. Out of the blue, someone ordered Mai's, and that was the message I got. I left work on time that day! Who cares if people thought I was nuts for taping it to my forehead? Hopefully they got the message, too.

I have actually attached the fortunes most dear to me to the steering wheel of my car. Right as I was about move to California, doubt and apprehension started to creep in. After a night of drinking, a group of us headed to Mai's and my fortune read, "It's time for something new." "Sure is," I thought. Then, about a month later, I was about to give my two week's notice to my boss. The night before, I had eaten at Mai's with my friend, Tako. My fortune said, "It would be smart to accept the next proposition you receive." I initially laughed thinking I was being told to take home a hooker. The next day when my boss offered me a job in the LA office, I accepted, being fully aware I was going to hate working there. Better to go to LA with a job than without one. The final weeks before my move were super stressful. Work was heating up, and emotional strain between family and friends was killing me. I was trying so hard to do all of the right things. You guessed it. I ate at Mai's and my fortune said, "Keep up the hard work and you will be rewarded." With tears in my eyes, I thought, "I fucking hope so." So far, each day in LA (minus about five) has been pretty bliss-filled…minus the traffic, of course.

As of late, I've been living the "only conventional in LA lifestyle" that hard working nine-to-fivers scoff at but crave. I have been wondering if I'm doing the right thing, and how I should best direct myself. Naturally during my last trip to Houston, I ate at Mai's. When I opened my fortune it read, "You create your own stage. Your audience is waiting." I laughed and thought, "Time to get cracking on that book you want to write." Then I was surprised by an event in the airport on the way home. I got a call from an extra's casting agency I had registered with months ago. The casting director asked me if I was available to work the following week on a feature film starring Cameron Diaz, Kate Winslett, Jude Law and Jack Black. I was stunned and jumped at the opportunity. I wound up working for five days with a happy introduction to the other side of the business. I gained huge experience and met Brad Wilder (and his very nice team) who is Reese Whitherspoon's make-up artist. I had that moment where I remembered being in my bedroom as a little girl, playing dress-up and imagining what it would be like to be in a Hollywood movie. I had no problem with that camera being in my face, let me tell you. (I fear you will never see that footage...that's another long story.) You better believe I'm carrying that fortune with me at all times right now!

I need to find out what fortune cookie distributor Mai's buys from and see if they have a direct mailing program...you know, a Fortune Cookie of the Month club. Plane tickets are expensive, people!

*He he he...Standing next to Kate Winslett this past week made me laugh. When I was eighteen years old, I lost my virginity. As the miraculous event was taking place, *Titanic* was playing in the background. I so wanted to turn to Kate and say, "I should have known that relationship was going to sink just as fast as that ship. Thanks for the warning." Alas, I did not.

As you were.

Sunday April 23, 2006
Relationship Leftovers

Today while folding a shirt I realized that I hadn't purchased it, I had stolen it. I had stolen it from the last guy I dated for silly reasons. The amorous reasons of loving that shirt had faded, (more like had been blacked out with a huge Sharpie) but I still I folded it in a certain way, the way that guy folded his shirts. I have actually picked up the way he folds shirts, as I like the fact that they wrinkle less and save space.

I got to thinking about myself and what I have truly been left with over the years from the dudes that have sauntered in and out of my life. This is what I have come up with.

1) Never date a guy whose father openly talks about how he hates the guy's mother. This guy will have anger issues. If he can't or hasn't dealt with them, you'll get to.

2) Some guys will actually sleep with your friends. Find better "friends."

3) Just because you share a lot of the same interests doesn't make the fact that he deals blow ok.

4) Men who tell you that they actually love you, but just can't date you and continue to fuck every girl in town, don't actually love you.

5) If a guy has a hard time telling you how many sexual partners he's had in his life, walk away.

6) If you aren't married to him, his suicidal tendencies aren't your problem.

7) If a man asks you if you are gay because you won't sleep with him, it is ok to kick him in the nuts. That's what an angry lesbian would do, right?

8) When a guy has rules for dating like, "Never leave a sure thing for a better thing," for the love of God, never be his sure thing.

9) If he looks way too good on paper, he's probably not so put-together in his own head. Proceed with caution.

10) A man covered from head to toe in tattoos probably has a lot of baggage, no matter how sexy he is.

11) Chefs are culinary artists. Artists tend to be crazy. Get it?

12) An "older man" doesn't really want to be your husband.

13) A man who tries to sell you drugs as a "dance-enhancement supplement" can be appreciated as a dance partner for life, nothing more.

14) If his mother tells you something like: "If you think you are going to take my baby from me you can forget it. You have been warned," followed by "It doesn't matter, he would never leave his mommy anyway," ask to be taken home that minute. (Even if that means being driven to the airport)

15) If a twenty-eight year-old man looks at you after seeing *Passion of the Christ* and says, "Jesus changed the world by age thirty," and decides not to spend the night, chances are you're about to be dumped. He might be about to start a crusade or something.

16) A man who has to spend more money on his wife being divorced from her than he did when he was married to her is more married to her than ever. Uttering, "Would have been cheaper to keep her," will assure you no second date.

17) A man who dreams of living out in the country away from the city life might actually wind up doing just that, no matter how hideous you find the idea.

18) When a grown man refers to his parents in conversation as "my mommy and daddy," it is ok to be grossed out and leave before the check comes to the table.

19) If a man thinks it's a great idea to live next door to his mother forever, he's probably not very ambitious.

20) If a man breaks up with you in an email, you should reply to him, carbon copying all of the people in your contact list. Be sure to go back through those stupid jokes he forwarded you and include his friends and family in your thoughts.

21) A man who accuses you of giving him The Clap without even knowing if he officially has it should be shot.

22) Men who think they are nice guys aren't always nice guys. (And just because their mother's tell them they are, doesn't make it so.)

23) When a man doesn't ever attempt to open a door for you, trust me, he will close one on you in a heartbeat.

24) Sometimes guys just want to fuck. Deal with it.

25) A man who NEVER invites you to HIS home should not be dated.

And you thought I was going to go on and on about all of the warm things I remember about old boyfriends. I'm optimistic, but for fuck's sake, I'm a realist. I'll get all mushy when a guy proves himself worthy of such mush. ;)

As you were.

Sunday April 23, 2006
When All the Work Is Done, There's Always Laundry

My apartment building has a sign on the laundry room door that says, "Last load at 8:00 pm."

This makes me a little peeved because I'm a night owl, and I like to do laundry in the middle of the night. I assume that we aren't supposed to do laundry in the middle of the night because the washer and dryer might make too much noise, but I live directly across from the laundry room, and the sound is no more bothersome than any other apartment building noise.

I find it funny that the management will control things like laundry times, yet they won't control other things that might not be noisy, but certainly be a bother. What could be bothersome, you ask?

Let's see:

1) The overpowering odors of neighbors' food and smoking accessories that creep into our apartment.

2) The fact that we are only allotted one parking place, when we have a two bedroom apartment and there are empty parking spaces in the garage.

3) They must love to hear lovers quarrel. I must be the only one who gets tired of being rattled out of my sleep by, "Fuck you, fuck you, bitch! Knowing you, you probably sucked his cum down like a milkshake," coming from the courtyard.

4) Is it too much to ask that our sink not back up just because the man next door uses his garbage disposal? I'd rather hear the washing machine than walk into my kitchen to find vichyssoise spilling over onto the floor. If we aren't supposed to put food particles in the garbage disposal, why were they installed?

I wonder what would happen if I left my laundry on their doorstep with a note that said: "You must want to do my laundry since you are telling me when I can and can't. Easy on the softener, please."

More than anything, what bothers me is that I am such a stickler for rules and guidelines that I feel guilty sneaking in there to do laundry at 3:00 am. I'd hate to upset the manager. They are really nice people and we have a great apartment at a great price in one of the best neighborhoods in town. If one of them came and scolded me, I'd feel about an inch tall. (Shut up. I know I'm short as is. Let's move on.) And that ticks me off as well. Why is it that at the age of twenty-six I still feel like I live in a dormitory?

"*Last* load at 8:00 pm," huh? Well good thing my *first* load doesn't start until 8:30 pm at the earliest, right? If they really want us out of there at 8:00 pm, then they should put a lock on the door.

Gotta' go put the last load in the dryer.

As you were.

Sunday April 23, 2006
Tossed by TSA

On the eve of departing for vacation in Maui, I have begun to pack. I guess you could say I have begun to repack. I never completely unpacked from my trip to Houston two weeks ago.

In fact, my pink suitcase has been napping on my bedroom floor while its contents are slowly picked through. I only took out what I needed. Frankly, I'm a lazy bitch, and I knew I would just be shoving most of the same crap right back in it tonight.

As I began to move things around I noticed a piece of paper in my bag that I didn't recognize. It was a "Notice of Baggage Inspection" from the Transportation Security Administration. Eww. Creepy. I find it very unsettling that some person I don't know opened my bag and went through it without me present. At least they were kind enough to leave a little note. I know they are trying to keep people safe, monitor drug trafficking and whatever else, but I can only imagine what they thought when they opened my pink bag:

Q: "Holy shit, this bag is perfectly packed. I wonder if she has this bugged so that she knows if even one thing is moved out of place?"

A: Guess not, since I didn't notice the government note until two weeks later.

Q: "Does this girl really need this many different bottles of perfume?"

A: Yes, and trust me, you do, too.

Q: "Two bags of toiletries?"

A: It used to be three. I've learned to consolidate. Fuck off.

Q: "I see bras but no underwear..."

A: Do the math.

Q: "How old is this girl? I see birth control pills, but this is a Rainbow Brite Journal."

A: I'm old in the loins, but young at heart.

Q: "Who travels with four jars of Smucker's Red Plum Jam?"

A: I live in Knott's country and can't find it anywhere in town. It's my favorite. Friends keep me stocked!

Q: "Does that shirt really say, 'Fuck y'all, I'm from Texas'?"

A: Uh...yeah. Take it as you will.

I couldn't help but wonder if people ever find that they have lost anything after one of these checks. I don't travel with anything expensive, and if I did it would be in my carry-on anyhow. One thing that bothered me is that the notice was in English on one side and Spanish on the other. Where was the representation for all of the other languages? I'm sure my non-English speaking Romanian neighbors would wonder what the hell was going on in their luggage if they opened it and noticed that it was slightly tossed. If they are going to go so far as to alert people who speak English and Spanish, couldn't they just print up an informational pamphlet like Sony does for its electronic products?

It's the least they could do since they've taken away silverware on airplanes and made our security clearance time at the airport about three hours longer than it should be. It's too bad that people complained about being felt up during the body search. Whatever does a body good. You paid for it after all; might as well get yours.

Bub-bye...

As you were.

Monday April 24, 2006
YOU Do the Math!

My friend Deb says that she thinks she likes boys more than math.

I say boys and math are the same; just problems.

Then I realize that I have never had an orgasm doing math.

Deb always has been faster at solving logic equations than me. I guess that's why she's the one going to grad school in the fall. ::sigh::

As you were.

Thursday May 4, 2006
Flying Really Sets the Mood

Headed to Maui:

I knew I was on a real vacation when I boarded a sparsely filled Continental Flight to Maui and instead of getting one First Class seat, I got three coach seats all to myself. I set up a little bungalow made of all the extra pillows and blankets from my empty row. It was cool and quiet. There were funny announcements made about going to Maui for engagements or perhaps divorces, and peaceful Hawaiian music played for a while. The flight attendant brought out the meals (that's right a full meal) consisting of little pizzas, macaroni salad, kettle chips and Pepperidge Farm Cookies (a blissfull carbohydrate overload). I snuggled down, all wrapped in my cocoon with my book and ginger

55

ale fizzing on the tray next to me. The flight attendant walked past, stopped and said, "I have never seen this." I'm a short pistol and am able to stretch out completely across the row. Upon arrival, Denise traditionally greeted me with a pretty set of leis before we jumped in her Jeep. I was in a balmy paradise!

Headed back to Los Angeles:

I knew my vacation was over when I arrived at the Maui airport a week later to see a long line of freshly sunburned, hungover, depressed looking people standing next to these plastic, waist-high barricades of yellow, featureless Candyland men with the message: "USDA Quarantined Area Do Not Cross" taped to them. That was comforting. I was somehow loaded down with extra stuff to carry on, and checking in took FOR-FUCKING-EVER! They combined two flights and about eighty people bound for Houston were suddenly hating the ten people they felt were responsible for delaying their flight two-and-a-half hours in Los Angeles. I was saying silent prayers that I might luck out and have at least one empty seat next to me. No. I did luck out that I was sitting next to two gay filmmakers from Colorado working on a documentary called, "Flying the Ama." Or was it "Sailing the Ama?" I couldn't move for five-and-a-half hours. THEY DIDN'T FUCKING FEED US!!! I was way too warm and so uncomfortable! Upon arrival, my friend Ryan picked me up, only this time I was the one giving gifts of pick-up appreciation (Oh, shut-up. I gave him a Hula Girl for his dashboard...gutterbrains). I was saddened to see that LA's June Gloom arrived a month early. I flew into a congested bowl of pea soup. Ugh.

What to do, what to do...Better go to Chicago at the end of the month for Tako's birthday...

As you were.

Thursday May 4, 2006
Like a Fish Out of Water

I'm twenty-six years old.

I pretty much know my likes and dislikes. I will not lie; I'm still learning about myself. Vacations are sometimes the best places to see new sides of yourself.

I found myself being asked, "Do you want to go snorkeling?" by Denise as we sat at a bar in Maui called, of all things, Nachos. (With the crap ass Baja Fresh Mexican food in LA, I wasn't interested in seeing what Maui had to offer in that department at all.)

No one had ever actually asked me if I wanted to go snorkeling, certainly no one who fully planned to take me snorkeling with in the next forty-eight hours. She followed her first question with, "You know how to swim, right?" Well, yes I KNOW how to swim, but I'm not sure that I'm a strong enough swimmer to get out in the middle of the fucking ocean and survive some crazy current. I had these flashbacks of being in High School at the Naditorium, out of breath as we were instructed to swim lap after lap. I sucked! I still remember the day I got out of the pool and asked Coach Wiley if I could just be the swim team manager. Thankfully, she said, "Sure." (She knew I sucked as well and that there was no future Olympian in me) Back to my Mai Thai at Nachos: "Yeah, I can swim," I told Denise nonchalantly.

The next day we went and picked up my "gear." I can't lie. I didn't really want to get out of the Jeep. I just wanted them to say, "I'm sorry. You're too short to snorkel." I would have been fine with that, but no. The guy behind the counter said, "You have the smallest foot. Here, take this gear for free and bring it back within a month." Christ.

We headed to Honalua Bay. Actually getting to the water was a feat. We parked somewhere on a narrow road and began the hike down into the tropics. We had to pass through this steep, magical jungle, cross a bubbling stream and then scale a rocky area just to put our feet in the water. I must have looked like a total retard, because the second I got near the water, a couple getting out offered to help me get in. He smiled, extended his hand and said (like a father teaching a child to walk), "Come on in. You can do it." She said, "Don't worry, those fish never let you get that close." He chimed in, "Remember, little fish don't eat bigger fish." Denise didn't make me look any better by adding: "It's her first time." It's a damn good thing I look like a twelve year-old when I'm wearing a bathing suit and no make-up. I felt like one.

I was in the water with my fins, mask and snorkel on. I had to get coordinated. Naturally, I wanted to breathe through my nose, and as I would try to inhale, I would only suck the mask tighter to my face and cause myself to gasp harder through the snorkel. There were some slapstick moments where my mask wasn't tight enough, so water would come in. Then I would pull my head out of the water, fling it back too far and inhale water into my mouth because the spout of the snorkel was now in the water. Lord. I was so out of my element. The water close to the shore was actually murky, and the rocks were covered in green scratchy shit that kept me shuddering with every touch.

"This is beautiful, serene and I will be amazed with what lies beneath." Oh fucking Christ. What does lie beneath? ::shudder:: What if there is some lost, huge fish that decides that I'm it's mother and that I need to nurse it or something? What if I see a dead body weighted down by a lost VW Bug?

Denise kept saying, "You have to relax and swim out a little farther where the water is clear." Right. With each kick the shore was getting smaller and smaller behind me. I could hear my breathing which reminded me of being on a respirator. "Oh, God. I'm going to wind up on a respirator if I'm not careful." Slowly, the water was clearing and there were a lot of fish about several feet below me. It was pretty exciting to get that close to some of those beautiful creatures. I felt like I was in an aquarium. That came to a halt when I saw that there was an eel just below me. "Welp, it's been real and I'm out. Late, yo." And I swam back to the shore.

When Denise made her way back, she asked if I was ok and said, "God, you took off swimming like you were in a race!"

I told her about the eel, and she laughed while I tried to catch my breath. I was the one laughing actually, wondering if I would have become a swimmer had they just put some eels in the pool. Doubtful.

*Oh...the amount of time I was actually in the water amounted to about ten minutes at the most.

I liked snorkeling. I even did it more than once while I was in Maui and would like to go again, just under my own conditions: clear water, no algae, no crap floating that might get in my ears...I tell you what, if you'll just put some plastic fish in the bathtub, that would be great. Thanks.

As you were.

Friday May 5, 2006
Sandblasted

Napili Bay is my favorite spot in Maui. I spent as much time there as I could get away with. The bay was close to Denise's house and had a perfect tree for me to park my stark, white ass under with a book all day if I felt like it.

One of the days Denise and I went together to park, sit and read, my breath was taken away when, out in the distance, whales were spouting water into the air and playing about. Seeing those whales having a ball in the waves unleashed my inner child. Armed with SPF 50 w/titanium dioxide, we hit the water and began to body surf for what wound up being about three hours. I've never felt so alive and free! We sounded like little kids: "Oh, here comes the big one!" We giggled and screamed like school girls. Ok...maybe that was just me. Fuck off.

The force of the waves was amazing. I don't know if I'm lopsided or just completely out of shape, but I was thrown around like a rag doll! I can't count the times I came up on the shore sideways, backwards or upside down. Sometimes I would just hold onto Denise and let her guide me like my mom used to when I was a kid. My bathing suit spent more time clinging to my neck than covering my ass. I had a serious collision with a middle-aged man and his boogie board in which awkward contact with body parts was made. He jumped back, like, fifty feet, apologizing. I laughed and just asked him to help me up. Then I pulled my bathing suit back into place as a boat-load of sand fell out. We had polite chat for a moment or so. He was from Chicago...blah blah blah...then his wife showed up and he scurried away.

Sand...Dear God...sand. The sand at Napili Bay isn't fine. It's a much more hearty-very granular. I began to realize that it wasn't leaving my body. It was sticking...to my scalp, to my sunblock, in my suit and in my naughty bits...places where God never intended light, man or thought to venture...

::sigh:: This may be more than some of you can handle, but I will gracefully say, being on my period during this trip was a good thing. I was plugged, which helped filter some...but not completely. Please, squirm. I did.

I have friends who participate in the cleansing of the colon; the high colonic. I can say that I now have as well. I had an anal sandblasting that I'm still kinda' recovering from. I'm walking better now, thanks for asking.

In the shower that night I shampooed, conditioned, scraped, combed and rinsed my hair for about forty-five minutes. That shit wasn't coming out without a fight. Sitting on the couch after my shower, I was still scratching sand loose. I had experienced the exfoliation of a lifetime.

I'm still finding sand in places that it shouldn't be...like my lip gloss palette, my suitcase and yes, my HAIR!!!

No lie, I loved every minute of that afternoon. If it wasn't for the fear of skin cancer, getting sucked out to sea or having my neck broken by one of those rad waves, I'd still be in the water right now. If I sit very still I can still feel the motion of the waves knocking into me, a feeling I used to love after a long day at the beach as a child.

As you were.

Friday May 5, 2006
Let's Get Necked

I love going to the drum circle in Venice Beach on Sunday evenings in LA, so when I got wind that there was a Sunday night drum circle in Maui, oh, I was IN! A drum circle setting the sun is like going to church for me.

There was a catch...it was on a nude beach. So what? I don't care. I don't have a problem with nudity. I love nudie bars; why wouldn't I love a nude beach? My hippie mother had me out at Hippie Hollow in Austin in 1979. I have an eighty-something nudist uncle in Northern California. I'm cool with the skins!

(After my experience in the sand the day before, I didn't understand why people were so eager to get down in the sand sans loin cloth, but I'm a weenie, so whatever)

Getting to the nude beach was a bitch. I understand that in order for it to be a nude beach, it must be secluded and not visible from the road, etc. However, I really wish I would have known I would be frickin' rock climbing to get to the neckedness and the drums. I realized that the childlike feeling I had in the waves the day before was all in my head; I nearly blew out one of my knees carting my ass over the last big step.

The drums: ehh...not as amazing as the two-hundred plus crowd that is drawn to Venice Beach, but the overall atmosphere was pretty awesome.

Ok...Let's get down to it-the people who were baring it all. I was surprised that more men were completely nude than women. There were more people clothed than not clothed. And here were my thoughts:

1) Why does a huge fat man think that it's a good idea to stand facing the water and do yoga completely naked? No one else was doing orifice exposing stretches in front of everyone!

2) My favorite naked male had to be the hot, tattooed, well-hung man with his two kids building sand castles and body surfing. Not only was he strutting around with the "I'm hot, and I have a huge cock" walk, but he also had the offspring to prove that his piece worked not once, but twice.

3) I don't know if it's the maternal instinct in me (dear God, do I have one of those?) or the nanny in me, but I just didn't like the fact that there were kids on this beach. It's one thing for adults to be nude and to respect bodies, but there was just something creepy about a naked man fucked out of his mind on God knows what dancing around someone else's kids on the beach. People who might harm children are anywhere and everywhere.

4) I saw a penis that was so small it looked like a sausage medallion. My hat goes off to him for being willing to just let it sit out there. That's right, sit. Lord knows it wasn't hangin'. Denise made me laugh when she said, "I don't even think he could hold it to pee." A friend of mine said, "Maybe he's a grower, not a shower." No. No way. He lost that thing in the war...

5) The only thing being sold on this beach was massage services. Now that's great. Get necked, get exfoliated by the sand and get a massage. The man had a sign that said, "Great Deals." "How great?" I wondered. I bet that man made no money, but had a great time.

6) I saw only beautiful nipples on the women who bared the breasts. I have a thing against ugly nipples. I just find people unattractive if they have nasty nipples. Kudos to you ladies.

7) Ahhh...Droopy cooter. One very thin older woman was wearing this pastel net cover up, (imagine a basketball net, but in Easter colors) and it didn't cover anything. Boob check...nice for her age. Skin-a little weathered and spotted. Cooter check...Oh hell, that shit was just hangin'. Gross. I think Denise's boyfriend, Bart, was the one who used the term "bat wings."

8) The area where the drum circle was gathering was under a tree with huge, low-hanging branches that rested on the sand. There were actually completely nude people just plopping their bare butts directly onto the branch, right there rubbin' the tree bark. Hello? I take it the sand doesn't hurt your skin at all??? Lord.

Denise said she would go back. It really was a nice beach area. The people were nice and very accepting. The overall mood was great.

*Note. Denise and I were not nude. I was in linen pants, a long sleeved shirt and dark sunglasses, reading "Harper's Bazaar." There isn't enough sunblock on Earth to really prepare me for total nudity on the beach. Total nudity for me is reserved for showering and sleeping.

As you were.

Friday May 5, 2006
Sleeping with Strangers

While in Maui, I stayed with my friend Denise and her boyfriend Bart. Denise is my age and her boyfriend is slightly older. He's been living on and off the island for about fifteen years and is pretty set in his ways. Denise and Bart are enjoying the trials and tribulations of not only being in a romantic relationship, but working together, as they have just birthed their own tile installation business.

Bart has a slightly younger brother, Doug, who has also been living on and off the island for fifteen years during which time he has lived predominantly with Bart. He has not dated in a LONG time. Doug is currently awaiting the completion of the apartment unit next door to Denise and Bart so he and a friend can move in together. Until then, he's occupying space at Denise and Bart's. They have a two bedroom apartment, but one of the bedrooms is functioning as an office so guests stay in the living room on the couches. Denise asked me, "Are you going to be ok sleeping in the same room with Doug?" I did a quick brain scan of the most drunk days of my early twenties recalling nights where crashing next to people I didn't know wasn't an issue in the slightest. "I've slept next to people I've known less, D," I casually replied.

Frankly, Doug puzzled me, and I was surprised that Denise could handle having him in the house. He doesn't work unless he has to. If he's not working he's either fishing, getting glazed, drinking rum, hanging out with Bart or sleeping. No joke. In any other similar case, I would have slept with one eye open, waiting to whack the crap out of a sleazy hand coming across the imaginary line of privacy in a 10 x 12 room. In this case, the only thing that wasn't safe from Doug was probably the refrigerator. Naturally, I couldn't help but wonder what kind of woman would ever want a guy like him.

Doug, however, surprised me. He turned out to be really funny. He actually expressed this face of raised eyebrows and forehead with pursed lips that was your cue to laugh at his jokes that made him look like a little old woman. You wouldn't expect a single middle-aged man to change the channel when the "Girls Gone Wild" promo comes on, but Doug did, saying, "I'm sure all of their fathers are so proud and are picking up the phone to buy two copies." He also said he'd give up the wacky weed if he was a father, but in order to that, duh, you gotta' give it up long enough to get off the couch...

Upon my departure, eyes squinting and glassy, he stood up, gave me the most disconnected hug and said, "Hungry? Grab a Snickers," and handed me a King Size Snickers bar. I laughed and bid my roommate farewell.

It wasn't until I was on the flight home reading the, *Self-Made Man*, by Norah Vincent that Doug's ways made sense to me. In this book, Vincent retells her account of living as a man for eighteen months. She did everything from changing her physical appearance to joining a bowling league, dating, working and joining a male support group. The activity most interesting to me was that she lived dissembled as a man in a monastery. She discusses the dynamics of personalities and the relationships between the monks. One of her major observations was that even though these men had chosen a celibate life, they were still, in fact, in relationships with each other, co-existing together for the duration of their lives. They may have sworn off romantic relations, but companionship was still a necessity.

It suddenly dawned on me. Doug is a monk, a Hawaiian Monk! He lives a modest, essentially celibate life, (I have chosen to believe this) yet he still wants the companionship of his friends. Thank God he's not out trying to lay every woman in town. Then again, Maui is small and he's been there for a long time...maybe he's run out of options. He has everything he needs.

Holy fuck!

My vacation was more spiritual than I realized. I was sleeping next to a monk, and that's not weird, right?

Shit, I hope I wasn't farting in my sleep. Oh crap, I was in my bathing suit in front of a man of the cloth. Granted it was plumeria print cloth, but still...Forgive me father for I have sinned. I am a mere mortal and know not what I do...

As you were.

Saturday May 6, 2006
With an Oink Oink There and a Meow Meow Here...

As if dating isn't unappealing enough in 2006, my friend Denise made it worse for me. I think she was trying to make it better, but I have only become more confused and even less motivated to make an effort.

While chatting about everything under the laid-back Maui sun, Denise and I started talking about relationships. Somehow the conversation turned astrological, and she pulled out this huge Bible of Astrology.

She started shooting all of this info at me that didn't really make a lot of sense. She said that because I was born in the year of the lamb, my best matches are people born in the year of the cat, horse, and pig. What? And here I just thought I was a Libra. It got more detailed. There were specific astrological signs and years of birth that fall into these barnyard categories.

It's already cheesy enough for me to think about snickering out the question, "So, what's your sign?" to some dude like it's groovy 1972 at Studio 54. I'm not sure I have enough time to sit and do a total breakdown on someone. I'm worried enough about whether or not I should bother remembering his name, much less whether or not he's a Leo, Cat born in 1975...

All I know is that I've dated some real pussies, horses-asses and chauvinist pigs already, and being told that those types are my "best matches" really makes me value my evenings at home alone.

Where's a nice, intelligent, handsome, witty, loyal, ambitious mouse for me to give some of my gentle lamb lovin'?

Perhaps I should consider hiring a psychic to hang out with me, doing readings on prospects, reporting back to me while I sip pretty drinks, instead of wasting my breath talking to dud dudes...

As you were.

Monday May 7, 2006
Not Quite Like Clockwork

I finally saw the movie, *A Clockwork Orange*. I'm still not sure what to think. I'm boggled, really. I usually dig artsy films, yet I'm kinda' stumped about this one. Have you seen it?

This is what I got from it: Bad boy Alex DeLarge goes around raping and pillaging, gets caught, goes to jail, is sent to a rehab facility and brainwashed with Pavlovian-style exercises until they set him free. Things that used to make him supercharged with power now cause him to be ill, which leads to his demise. Everyone has turned on him. Hooray. Add in all the unique characteristics like the drugged milk, the whacked out costumes, the bizarre rape scenes, his love of Beethoven and the eye clamps and that's when it goes from what could be an action film or after-school special to some abstract seventies chic Kubrick film.

Got it...

Now, I'm stumped because I think that part of society that LOVES this film wants other parts of society to "not get it" so that they can feel superior or something. Example: Guy who used to live in the dorms: He used to watch it all the time. This movie isn't one that you can just pop in on and catch forty-five minutes of just for the humor. I would see him watching it in the main lounge and would ask him about it. "You probably wouldn't like this very much," or "This probably isn't your type of film," he would say. Uhhh...If I can love David Lynch/Mark Frost productions, I think I can take on Stanley Kubrick.

Right after I finished the movie I spoke with my Main Gay, Josh. I said, "I just watched *A Clockwork Orange*. I don't think I get it." I expected him to say that it was pretty bizarre, but instead he said like I was riding the short bus: "You don't get it?? I love that movie. It's fabulous." Ok...whatever, Josh. So the gay vote is in. He did admit that it was "kinda teen-angsty."

Then I was reminded of a college friend named Tim V.-a Residential Advisor in the dorms who dressed as Alex DeLarge for Halloween once. Hmmm...A guy in charge of looking after a co-ed dormitory dressing as a rapist for fun...Good thing Tim V.'s a doctor now. I wonder if he had to disclose such a thing to the Medical Board?

What puzzles me the most is a waitress I remember from a pub in Houston who had a tattoo of Alex DeLarge on her forearm. She was one of those Emo's before emo was emo with a lower case "e." At the time I thought it was odd, just because I thought it was odd, but now I'm disturbed. Why would you put a permanent picture of a rapist on your arm? I wonder if she's got Osama bin Laden tattooed on her back now?

Is the allure to this character the fact that he falls, or that it is safe to be attracted to a bad guy if he is taken down? I'm not seeing the hero here...

My hero in this movie is the man with the tiny flashlight in the scene where DeLarge has been taken into custody. Damn, I could never do what he did. And I know how many takes go into some scenes. Watch the film and you will understand. Or maybe you won't...

I think I'm so jaded by society today that this film just doesn't have that, "Oh my God!" effect on me. I'm sure if I was seeing it on its release date decades ago I might feel differently. One thing is for sure-I will never listen to Beethoven with the same pictures in my mind again.

As you were.

Monday May 8, 2006
The Answer Is Blowin' In the Wind

Conversations with my mother are always gems. No topic is off-limits, and you never know where one might lead. (Hmmm...wonder where I get it???)

Yesterday was no exception.

My mother and step dad are over fifty-five and have a large group of friends who are older senior citizens. They are very active people who travel, ride motorcycles, get together to work on projects of all sorts and cook. Sadly, well, here and there people are starting to kick off.

Their parents are also venturing into their eighth decades and both my mom and step dad are dealing with the trials and tribulations of health care, future planning, etc.

Mother and her friends have been visiting about what they want to happen to their remains. Truthfully, this is not the conversation I want to have on a Sunday evening before going to bed, but as per usual, I was left not with macabre emotions, but chuckles.

My mother has not only figured out what she wants done with her remains, but she wants to market the idea. Good ol' Momma, gotta' try to make a buck. If you've ever visited our home, you know that the back patio has a lot of character. Mother has quite collection of yard decor that hangs from the trees, sits in the potted plants and in the flowerbeds. Yeah, it's a lot of crap really, but it's her crap and she displays it well. She loves wind chimes and they are all over the place. *My favorite ornament is the foot-tall stone lady frog which my mother painted green and pink...What's pink on a frog you ask; her nipples, of course.

"Me and Phil (short for her childhood friend, Phyllis) want to be put in wind chimes so we can hang out with our kids, family and friends. We'll get to travel, chill on the porch during cook outs and we get to yell when the wind blows. We can look out for our families by protecting the yard. The chimes will be very well made. It will save so much money on funerals. Funerals are a tradition that is so archaic. I want something much more meaningful and modern," my mother spouted.

I honestly think it's a pretty cool idea, but I couldn't help thinking of all of the funny situations that could arise:

1) I'm trying to have sex, and there in the background I hear my mother howlin'. Not what I want to think of during sex. I'd have to convince myself that she's cheering me on, and this whole stream of thought is just fucked up.

2) What if someone steals or vandalizes my momma? I mean, really. Well, the joke's on them if they make it out of the yard with her. She can be a real mean cookie if she gets her knickers in a bunch.

3) What if I move and forget to get her out of the tree? Holy Christ. I can just see getting off the plane in a new state or country and thinking, "Oh my God...Momma..." It would be like *Home Alone*. She'd be causing all sorts of mayhem in order to get to me.

4) I'd feel really badly if the birds doodied all over her. I HATE yard work and the idea of having to get out there and scrub shit off of her a couple of times a week just doesn't seem like resting in peace. I can just hear her now..."Robin Amber...I wiped your ass for years, the least you could do is shoot me with garden hose once in a while."

5) Now let's assume that this happens and I'm the best daughter ever and I keep her well preserved. I'm going to get old one day, too. Am I supposed to will her to someone when I go? "And to my dear god children: Here are some VERY expensive wind chimes, that serve as an urn to my dearly departed mother." Uh-huh...the gift of death. How lovely. That's just fuckin' creepy.

I have no idea what I want done with my remains, though I do think about it. Some other people in my family have thrown out their ideas:

Step dad: He doesn't care where he physically goes, but he would like a jazz band to play at his funeral.

Gumma: She claims that she wants to be cremated and shot off into the atmosphere either from a rocket or a firecracker.

Damn. Wind chimes, jazz bands and fireworks...I'd better think of something good.

I may not know how I want to be memorialized, but I do know how I want to be remembered.

Ahem: I want to be remembered as a woman who loved with abandon, laughed too much, was brutally honest and made a difference in the lives of children.

As you were.

Friday May 12, 2006
I Do Believe the Temperature of Hell Is Dropping

I've been showing serious signs of needing to go back to work on a more regular basis:

1) While nannying I got completely annoyed that the two-and-a half year-old colored on my area with an ugly color during sidewalk chalk time. I remember why kids shove each other on the playground. Why, if I wasn't paid to take care of that lil' monkey...

2) I cried during the recently aired *Legally Blonde 2*. (Shut-up) Sally Field should never be the bad guy. She was Gidget for Christ's sake. And who doesn't love a homosexual Chihuahua in drag on Capital Hill?

3) I have been considering going back to school. I decided on a Master's Program at Princeton called Media in Modernity. Uh-huh. Sure. What's fifty grand a year in tuition and living expenses? If you're going in debt, go deep I say.

4) I washed my car. If you know me, you know that it takes months for me to get around to doing that, and that's when I'm driving everyday. I only drive about two days a week now. *I only paid $7.99 for the hand wash and wax. My coupon was only valid for another week. That's right. I said coupon.

5) I cooked a meal. Dinner. Yep, stuffed ricotta cheese chicken breasts with a basil marinara sauce and bow-tie pasta with spinach/sun dried tomatoes. Yum. Hello? Are you ok? Open a window. Get some fresh air in here. You fainted. I know. It was hard for me to believe, too. *I even cleaned the kitchen as I went so when I sat down to eat, the dishes were all already in the dishwasher! Snaps for me! Eeeeee.

::sigh:: I'm starting to hate myself.

As you were.

Saturday May 13, 2006
Yeah, Happy Mother's Day...

I have always loved going to get the mail. When I was little my dad would drive to the post office and hand me the key to his post office box. I was allowed to get out of the car and go get the mail all by myself. It felt like an important job since there was a key that I had to use to unlock this private metal box at a government building. To this day, I absolutely love the fact that I live in an apartment building where I have to use a key to open my mailbox.

Perhaps as a result of not having much to do, my paternal grandmother would go to the post office several times a week. As I recall, she rarely put mail out for the postman to pick up. She wanted to make sure that it GOT to the post office, as if that ensured that her mail would actually get delivered. I'm sure that ritual of hers is why I find myself often walking my mail down the street to my local post office. I'd like to think it's because of the extra exercise I get from the ten minute walk, but I have to admit, I still get that rush of that "official feeling" pulling back the steel door as I drop off my intentions.

However, I would rather go to the DMV or the gyno than stand in line at my local post office in order to mail packages. I try to see the adventure in it keeping my natural sparkle and bounce about me as I stand in that line that usually strings out the fucking door. My favorite people in line are the ones who just need to buy stamps. Don't they know there's a machine in the lobby??? Christ! It's hard to keep myself from yelling, "We all know!" when people in line talk audibly about how long the line is, as if they've never been to The Los Feliz Village Post Office before. It makes me even more tickled when they give their inane commentary about how the post office could alleviate the congestion and speed up the process, as if there are hidden microphones and representatives listening in from the imaginary Postal System Suggestion Center. In this highly automated society, trust me I'm pretty sure they know how they could speed things up, and I'm thinkin' they've just said, "No, thanks. Sorry, America. We're just not that interested."

During my latest visit to the post office I was, as per usual, amazed at the line and doing everything to keep my mind off the wait. I counted the number of people ahead of me: eleven. I listened to a man on his cell phone and imagined that he wasn't really talking to anyone-just pretending he was so he wouldn't have an anxiety attack in line. I watched a fly buzz around in a perfect square pattern at eye level to the man ahead of me for about ten minutes. The man never once seemed to notice that the fly was there. I watched a child in a stroller thumb through a magazine and marveled at her thick head of hair. I then realized that she was autistic and stopped staring so her mother wouldn't feel uncomfortable. I examined the veins in my hands; yep-still there and still doing their job. I checked my packages to make sure the addresses were correct and that they were sealed about three times. I counted how many seconds went by between deep SNIFFs as the man behind me must have had a horrible cold: it varied between two and four seconds.

Just when I thought I couldn't handle one more SNIFF, a postal attendant bellowed, "Next," and it was my turn. Pumping up the charm to brighten her day, I headed to counter. When she asked how she could help me I smiled and said, "I'd like a cheeseburger, fries and bottled water." She laughed and said, "Honey, me, too." She saw that

I was sending something to Hawaii and we talked about her favorite trip to the islands. I offered her praise for working on her usual day off. The birds were singing, the sun was out and trumpets were sounding off...and then...while our beings were connected as we both held the opposite ends of my receipt, she said...she said...with the most genuine and loving voice, "You enjoy YOUR Mother's Day."

Eeeeerrrrkkk...Uhh...You betta' back the fuckin' truck up. Did she just wish ME a Happy Mother's Day as if I'M a mother? What in the hell about me says that I have produced offspring? I mean really, what the fuck was that??? All I could say with a confused half-grin was, "Yeah, Happy Mother's Day..." As I walked out, I was thinking about our exchange and not once were children brought up. Oh my God...I need to get my eyes done. I know it. Those little lines aren't so little anymore. My hips are not that fuckin' wide! I'm going to start calling FedEx.

You know, I've got some great ideas that would really speed up that line and ease the congestion at the post office...

*Call your mothers or who ever was a positive female influence in your life.

As you were.

Saturday May 13, 2006
What I Know Now

During a very annoying and traumatic, yet thankfully short-lived laptop meltdown and extended computer scan, I picked up a book I purchased called, *What I Know Now,* edited by Ellyn Spragins. It's this compilation of mini interviews and letters from influential women of our society and recent American history. The women were asked to write a letter to a younger self knowing what they know now. By the time I had read the first four entries, I was ready to stop reading and start writing. Granted most of these women are over thirty-five and have done things that have warranted national attention, but I think it's important to reflect on life and keep tabs on oneself no matter how old you are or what you have done. So, I did just that. I put down the book and picked up a pen. I'm sharing this because I encourage you to do the same, even if you aren't prepared to share it publicly just yet.

I wrote this letter to my eight year-old self.

"Hey Little Lady-

You are living in turmoil. I see you there, all curled up in your bed, holding Cupcake (my childhood pet of fifteen years, a miniature poodle) next to you in the dark, wondering if your parents are actually going to follow through with the horrific threats they are screaming as they beat the hell out of each other once again. I know it's scary. I know you do you best to project the picture of that perfect child attitude at school in order to make sure you never look weak, never look poor and never look ashamed.

These awful stresses will come to you more than I care to share now, but I have good news for you. You are lucky-charmed almost. Somehow, by the grace of God, you will always be in the presence of someone who will suddenly say just the right thing when you need to hear it most.

Honesty, integrity, open-mindedness, an amazing sense of humor and faith will become your internal guides to finding the greatest treasure in the world: a strong sense of self-worth and being.

The journey and adventures aren't over until the last breath leaves your body. You've got so much love and laughter to experience. The sources from which they come will surprise you. All things really do happen for a reason. People truly do come into your life, even if it's for a shorter time than you hope, to show you something. Keep a mental notebook and pen ready at all times!

Never live unconsciously. Never live in the darkness of secrets. Get up everyday knowing that you have a purpose, even if it's just to pee. Watch out for your lazy streak. It will cause you to miss out on a lot of fun if you aren't careful.

You're going to realize (and forget and realize again) that your personality is pretty bold and your humor is quite raw. You may only be five feet tall, (sorry to say, that's all the height you're going to get) but you stand about seven feet tall when you open your mouth. Despite what you think, people notice you and take what you say seriously. Know your audience.

You will fall in love a lot and have your heart broken more than once. The good news is that you will start picking better men as you get older. Simply settling will not be your style.

By twenty-six, one of the greatest things you will be able to do, is find something good to say about every person you meet. You will be well-liked, not because that is your goal, but because you are likeable. You are genuine. You are special. You will make amazing friendships.

You will make a difference in the world around you in your own way, seemingly on accident.

I know that's a lot to imagine as you sit in your dark room holding Cupcake close to you trying to ignore the senseless war raging down the hall. Yet, believe it or not, that awful repetitive scene will shape you, and help you deal with every situation and decision in life. I think you start getting pretty good at it, too.

Chin up.

With love and a little knowledge,

Your twenty-six year-old self,

The Bean...You're going to love how you start to call yourself this."

As you were.

Monday May 15, 2006
Heavy Stuff Happens

I had just put in the movie, *My Life Without Me*, and I sat down to go through my emails. I read that a guy I had known from afar in high school had lost his wife and the mother of his children to an accident. She was walking, had a heart attack, fell, broke her neck and died instantly. She was twenty-six. I'm twenty-six. I go on walks. I thought walks were pretty safe, safer than jogging, anyhow.

My Life Without Me is about a twenty-three year-old married mother of two who finds out that she only has a few months to live. She makes a list of things she wants to do before she dies.

While realizing that my former classmate/community member may not have had such a list I was even more compelled to think about what I would do if I knew I was going to die shortly. Shouldn't we live somewhat like this everyday to avoid stagnation? I also realized that as of the last year, I kinda' have been living as if each day was my last. I have been traveling, playing with make-up, watching the sun set from hill tops and writing my heart out more than usual.

Alas, I'm forcing myself to think as if I might have only three months to live. What would I do? If I was physically capable I would:

1) Find someone to wash my hair everyday.

2) Read more books.

3) Be naked outside just for the hell of it.

4) Color with crayons and play with Play-Doh.

5) Volunteer at schools.

6) Eat whatever the fuck I want, whenever the fuck I want, even more often than I do now.

7) Learn to ice skate.

8) Write even more.

9) Hold hands with everyone I have a face to face conversation with, so that they feel humanity and know that they are important.

10) Drink Abuelita Mexican Hot chocolate with breakfast every morning, a lemon drop martini with lunch and a glass of wine with dinner every night, if I felt like it.

11) Wake up to Willie Nelson music every morning and fall asleep to house music every night.

12) Lie in the grass more often.

13) Get some sun.

14) Call boys that were good kissers and ask them for one more kiss.

15) Sit in my mother's lap.

16) Mow the lawn for my grandparents (and I you know ABHOR yard work).

17) Admit what I am really thinking about when I have orgasms during sexual intercourse.

18) Write my little brother a letter. He might actually read one of my letters if I was dead.

19) Sleep whenever I felt like it, even more than I do now.

20) Take a trip to Europe.

21) Push to publish a book.

22) Do some stand-up comedy.

23) Tell off a few people who I find myself having bad dreams about.

24) Decide what I want done with my remains.

25) Make sure my photo albums and journals are all labeled and preserved.

26) Have my eggs frozen and donated to people who need them.

27) Ask to sit in the cockpit of the plane during a trip.

28) Have one really stunning black and white photo taken of myself for my friends and family to have to remember me by.

29) Sit with each of the children I have worked with over the years and give them one more heaping spoonful of love, encouragement and advice.

30) Sleep on fresh sheets every night.

31) Begin to learn to play the drums and read music.

32) Learn to Tango.

33) Clean out my apartment. No one should leave a bunch of crap behind for people to have to cull through.

34) Host dinner parties every week.

35) Learn to pee on the side of the road. I just can't do it.

I think I'm pretty simple.

What would you do?

*Dedicated to the memory of Miranda Twitty and the Twitty Family.

As you were.

Tuesday May 16, 2006
In Robin's Nest...

::sigh::

The following might seem strange, absurd, shocking or unnecessary to share, but I find it truly humbling and if it can happen to me, it can happen to you...

I woke up the other morning naked as the day I was born, and sauntered into the bathroom, scratchin' my ass.

I sat down on the pot, still a little squinty-eyed and began that oh so wonderful "First Morning Pee." My gaze fell towards my lap, and I noticed something strange...

**Now, here's where things get a little hairy. Literally. So if you don't want to know some deep details about me, run away now!

Nestled in the very small amount of pubic hair I keep was something tiny and plastic. "What the fuck?" I thought.

Trying to get my eyes to focus, I plucked from my loins an itty-bitty...earring backing?

Yeah...it was the backing to an earring...you know, the clear plastic tubing kind?

I can see how this might be odd for some of you to imagine, but the part where I get uncomfortable is remembering the last time I actually wore a pair of earrings. It was mid-February of this year, and I was in New Jersey! I've been to Texas and Hawaii since then, making stops here in California in between. I do bathe; several bubble baths a week in fact. I shave. I do laundry!

Ummm...Where exactly has this lil' guy been hiding since February?

Needless to say, there have even more cutbacks around the little office.

Arg. What worries me, though, is that I haven't seen the earrings that go with that backing since New Jersey either...Eee-gadz!...

I never cease to amaze or belittle myself.

As you were.

Thursday May 18, 2006
Supermarket Sweep

You just never know when competition is going to arise in life. Sometimes it happens and you don't know that you are a part of it until it's over. I experienced this at the grocery store recently.

My roommate was going to be cooking for both of us and I thought I should at least make a salad to add to the meal, so I walked to the Albertson's around the corner to pick up some fixin's.

I grabbed some field greens, an avocado and some cranberries. I made a pass by the wine, decided that a bottle of Shiraz was in order and headed towards the checkout lanes. I think I've listed about four items, right? Express Lane, here I come.

Just as I was nearing the checkout lane, you know, right in front of the end cap with the magazines and bottled cold drinks, I saw someone zooming towards me. This tall woman in athletic apparel literally cut me off at the pass. She put her handheld basket

71

on the belt and stood there like she just planted a flag on a piece of unclaimed land. She wouldn't look at me. She stood with her back to me, stiff and tall.

I'm not usually the type of person to initiate or promulgate confrontation, but something came over me and I stepped forward about six inches away from her. And into the middle of her back (because that's where my face leveled off), I whispered, "She won."

She spun around and looked down at me, hissing, "I heard you."

I replied casually, "Oh. I'm sorry. I wasn't talking to you. I was talking to the invisible people who missed the photo finish of the imaginary race we were running."

She looked like I had just farted on her leg, (which was my next move if she didn't get lost) and as she gathered her items to leave the lane, she said with disdain: "Whatever. You don't have to be so sarcastic."

I smiled, moving out of her way, putting my items on the belt and said, "Sarcasm would be if I congratulated you on your win, Ma'am."

The cashier witnessed the whole thing. (He's this adorable, hot, young Latin gay man). As I approached the register he grinned and said, "Oh honey, YOU won. I don't know who that bitch thinks she is."

Aw, snap.

Chill the fuck out people!

As you were.

Thursday May 18, 2006
Now, That's a Party!

I don't normally go to the movies, as I have a very beautiful love affair going with Netflix.com. For the cost of one movie ticket, I can see almost as many movies I want in a month from the comfort of my couch. However, last night I really wanted to GO to the movies.

I've been itching to see *Keeping Up With the Steins*. It's a movie based around the outrageous costs of the Bar Mitzvah in the Jewish culture. *In case you don't know, when a Jewish boy or girl turns thirteen, he/she has the right to go through a special ceremony called a Bat Mitzvah (for girls) or a Bar Mitzvah (for boys). The ceremony commemorates the change from childhood into adulthood. During the year they are supposed to perform a mitzvah...a good deed as a sign of charity, etc.

The cost of the ceremony is nominal, but the costs of the party afterward can get completely out of control! Often times, the mitzvah seems to get lost in the matzah balls as the focus becomes about how extravagant it can be. I feel a very strong connection to this movie as I was a live-in nanny in a Jewish home with three children. I have to admit, by their family socio-economic social status, they kept their children's bar/bat mitzvah's pretty modest. However, I spent a couple of years hauling kids to and from these little kosher shindigs. Families renting out entire sports stadiums, bars and having amazing bands and over the top parties were just a matter of fact.

I've always had this odd fascination with these ceremonies. Mexican girls have Quince's and Polynesian women get their legs tattooed. What do little white girls get? I guess we get our periods. *I just thought about it...Maybe I became Catholic so I could at least have a move, you know, that whole Sign of the Cross thing is very powerful looking when done at the right time...huh...

Anyhow, I got to the Burbank AMC and bought my ticket and headed into the theatre. It was empty, but the lights were still up. I took my seat: low, center and comfy. The movie started. Still no one there. How awesome was that? I was the only person there! I'm not sure what it said about the film, but I was stoked. I laid down. I sat up. I moved seats. I ANSWERED my cell phone and said, "Oh, I'll have to call you back, I'm screening a movie in my private theatre...Muah." I even got up and danced during the party scene of the movie. When it was over, I waved to the projectionist and yelled, "Thank you!" He flashed the lights at me and I walked out feeling like a million bucks!

I figured out what little white girls get. They get to grow up, move to Hollywood, quit their jobs, play on movie sets, travel around the country and have movie theatres to themselves, all while living on unemployment. Now, that's an American adult dream for as long as it lasts.

In the name of the Father, the Son and The Holy Spirit, Mazol tov to me.

*Oh yeah...The movie was really good-heartwarming and funny. And speaking of matzah balls, there's a scene in which you get a quick glance at Gary Marshall's old saggin' set as he gets out of a hot tub! Oy vey.

As you were.

Thursday May 18, 2006
Sir Licks-A-Lot

He's creepy. He's got a fetish. He's lurks in parks, playgrounds and fast food restaurants.

He's The Foot Licker.

Yes. That's what I said.

If you didn't think we could fit anymore of the most bizarre and disturbed people into Los Angeles, you were mistaken, my friend.

Apprehended after being identified by his victims, some man I don't give a shit about enough to learn his name, has been taken off the streets. He was posing as a commercial agent and approaching children on playgrounds, etc. telling them that they could be eligible to be in a TV commercial for footwear if their feet were just right. This pervert was telling the kids that he just needed to examine their feet. When the children would take off their shoes, HE WOULD LICK THEIR FUCKING FEET!

We do the best we can with kids. We try to prepare them for people who might want harm them by doing really inappropriate things to them, but does it ever cross your mind to tell a child, "Now if a man (who, by the way, was dressed up like a modern-day pimp) approaches you and asks to see your feet, scream FIRE and run away as fast as you can." Uh, NO. So, thank you, Sir Licks-A-Lot, for giving us one more thing to add to our list of fears to impress upon our children.

Can you imagine those children's dreams at night after being attacked? *Can we call that molested? Oh, ok, violated. Can you imagine having to comfort your child when he comes into your room crying, "Oh Mommy, there he was trying to pull me by the feet into a dark hole in the ground. He kept saying that he had to have just one more taste." Dear God. That's just moronic.

See, in the old days, when a child would suck his thumb or a mother would be trying to wean a youngster from breast feeding, it was common to put something really nasty tasting or smelling on the thumb or nipple. Perhaps if children went around with garlic or shit smeared on their feet, this would keep The Foot Licker away. But then again, don't children's feet already smell like wet goats? Damn, this guy's more deranged than I realize.

Well, then there's only one solution: shoes that lock! No more learning to tie shoes or getting away with Velcro; we're getting combination locks for all kid's shoes. Just think-it will save them so much time in middle school when they start moving from class to class and have to have a locker. If four year-olds today can navigate the Internet, why not a combination lock? Works for the feet; might work for the pants and the mouth. Oh heck, let's just get little Billy a nice suit of armor for his fifth birthday. He'll be the coolest kid in school!

I wonder if he was thinking: "How many licks does it take to get to the center of a second grader?" as he licked them...

::shudder::

As you were.

Friday May 19, 2006
I'm a Little Teapot

The following three states of being cause similar levels of aggravation:

1) PMS

2) Having a head cold and craving food that you wind up not wanting when you finally eat it because it's not what you really want after all, and you can't even taste it.

3) Being stuck in traffic in a dead spot where you get no radio/cell phone reception for about forty-five minutes when you're just trying to travel six miles.

Today I was lucky enough to experience ALL FUCKING THREE AT THE SAME GODDAMN TIME!!!!!!!!!!!!!!!

::said in a Karen Walker whisper:: There. That feels better.

As you were.

Friday June 9, 2006
What Wispy Chakras Cause

If you know me, you know that I believe that all things happen for a reason.

I had a series of experiences during my visit to Chicago that have turned my head in a new direction:

1) A complimentary aura and chakra reading at a trendy boutique in Wicker Park on my first day in the city left me with a lump in my throat and a question mark looming over my head. *Just a note, your chakras should be tight orbs not "wispy nests."

2) I found a gem called "Jewel" that not only sells Abuelita hot chocolate in single servings, but also sells my favorite: Smucker's Red Plum Jam. Do you know how many people have been shipping me jam???

3) Did you know that there are these underground tubes that carry humans to and fro with ease and efficiency? I was stunned. It was cheap. With one monthly car payment I could ride "The El," as they call it, for an entire year and not have to stop for gas once!

4) I met a REAL Bond Girl at SAKS on Michigan Ave.! Sherri G. at the Bond No. 9 fragrance counter lifted my spirits with spritzes of the line's amazing scents. I'm loyally bonded to her for life. 007 needs her as his secret weapon!

5) Around 4:00 am on a Monday I realized that I was still out dancing with Tako in a club packed with people ranging in age from people my parents age all the way down to club kiddies. It was a Monday...The same ritual could be had EVERY night of the week. House music...ahhh...everywhere.

6) Many know me as Bean. While sauntering down Michigan Avenue I stumbled upon this gigantic silver bean. It was like a homing device that screamed, "Elsa Peretti, eat your heart out!" I still have no knowledge of its significance, but it spoke to me with its gleaming opulence and smooth demeanor.

7) My mother's childhood best friend's daughter, Amanda, lives there. We are almost the same age. The two of us went out for drinks, and after a few refreshing Sapphire and tonics, the Texas twang was out, loud and proud. We shared tales and laughed, probably much like our mothers once did and still do.

8) Homeless men in Chicago are the most honest people. While leaving a bar, a homeless man asked me for some money. I said that I didn't have any cash. He said with the utmost articulation: "Bitch." I was surprised, as most homeless people would just walk away, and said, "Did you just call me a bitch?" He replied, "Yes." I looked him straight in the eye and said, "Well, that is just tacky." I walked away feeling like Charlotte York from "Sex and the City"...

9) Homeless people in Chicago are also comical. As I walked home carrying a large pizza, I passed two men sitting outside a bar begging for money. When they were behind me I heard, "Nothing like a hot girl carrying a pizza. Hey, pretty lady, can I have a piece of your hot pie?" I couldn't help but laugh...and turn and say, "Oh behave," like Charlotte York again, only I was in Chucks and not Monolos, but whatever.

10) Eating alone at Go Roma, I was given my order number. The card I was handed had a saying in Italian on it. Translated it said, "One who wants too much holds nothing." It made me think a lot about what I want in life. I still haven't decided completely, but I did gank the card and am holding on to it.

11) While walking to the train, I saw a woman inside a store. Over her shoulder was a canvas Trader Joe's grocery bag. I did a one-eighty and went into the store to ask her where she got the bag. Trying not to be too obviously condescending she said, "At Trader Joe's." Duh... "Is there one here in Chicago?" When that simple, powerful, "Yes," came out of her mouth, I heard angels sing out.

It was all clear...I could live here.

Tako offering me a place to stay and the cheapest rent imaginable sealed the deal. Out of eleven trips this year, Chicago was the first place with the right energy, the right comfort and the right mood...at least for now. I sense some balance.

So, I'm moving to Chicago at the end of the month unless something miraculous happens, of course. Everything is for sale.

Like Willie Nelson, I'm on the road again-the road to Find Out, as my biological father used to say...

Uggg, two-thousand miles of driving across what, six, seven states? No one said it would be easy...

As you were.

Friday June 9, 2006
Happy Birthday, Johnny

Today is Johnny Depp's birthday. Let us have cake and rejoice.

God gave that man the most expressive set of eyes on the planet and he puts them to the most amazing use.

::sigh::

Male or female, you know you all appreciate his work and want him to kiss you like he kissed Amy Locane in John Waters', *Cry Baby*. Don't lie...you know you do.

As you were.

Friday June 9, 2006
Hello Karen, Earth to Karen

I have lived in my current apartment building for almost a year-and-a-half. I haven't gotten to know very many of my neighbors. It's just not a building architecturally conducive to socializing.

The other day, however, while walking out the front door, I was able to have a conversation with a girl who lives here. Her name is Karen. She lives on the third floor and is an actress. We agreed to keep in touch and thought it would be great if we could gather the people in our building for a meet-n-greet as no one seems to know each other.

As it was my best friend, Alba's, birthday, I was in a hurry to get a piece of See's Candies Cake from The Alcove in her honor. We parted ways. After returning and devouring the cake, I decided that I would take that next step and head up to the third floor to give Karen my number. If there's one thing I know about this town, the effort of intent lies with yourself.

When I got to the third floor I realized that she was home. She answered the door, happy to see me and we chatted a little. I complimented her apartment and even went inside to see if she could see my apartment from her window, which she could. We agreed that we should get together for drinks sometime. Great, I thought.

Two weeks went by. I returned from Chicago. My friend, Sarah Cole, came in from Nashville and as we were leaving the apartment to go for a long walk through Griffith Park, I saw Karen walking towards us with a friend. I prepared the smile and eye contact, only to be completely ignored as she walked right past us, bumping into me on the way. I know Sarah C. and I are intimidatingly hot in Lycra, but really...

Today was the icing on the cake, so to speak, as my friend Tracy and I decided to go to The Alcove for a slice of that divine chocolate lust in buttercream frosting. As we were leaving I saw my neighbor from across the hall, Karm, and we chatted. Our chat included how oddly Karen had acted. He laughed and shrugged it off as LA's special way of attracting the brightest bulbs.

I swear to God, they must be filming me for an episode of "Girls Behaving Badly" or "Candid Camera," because as Tracy and I walked into The Alcove, behind the counter stood who else, but Karen! She looked at me with the most perky expression and said, "Welcome to The Alcove. The menus are right here."

I turned to Tracy and said, "Oh my God! That's Karen, the neighbor I was just telling Karm about." I made a point to have my order taken by her. She and I exchanged pleasantries and still...nothing. Not a single glimmer of recognition in her eyes. How in the hell can you not remember a person that was in your fucking apartment? I wonder how many men think she's a total bitch for not remembering sleeping with them, or if directions on how to get home at night are written on her hand. Did I say something that put her off?

The only thing that could top all of this is if she calls me once I'm already in Chicago and wants to grab those drinks. I think she's been grabbing more than drinks...

I seriously hope this is an example of the Phoebe/Ursula issue "Friends" entertained us with for years.

Who could forget this face? I mean, really...

As you were.

Friday June 9, 2006
It's So Hard To Say Goodbye...

To my couch!! Though it made the move from Houston to Los Angeles, it's not going to be able to make the journey to Chicago. The cost of driving or shipping my furniture is just not in the budget.

Many of you have seen my couch. It's from the seventies, slightly curved, about ten feet long, covered in a soft, velouresque golden fabric and in really good condition. At first glance one might say, "God, where the fuck did you get that thing? How old is it?" When I look at it I see safe, happy childhood memories.

Sadly, these memories were NOT in my parent's home, but in the home of one of my dearest friends to this day, Sarah Cole. Her family lived on the street behind ours. When I was about eight years old I went to Sarah's house for a birthday slumber party. What I found inside their home was so foreign. Her parents were very loving to each other. The house was pretty. The furniture matched. Both of her parents participated in her birthday fun and slept in the same room. There was a sense of peace and warmth in her home. I remember us gathering in their formal living room (a room I had never heard of) to watch her open presents. I remember sitting on her couch and looking around at how nice everything seemed and thinking: "I want this. Why isn't my house like this?" I remember rubbing my hands over the soft fabric and feeling so safe and happy. Her mom handed out goodie bags for all of us to take home, full of candy and a lip gloss that I swear I finally used up about three years ago.

I'll never forget stalling to leave as long as I could that Sunday after her birthday. When my mother finally dragged me out with my head hanging, she stopped and bent down to my eye level. With her hand she lifted my chin up and said, "It's different here, isn't it?" I silently nodded. She got a little teary and picked me up and carried me home. My parent's marriage was a nightmare.

I was a guest in the Cole's home many, many times throughout the years and still am when Sarah and I are in town at the same time. Sometime in Intermediate School I began telling Sarah's parents that I fully planned to buy their couch from them when I got my own place. I think they laughed it off for a long time, but at the age of twenty-two and in my own apartment for the first time, I knocked on their door and handed them a check. It's been my sense and token of intention for a loving and peaceful home life since.

Alas, here I am about to pick up and move, unable to take my furniture with me. A part of me is weeping that I have to give up my couch. I got an email from a friend and what she said shook me a bit. She told me that she's going through a divorce and is losing many of her belongings as a result. It hit me that maybe it's time for this couch to help someone else achieve that sense of peace and warmth as she embarks on a new beginning. I think I might just be able to live without it.

As silly as it might sound to onlookers, I'm going to take a great photograph of this golden wonder and frame it. I can let go of the object, but I still need a piece of it with me.

It's funny what moving makes you deal with...

*As a side note, to my knowledge, The Coles still have not replaced the couch in the formal living room. Is it possible they might want it back?

As you were.

Tuesday June 20, 2006
Now Showing 108

Ok...I have something new that I find just disturbing.

I'm moving out of my apartment at the end of the month. Where I end up, fuck only knows, and that's a whole other topic I'm chewing on. I honestly believe that unless I was standing on the nose of a 747 in flight, my life could be no more up in the air.

Anyhow, my apartment managers are starting to show the apartment to prospective tenants. Fine. No. Not fine. I like my alone time. When I'm alone, most of you know I'm either naked or in my pink bathrobe. I'm no Betty Crocker Homemaker, (though I did make some succulent stuffed pork chops last night) so yes, the bed will be tussled like my hair. There will be no make-up on my face. Things will be scattered about. I LIVE in my apartment. If there is company coming, all of this will change as in *Cinderella,* all things will magically fall into place.

Now, when the doorbell randomly rings at 11:22 in the mid-morning, I am not prepared for the magic to happen. News flash: I'm the magic and unless forewarned, it doesn't happen. And what is the result? I open the door and there stand two men, staring at me with their mouths hanging open as I tie up my bathrobe. "Why, come right on in," I say. "I'm just going to slip into the powder room while you guys look around."

I really don't want to be here when people are walking through my place. I don't want to hear their comments about the decor, the way the light comes through the vertical blinds, the carpet in the bedrooms and especially not their excitement about the place. This is where I have found refuge, sanctity and comfort for over a year now. Unless I was out of town or about to go out of town, there wasn't a single night that I didn't sleep in this apartment since I've lived here.

I don't like to be randomly disturbed. I don't like people looking at my stuff. This town is full of morons who are just out to see what you are moving.

I feel like I should pee on the carpet and hang some Nazi garbage on the walls before the next random appearance of my apartment manager.

Pouting.

As you were.

Wednesday June 21, 2006
March 5, 1920 - June 14, 2006

My grandmother, Margaret Sue Patton Kilgore Hunt, passed away last week at the age of eighty-six. She was a daughter, twin sister, wife, aunt, mother and grandmother. Alzheimer's was the only ailment that led to her death. She is the first member of my immediate family to pass away. I will not be going to her funeral for absurd family reasons that are not the focus of this commentary. Because of her age and the length of time I have been preparing for her to pass, I was more relieved that she finally died. She was losing her dignity, something she would have hated to lose, second only to her vanity. I know where I get it. We are from The South. We are what we are.

Many things come to mind when I think of her. Here are some random rambles and thoughts:

I never knew my grandfather James (Jimmy) Kilgore. He had a heart attack and died in January of 1972. My parents married that May, and I was born in 1979. Sometime in 1983 we moved into my grandmother's house and my grandmother married the man next door who was also a widow. His name was Jesse Hunt. He also died of a heart attack. I remember my grandmother saying, "My husbands don't leave me. I bury them."

My grandmother had two sons and FIVE daughter-in-laws...I can't really speak for many of them, but on a first-hand account from my mother's experience, she was pretty protective of her boys to a fault...Let's just leave it at that.

I lucked out. I was the grandchild that saw her almost everyday. When I wasn't staying with my mother's parents, I was with Grandma Sue.

We had a lot of tea parties as I recall. She had this really neat collection of pieces of stemware and teacups that I adored. Correction: We had a lot of Tang and Sprite parties. She would fill a cute little teapot (white with red hearts) with Tang and fill my glass with Sprite. She, however, drank coffee...tons and tons of coffee. The last time I saw her alive, she had a cup of coffee in her hand.

Cinnamon toast accompanied our Tang parties. She knew just how to mix the sugar and cinnamon in a shallow dish for the best flavor. The secret was in buttering both sides of the bread before dusting it in the mix, then putting the slices of bread in a toaster oven. I can still smell it cooking.

I used to think that she invented the idea of suspending fruit in Jell-O. Her gelatin was amazing. She had this special way of mixing extra fruit juice into the liquid. She said that you had to do it when the liquid was just the right temperature. I have no idea what that is, but ehh...I don't eat Jell-O unless it's served to me.

She taught me to knit. I'll never forget how tickled she was by me when the phone rang during one of our kitting sessions. I followed her to the phone with my knitting needles in my hands. She said, "Robin A, you dropped a stitch." I began to look on the ground for it. She had to sit down she laughed so hard.

I owe a great deal of my love of cosmetics to her. She worked at Foley's Department Store. My dad and I would drive her to work, and on the way there she would put on her face. She taught me to put on my lipstick in a moving vehicle without a mirror. I will never forget the smell of her Avon cold cream that she kept in the fridge, or her perfume of choice, Oscar de la Renta. Her bathroom vanity area was my clubhouse.

I cannot remember a day when she wasn't up at 5:00 am, dressed in at least a button up shirt and slacks, a string of beads, her hair set and her face on, headed to the post office, the bank or the grocery store.

My grandmother thought it was perfectly ok to say the word, "Nigra," "because saying colored people was rude" and often mentioned that I "should never marry a Catholic, a Mexican or a Jew." I'm Catholic now. Everybody knows I love me a good Mexican and I don't mind if I Jew...

Entering her home was like entering a cafe. Before you could sit down you were offered every possible consumable liquid, and if you stopped by without four hours notice you were sure to hear the line, "Had I known you were coming, I'da baked a cake." Upon your departure, "You're always welcome at my house, at anytime of the day. I love you a bushel and a peck and a hug around the neck," was common. (I lived next door. There was always cake.)

She had some unique vocabulary words:

epizootie: I'm still not sure what this is, but if you didn't wash your hands, dry your hair after a shower, stay out of the rain, or cover your mouth when you coughed and about a million other things, you were sure to catch the epizootie.

boomtegoozle: I'm still not sure what this is either but once (at age four) I tripped over a tree root in the front yard. When I stumbled she said in this baby-talk voice, "Uh-oh, did you fall down, go boomtegoozle?" I pushed my glasses up on my nose and asked in all seriousness, "How the fuck do you go boomtegoozle?" I got a whipping for that from my mother...but no answer...

boople: Ahhh, this one I know. She used this term to describe flatulence. "Robin A, you'll have to pardon me, I have a case of the booples." ::sigh::

On the topic of virginity, I will never forget Grandma Sue explaining to me: "I was a virgin when I married your Grandfather Jimmy, as pure as the driven snow, but not without a lot of heavy petting, of course." Uhhhh...::shudder::

Narcotics: My grandmother and her circle of friends loved their medications. When one doctor wouldn't give them what they wanted, they went to a new doctor and lied about what they were currently taking, got what they wanted and traded between each other. Opening a Tylenol bottle at Grandma's house was a gamble...I remember some great pain relief, that's for sure.

Shitty people: The famous statement, "Well, I call a spade a spade unless I step on it in the dark, and then I call it a son-of-a-bitch."

She was like Snow White when it came to animals. Birds would land on her fingers, and she would risk her life for a stray dog. Tippy was the dog of hers I remember most from my childhood. That dog was so annoying, but she loved her and that's all that mattered.

The day I decided she was no longer the grandmother I cozied up to as a child, happened a few months before she went into the nursing home. I had to bathe her. She was feeble, still had a grip on her lucidity but needed help. I'll never forget how rail-thin she was, yet she still had this cute, girlish shape to her. She looked at me and said,

"I'm sorry I'm such a fright to look at. Please don't remember me this way." I told her, "Are you kidding? I can only hope that my breasts look that perky when I'm eighty." She relaxed, looking down at her chest and said, "Well, I have done what I can with cocoa butter." Walgreens. $4.99. Run. Get some.

I once took a boyfriend to see her at the nursing home, and she asked me in quite an audible whisper, "Where did you find him? He sure is pretty to look at," and began to flirt with him. Ehhh...I couldn't blame her. He was pretty to look at.

When I visited her last in Georgetown, Texas at the nursing home, I held her hands and told her that I was moving to California. I was scared that she might tell me not to go, but when I looked into her eyes, I could see how vacant she was. It was clear that she had left home long before I ever knew I would be ready to.

She was my grandmother. Her favorite color was orchid. She loved to watch "The Bold and The Beautiful." You never went hungry or thirsty at her house. If you had a fever she would press on your forehead so hard to feel it that you would swear it went away, just so she would let up. I can still hear her clear her throat. She was a beautiful woman, a poster-woman for those 1950's black and white photographs. She wasn't perfect. She had a wicked streak. She was my grandmother.

Margaret Sue Patton Kilgore Hunt: Born March 5, 1920 - Died June 14, 2006.

As you were.

"Be careful kissing boys, you'll get the epizootie." said Gram. I should have listened.

Wednesday June 21, 2006
One Man Show

While walking to the post office as I love to do, I was approaching the corner of Vermont and Franklin where I could see an elderly man, rather hunched over, waiting for the light to change.

He had Santa Claus white hair and a long full beard to match. He was dressed in brown slacks, a long-sleeved green/brown plaid shirt and those classic old person walking shoes in "tan."

As I got closer I wondered if he might need a hand getting across the street. The light changed and he wasn't moving forward, but he was shaking a bit.

Now near him on his right side, I could see that he was not in need of a hand at all, though maybe he was hoping I might join in; he was jackin' off right there on the street corner.

Through his thick black-rimmed glasses, his eyes twinkled at me. He looked so proud and determined. I just smiled and walked on by. Maybe his Viagra kicked in for the first time in a long time. He really wasn't hurting anyone-just enjoying the views, I guess. He looked like he was going to be keeping his hands to himself.

I live in Los Feliz Village. It's The Happy Village for a reason.

As you were.

Sunday June 25, 2006
New For the Summer Fashion Line...

The Fucktard.

Ever known a person who was a fucker and a retard all at the same time? Well now you can dress them appropriately so they are clearly marked for the safety of the public.

The Fucktard is made of a thick, suffocating, tight, elastic wool that is highly flammable and conveniently soaked in kerosene for your random combustion pleasure.

The Fucktard emits a pungent odor that lies somewhere in between sour grapes, rotting flesh and fecal matter from a motorized blower, announcing The Fucktard's arrival long before you see him/her coming through the door.

The Fucktard comes in tranquil shades of gloomy-gray, cunt-drip cream and butt-smear brown.

The Fucktard is great for The Special Fucktard Olympics where you can enter your Fucktard in such events as: Beat The Fucktard, Make the Fucktard Eat Shit and The Fucktard Toss.

If you've ever met a true Fucktard, you know you wish you would have seen them coming. So do yourself and others a favor by purchasing The Fucktard, a garment that helps save the Earth from suffering. It's tax deductible and makes a great gift.

Call me for pricing and shipping details.

::sigh::

That just felt good...

As you were.

Tuesday July 4, 2006
Leveled

Ok...so no, I didn't move to Chicago.

Instead, I stuck around Los Angeles to experience my first official Hollywood Burn.

The mayhem all started when I returned from Chicago and realized that I had a whole month left here to figure out what in the hell I was going to do. My roommate was ready to move out on her own, and I had to make decisions based on financial stability over desired location.

While fully preparing myself to move two-thousand miles and leave all of my possessions behind, I decided to continue the job search in LA "just in case."

I posted my resume on job sites and was approached to sell computer software, cell phones and my body. Oh, fuck off. Then one morning I got an email from a man named Mr. Level. He was looking for a personal assistant. He claimed to work for a big record company. He told me that the record company had just merged with a limousine company, for which he was the business development manager here in Southern California. Fine.

We communicated via email, then phone. He told me that he was looking for a thick-skinned gal to be a cock-blocker between him and the rest of the world, basically. Hmmm...Sure. Sounds just glammy, really. The job description was pretty cool. Work pretty much from home, making appearances at the office when needed. Attend functions with and for Level. Handle scheduling, field emails and telephone calls. Business travel. Run errands at the drop of a hat, you know, all the normal life-sucking PA duties. Got it. The benefits were great: full of industry perks, company car, full medical, paid meals everyday, expense account...

After conferring via email and phone, he asked me to meet him for a face to face interview. We met at a Coffee Bean and Tea Leaf on a Thursday morning. How very LA. It went well. He told me that his decision was between me and another girl who he was interviewing at three that afternoon. His final request was two-part. First he wanted me to write him a "heart and soul" email as to why I wanted the job. Secondly, he said he would give me a challenge, a sample errand to do later that day. Fine.

All of this seemed pretty amusing, as he was the first actual person to really take professional interest in me in a while. I wrote the "heart and soul" email and just before I pushed send, Level called with my errand challenge. He wanted me to go put $100 into his daughter's checking account within one hour at a Wescom Credit Union that would be returned to me the following day. Now, don't get me wrong, I saw a huge red flag with a person I barely know asking me for money. Momma didn't raise no fool. At the same time, I also considered how much money I spend on haircuts, fuck-me shoes, blue jeans, make-up and trips to Target on a whim. Taking a risk on getting a job for $100 didn't seem like such a big deal.

All tasks done. Level called me later that evening and told me that the girl he was supposed to interview cancelled due to car trouble and that she wanted to reschedule for Saturday. He asked if I was acting as his PA, how I would react to that. I told him that if she really wanted to be at that interview she would have taken a cab.

Later that night he sent me a congratulatory email, letting me know that I had the job. I was elated. Suddenly, all things were falling into place. I wouldn't have to pick up and move, I could keep my couch and I could nurture the relationships I had started over the past year in this town. The next day I went and made arrangements to stay in the apartment building with my neighbor who needed a roommate. I had begun communicating with Level's former PA. On Friday night I sent her a list of questions for her to comment on regarding the job. On Saturday morning my heart stopped when I read her response. She sent word that she couldn't answer any more of my questions just yet, as Level had decided to interview the other candidate. What the fuck?

I instantly emailed him a very professional memo asking him to please be completely honest with me about the situation. I heard nothing for two days. Then I got a one-line email stating that "He would call me later in the evening." Look, I know all about the theory of free beer tomorrow, and I knew that Borriqua wasn't going to be calling anytime soon.

Agitated and trying to keep my cool, I walked around like I had a loved one in the hospital undergoing major surgery for about a week. There was hope for the best, then prayer that they might make it through long enough to see another birthday, then the reality that they're dead and not coming back.

I can accept that I didn't get a job. I can accept that I lost $100. But I cannot accept someone going against ethical business practice. I had been Leveled, burned and emotionally flattened. I'm not done with the situation. I will report him to the BBB, and I found out there is an agency set up to protect people from such creatures in "The Industry" here in LA.

What amazes me more than anything is that we live in the same city, and if he's as public as he claims to be, it's only a matter of time before I run into him somewhere. I would love to stand in front of him, smiling, with one hand on my hip and the other extended and say (like Julia Sugarbaker in a low Southern voice), "Why, how convenient that we have run into each other like this. Why don't you just make this easy on yourself-reach in your pocket, pull out your wallet and give me my money back so I don't have to make a scene by reaching for it myself. I would hate to accidentally yank out more than just my $100."

For now I have just settled for sending him polite, weekly reminders via email that he owes me money. I'm sure his new assistant loves those!

So, here I am, still in LA, only slightly singed by my burns, wondering when the next ball of fresh hell is going to be hurled in my direction.

Mr. Level, what a cowardly fucktard.

As you were.

Saturday July 8, 2006
Baked Brain Dead

I hate hot weather.

After living in Houston for over twenty years, I don't just know heat, I know humid heat. It's the kind of heat where you find yourself showering several times a day, swimming while you walk down the street, and your glasses instantly fogging up as you step outside into the moist, hot air. Let us not forget the big, puffy, out-of-control hair...The styling tool known as the flat iron was invented for Texans.

Moving to a drier, cooler climate has turned me into an anti-heat Nazi. Much like a former smoker flips out at the tiniest waft of cigarette smoke, I now recoil away from high temperatures like they are laced with incurable diseases.

The heat in LA isn't anywhere near the same as the heat I grew up in, but after being quickly reprogrammed to only enjoy temperatures in the sixties and seventies, LA causes me to go dumb and useless when it hits triple digits.

Take the other day for example: The Object Of My Affection and I decided to go for a hike. I love to get out and hike around in the hills. Great! No. Stupid. It was 4:00 pm, over a hundred degrees and the smog layer looked like chocolate frosting across the sky. We were headed up into really high elevation and as my head started to throb and my hands started to swell, I had a flashback to a news story I saw last year, discussing how people who aren't trained in climbing really shouldn't do it in extreme temperatures. When I got a sudden case of the chills, I was done. "Why exactly are we doing this now? Fuck this," is all I could think. I was accused of being weak and not a soldier. I thought about it, and decided he was right. I was not a soldier, as I was about to leave a man behind. *Of course I did not. I did allow him to take a picture of my ass from behind in my Lycra workout shorts as we walked to the car. That appeased him. I was useless for the rest of the day.

Heat like this just makes me want to sleep, stand over the fan and drink lemonade. I find myself making every excuse to stay inside and stay horizontal. Intelligent thought and conversation are nonexistent. Anything that requires energy or creativity is awash. Daydreaming is even too warm of an activity. TV static snow falls in my mind instead.

The saving grace here is that it cools down in the evenings, and this heat only lasts a few months.

Damn. I'm a crabby bitch until Fall. Mmmm...How I long for sleeping with the windows open while cuddling under my beachwood pulp sheets, wearing sweaters and boots, sipping hot chocolate and feeling crisp air snap at my cheeks. Oh, how I cannot wait until the season of driving in a hot car that only cools down two minutes before reaching my destination, sweaty cleavage (shut-up, I do have some cleavage!), high electric bills, and dealing with extra deodorant is over. ::sigh::

I need a nap.

As you were.

86

Saturday July 8, 2006
Rosenblum

One of my favorite wines is Rosenblum Red Zinfandel. It's described as "juicy, with a streak of orange peel running through the thick, jammy flavors and black pepper and wild berry notes."

I discovered this wine in 2004 while being a barfly at the Twelve Spot in Houston where I used to sit, unleash my awful work day and admire my best friend as she bartended the night away.

Many amazing conversations about art, politics and love have been had over a glass of this wine. Many a boring conversation with countless, faceless males has been had over several glasses of this wine. But one of my favorite memories to this day involves two chefs, two hot chicks and a drive to Treasures, one of Houston's upscale strip clubs, and of course, this wine. Nothing is better than passing around a good bottle of wine, ghetto koozie-style in the car before an impromptu evening of stuffing singles in a dancer's g-string...

I opened a bottle last night with The Object Of My Affection. We enjoyed some boneless beef ribs in an awesome cherry BBQ sauce while watching...what the hell were we watching? Come to think of it, what happened after we ate? I just remember visions of juicy, wild-berry strippers dancing through my head. I awoke only to drift about in a fog until about noon today. The bottle was empty and The Object Of My Affection left for work with a smile on his face.

Oh, how I adore good wine, fun memories, strippers and of course, The Object Of My Affection. Oh, and beef... :)

*Side note-The two chefs insist that strippers taste like candy. They're chefs, so I believe them.

As you were.

Sunday July 9, 2006
I Should Have Stuffed HER In Dead Man's Chest!

Last night I joined two friends (Michelle C. and her boyfriend) to see *Pirates of the Caribbean: Dead Man's Chest*. We were stoked, despite the fact that I was running late, the lines were long and it was an 11:00 pm showing at Universal City Walk on a Saturday night. (Ugh. Welcome to a small piece of congested Hell, full of flashing lights, loud music, ghetto fabulousness and underpaid staff that have no intent or capability of controlling it. Sorry...I try not leave The Happy Village very often.)

The theatre was packed, seats were scarce and the excitement was building. The lights went down, the previews played and when the movie started, the crowd cheered. Yes! An active crowd. They always make the movie so much more enjoyable. Suddenly, we were all pirates awaiting orders from our Captain Jack Sparrow!

Disney, Jerry Bruckheimer, Hans Zimmer, Ve Neill, ILM...Let's face it...It just doesn't get any bigger and better than this. Pure magic was projected onto the silver screen.

The multitude of well-developed, unique characters and plot will leave your jaw on the fuckin' floor, drooling for the arrival of the third film. There has to be Oscar Gold in someone's midst for this...

Now...Thank God this movie was so mesmerizing, otherwise I would be recounting my thoughts on this film from jail. I truly thought I was going to go bitch-slap-crazy on the dingbat who sat next to me. When people go to the movies, do they forget that they are in public and aren't alone? Do people live so unconsciously that they just don't notice that when they laugh randomly for, oh, forty-five seconds during quiet parts of the movie they prevent others from hearing crucial lines. And I'm not talking a deep guttural laugh or tiny high pitched tee-hee-hee, I'm talking a huge, weird cackle that kept me from being able to turn my head and look at her. I actually leaned into Michelle C. and whispered, "What the fuck is this next to me? I'm scared to look at her."

Bizarro and her man devoured a small country's food supply and proceeded to pillage through the wrappers in hopes of extra tiny morsels that might have fallen down into the cardboard tray. "Oh my God...Why don't you pick the shit out of each other's teeth?? Maybe that would keep you quiet for a bit...," I grumbled to myself. "Focus on Johnny...Focus on Johnny..." I forged on, determined to stay lost in the story...

And when the bitch got on her cell phone and started quacking in a foreign language, I felt my head start snappin' around on my neck like Tyler Perry's *Medea* had invaded my body; I was so becoming a mad, black woman! Michelle C. and I locked eyes, both of us thinking the same thing: "Oh my God, she must die!!!!" Hello...How many cheesy "don't answer your phone" sketches have to be put in movie trailer previews before there has to be a phone check next to the coat check? Huh??? Tell me!!! I understand that you might have to take a call. You have kids that might have caught on fire at the babysitter's. You're wife might be in labor. Jesus just might reveal himself via cell during the climax of the movie...I know...but let me tell you something...If Jesus is calling during a movie, he just testing you to see if you have the courtesy to step out into the fucking lobby!!!!

Go see the film. Marvel at the make-ups. Feel like a Goonie when you leave. But for the love of all things Holy, conduct a small interview with the patron sitting next to you. Have them sign a "Will Not Be a Fucktard Agreement" before the lights go down.

As you were.

Sunday July 9, 2006
It'snot

What is it about this season?

I'm spending far too much time digging Goddamned huge crusty boogers out of my frickin' nose.

I get the cycle, really. Spring's beautiful blossoms have led to some allergic reactions and the typical runny nose here and there. The runny nose leads to the immune system kicking into gear. But, this arid climate is causing super bats to cling to the inside of my cave!!!! My breathing is off. My sleeping becomes compromised. I dream insane dreams and snore a tad. I wake up with my sinuses feeling like the Panama Canal as I drag shit out of it. I'm just waiting on the nosebleeds...With each inhale I feel the mucous membrane lining of my nostrils tightening, ever nearing the breaking point.

Now I know why my Grandmother Sue used to smear Mentholatum up her nose...

*We call it Vic's Vapo Rub now...

As you were.

Monday July 10, 2006
The Diet of High White Cell Count Champions

It's official. I have an infection of some sort. I'm listless, having sinus issues, swollen glands, scratchy throat. My eyes are burning in the sockets, and I'm whiny. I want to be three years old, following my mother around the house, crying that I don't feel good. I'm talking head back, mouth wide, lethargically whaling, barely standing on spaghetti limbs. A possible flop on the couch might just be in order. Feetie Jammies are a definite must.

I realized that something was definitely wrong when I didn't get out of bed yesterday until 1:00 pm. I was awake, but all business conducted was from the bed. I made one trip to the bathroom and fridge for cookie dough and cherries before feeling feverish and falling back to sleep. A second trip to the bathroom and fridge occurred around 5:00 pm, only this time I showered, thinking that would perk me up. (It didn't.) I still grabbed a handful of cookie dough and cherries and after consumption, I went back to sleep for a while.

I woke up a little later, hearing my roommate in the middle stages of a Sunday cleaning frenzy. The vacuum was zooming about. I was careful not trip over it on my third trip to the fridge. It dawned on me that I should probably eat something other than cookie dough and cherries. Naturally, I stood there, staring into the fridge with no healthy taste buds to guide my hunger. I settled for cottage cheese dotted with green grapes. I sat on the couch and watched my roommate scamper like a sprite with magic wands. He told me that I looked bad and should just lie on the couch. He's the best roommate ever.

Bored, I thought about food again. I decided to get crazy and whip up a pancake. I got insane and chopped up some peaches. Just before it was time to flip the lil' bugger I strategically placed the midget, bite-sized pieces in the gooey batter. Then...FLIP! I smothered her in butter and syrup. She was delicious.

Realizing that I still felt like shit, I knew it was time. It was time for a hot toddy. Here's the family recipe. I won't repeat it, so read it slowly:

1 packet of Thera-Flu
4 ounces of water
2 ounces of Jack Daniels
1 lemon
Honey to taste

Heat the water. Mix in the Thera-Flu and Jack. Squeeze in the lemon, and stir in the desired amount of honey. Drink and repeat if desired. No operating anything more important than the TV remote control. Pass the fuck out.

And I did.

And six hours later I'm awake, wondering why The Object Of My Affection didn't call me today. Oh well, at least I have a self-induced, warm fuzzy feeling. Mmmm...time to feed my sickness...round four...cookie dough and cherries...

Would somebody pick me up and carry me to the fridge? Puh-puh-puh-pa-leeeeeze?

Eh.

As you were.

Thursday July 19, 2006
Move Over Ms. Daisy, Mr. and Mrs. Crazy Need a Ride

As the misery/adventure of searching for a decent job that is real and worth my time continues in Los Angeles, I am brought to my knees in laughter when I see a job posting such as the one below. Not only does this city draw the most ruthless, soul-swallowing and free-spirited people to live here, its reputation also beckons those types of vacationers.

Taken straight from Craigslist.com:

"I am visiting Los Angeles on vaction. My wife and I are looking for a personal assistant/driver, who will available on a full time basis to run errands, drive us around, pour drinks, set beach chairs, etc. Preferably someone who is not prudish, who can arrange for entertainment as well. Knowledge of stripclubs, masseuse, and swingclubs would be great, as we are on vacation, and ready to PARTY!! You don't have to go in, just know where things are, and drop us off. We would need you days, and nights as our driver. We will compensate for gas and expenses. We are very honest, and open, and looking for our assistant to be non-judgemental, a little wild at heart, and very discreet. Looking for someone who has already tried most things, and is not puritanical. This is for the month of August only. Please let us know what you can do, and what you know in your response, and be creative. Only for the serious....rude, judgemental types, please do not respond. We would like if you had a large vehicle, and we could pay for gas, but we would also rent a car for the month, if you are the right person for the job. Compensation: $10-15 per hour plus gas also tips and bonuses."

What I find most depressing about this: It doesn't bother me in the least and there's piece of me that wants to respond. I mean, really, what am I going to be doing in the month of August? And I was offered a marketing position for one of the hottest all-nude clubs in LA last summer. I can set up a beach chair with the best of them. And who is more creative than moi?

"Only the serious need apply..." I bet they are some uneducated, lottery winning, skanky, inbreds who think LA is the hottest vacation spot ever. I wonder if these people realize that they are setting themselves up to be robbed, murdered and dumped off of Mulholland Drive, never to be seen again? Idiots.

As you were.

Along Came A Spider...

He's Caucasian, thirty-eight, gay, a recovering drug addict, loves his Valium, wears ear plugs around the house, loves to clean, smokes clove cigarettes, believes in drinking baking soda and water to calm an upset stomach, collects huge antique furniture, practices the Hindu Faith, naps more than I do and is currently reading Kim Cattrall's book about the female orgasm. And at 10:30 pm last night he appeared in my bedroom doorway in his Queen Helene Mint Julep Mud Mask and said with his voice high and trembling, "Hey, sweetie...Are you feeling particularly Texas tough right now, because, Houston, we have a problem."

He is my current roommate.

I picked up one of my shoes, knowing what he wanted me to do. I entered his bedroom adorned with his heavy shrouds and draperies. He lead me to his computer desk. Like a child afraid of the monsters in the closet he said in a whisper, "Do you see it?" I stood with my hands on my hips, squinting at one of his decorative fabric wall hangings, "Where is it?"

"Here," he said, clicking on a flashlight. And there, on his piece of art building a cottony, dense nest, was a big ol' nasty brown recluse spider with a sack full of eggs just waiting to infest the world. I got up on a chair, then the desk and leaned in a little for a closer look: "Oh Lord," I said as my arm instinctively slammed my shoe into the nest. A shrill shriek was released behind me and when I turned around, there was my roommate with his hands over his face, squirming around like I threw period blood on him. "Oh my God, sweetie. I knew you would be able to do that. I just can't kill things. Oh, I am so sorry you had to do that. Oh, that's just too much nature for me today. Oh, my God, honey get down from there. I've got to wash that immediately." He helped me down off the desk and hugged me: "I'm so lucky to have you here."

Flustered, he began to scrub his wall hanging feverishly in the kitchen sink. I couldn't help but laugh my ass off at the whole scene. He kept recounting what he had just witnessed, "You just looked that monster dead in the eye and said, 'Oh Lord,' and thwap; you just took that beast and her babies out. It's true what they say, 'Don't mess with Texas'...Oh my God...You're totally Spiderwoman. I still can't believe you did that."

And then as quickly as the moment had arisen, he hung his fabric wall art and finished his mud mask ritual and the moment was gone. All was quiet. But one thing remains; I'm still the household superhero.

As you were.

✳ **Thursday July 13, 2006**
The Happy Village Doctor

I've said it before and I will say it again: Los Feliz Village is one of the best areas to live in Los Angeles. Everything you need to live comfortably is within WALKING DISTANCE!

Today, I am convinced there is a God, because when I woke up for the third day in a row with tonsils so infected and swollen that I couldn't breathe or swallow normally, I knew I had to go to the doctor despite the fact that I don't have health insurance. I've *knock on wood* been incredibly healthy this year despite my abundant travels and crazy lifestyle. (I made it through Vegas, Maui, Chicago, Houston and NYC/New Jersey without catching more than a few headaches [especially from the uber fucktard in New Jersey] and hangovers.) I am due for a little illness. But when I get sick, I get SICK. The Thera-Flu and Jack Daniels just weren't cutting it anymore, though they are going down easier and easier...I can't lie...

I remembered that there is a doctor's office on the corner of Hillhurst and Ambrose, only a two-minute walk from my front steps. I got out of bed and walked over about 8:30 am. I was sixth in line and by the time I had filled out my new patient paperwork, I was already in an examination room. Before I knew it, Dr. Michael Burton was in my presence, giving me a once-over. I told him what was wrong; he looked at my throat, grimaced a tad and said, "I notice that you don't have insurance. I will give you a weeks worth of penicillin for free. If you don't feel better I will call in a prescription. Until then gargle with warm salty water and eat lots of Jell-O and ice cream." I think I may have thrown my arms around him and kissed him. I can't quite recall. I had a fever; parts of the day are blurry...

I got to the counter, awaiting the damages and the receptionist said, "That will be $139.00" "Ouch," I thought, handing over my debit card, "but at least I got free meds." She ran my card and handed me the receipt to sign. The total was listed as only $39.00. I showed it to her and she said that it was correct. I had misunderstood her! $39.00? Are you kidding me? $39.00 won't even fill up the gas tank in my car! Hoorah!

I've already taken the first day's dose and I feel 75% better. Ben and Jerry's Brownie Batter Ice Cream isn't hurting the cause at all, I'll tell you that for sure.

Who really needs employment or health insurance when you live in The Happy Village?

Go see Michael Burton M.D.

2101 Hillhurst Ave., Los Angeles, CA 90027 (323) 664-2931

He's open SEVEN DAYS A WEEK!

As you were.

Thursday July 13, 2006
Sephora's Insincere Squiggle

[:::::SIGH:::::Robin lets head hit the keyboard, as yet again, another business entity in Los Angeles disappoints her.]

I went to check the mail and amidst the junk mail and bills was a flimsy postcard addressed to me from Sephora. You know what Sephora is. It's that wonderful store where a million cosmetic, skin care and fragrance brands come to mingle together for an exhilarating, one-stop shopping extravaganza. Sounds dreamy, huh? Fuck that.

The postcard read:

"6/2006

Thank you very much for your application of employment with Sephora.

We had a number of qualified candidates for our opening and would like to let you know we have selected another candidate whose qualifications most closely match the requirements for the position.

We will retain your resume on file and will contact you should we have a position in the future for which you may be considered.

I would like to thank you again for your interest in Sephora.

Yours Sincerely,

[Some encrypted squiggle]"

Ok...What? Yes. At one time I did apply to work for Sephora. I even interviewed with them. I patiently waited for a response, followed up a week later by phone and was hung up on twice. I figured it was a lost cause. Irritated with the unprofessional manner in which I was treated, I let it go and moved on.

Just for the shits and giggles of it all, I went back and looked at my day planner. I interviewed with them at the beginning of January, 2006. It's now mid-July people! THAT WAS SIX-AND-A-HALF MONTHS AGO! WHY AM JUST NOW HEARING FROM THEM???? Do I really believe that they took that long to place a few sales people? No fucking way.

I love Sephora and don't get me wrong, I won't stop shopping there. It does have the things I want in one location, but I have never been helped by a single person upon entering the store. The employees just move about like retail robots doing their assigned task for the zone that they are in at the time. There's the greeter: "Hi. Welcome to Sephora." The floor person: "Hi. Let me know if you need help finding anything." And the cashier: "Hi. Did you find everything ok?" If I could reach out and physically hand you some lipstick in a bag while blasting some techno music at you right now, I would have just completed a virtual shopping experience at Sephora for you. Woo...

SIX-AND-A-HALF MONTHS TO RESPOND FOR A RETAIL POSITION THAT PAYS AVERAGE PAY???

What makes me want to poke their eyes out more than anything is that little encrypted squiggle signature...I can't call and chew them out. I can't report them to the corporate office effectively with a squiggle. There is nothing sincere about a squiggle!!! Fuckers.

I would really expect more from a company that stems from such big names as Moet Chandon and Louis Vuitton...

Scrubs...

Am I really living this life? Sometimes I wonder...

As you were.

Friday July 14, 2006
Calling The Ol' Roley Poley

My cell phone number has been mine since 1998. I have refused to change it and have been with T-Mobile since the Aerial days. I have had very few problems with my service, and let me tell you, if I ever have to call the company for anything at all, they see that I've been a customer since 1998 and I get the princess deals, free bonus minutes, extended warranties and all that jazz.

What I have found to be an issue over the years is that my cell phone number is very close to several business numbers. Calls come in consistently for a Holiday Inn in the Clear Lake area of Houston. I cannot count the number of phone calls I have gotten at all hours of the day and night asking for room rates, specials and to speak to the manager. The first couple of times I just said, "Oh I'm sorry; you have the wrong number." But after a while I just started to have fun with it. If they are dumb enough to give their credit card number to me when I have answered the phone at 3:00 am with a sleepy voice and without saying, "Thank you for calling the Holiday Inn. How can I help you?" then they deserve to have their identity threatened. It turns out that about a trillion business cards and marketing material were misprinted and distributed. Good thing I'm a nice person: I always tell every person who calls what the correct number is. At one point I called the hotel in question and explained the issue. The manager said, "Oh my God, you're Robin Kilgore. People call here asking for you all the time." So I guess a bunch of people I have given my number to are dumb, as they do answer the phone at the hotel by saying, "Thank you for calling the Holiday Inn. How can I help you?" What morons actually ask for me once they hear it's a hotel?

Another set of calls I receive are about pet grooming and pet grooming supplies. I haven't ever figured out what the business name actually is because I usually laugh at the callers. When I hear: "Do you do German Shepards," at 8:00 am on a Saturday and respond, "No, but I've had myself a few stallions," they usually hang up.

Some fucktard out there is in a lot of trouble with creditors and/or the law, because I get quite a few calls for a Gerald Whitaker. "Are you sure this isn't Gerald Whitaker?" I get probed by countless callers. Do I sound like a man? One Friday afternoon I got asked if I was sure I wasn't Gerald Whitaker one too many times by the same woman. I told the woman to hold on, then after a minute of me rubbing my phone on my pants leg, I said to her, "Did you hear that? That was the sound of me rubbing my phone on my vagina. I'm sure I'm not some fucking man named Gerald Whitaker!" She hung up, and I haven't heard from her since.   ::tears dropping::

This morning I got a call that is currently my favorite and will be for a while, I imagine. At 6:34 am, my cell phone rang and a deep East Texas drawl came swooning through: "Is this Roley Poley?" I chuckled a bit. For an instant I thought it was my Main Gay Josh, who I have been prank calling at work recently because I'm unemployed, immature and a loser (and because I love hearing him gasp when I call him a cuntface). I realized that it wasn't and just laughed and said, "Are you calling me fat?" The man apologized and said all nice and slow, "This must be an old directory," and hung up. What the hell kind of business is called Roley Poley? Hmmm...maybe it's the pet grooming place....I don't know, but it was kinda neat to hear a familiar-sounding accent on the other end of the line.

94

Speaking of prank calling Josh, it's just about that time...heh heh heh heh...

As you were.

Sunday July 16, 2006
I Heart My Anteater

My friend Ziggy is a self-proclaimed Anteater. That's right. He's uncircumcised and proud of it. In fact, he might just introduce himself as "Anteater not Mushroom" when you meet him.

More than anything, uncut men tend to take a lot of flack for their extra baggage. It is often assumed from those urban legend-style horror stories that an uncut penis will give you nothing but grief, like grody infections. The reality is that cut or uncut, if it's not a clean penis in a clean vagina, you are both human Petri dishes for cottage cheese and slime. Granted, uncut men do have a responsibility to pay a tad bit more attention to their genital hygiene, but how hard do you really think it is to get a man to pay more attention to his dick?

I have done some research. Surveys say when it comes to what most women prefer- the cut or uncut penis, the answer is simple: It depends on what they have had more experience with. Whether a man has been cut or not depends on several things: cultural influence, religious influence, parental influence, etc. Chances are, (in America) if you live in a very Jewish, Christian or basically Caucasian area, you're in Mushroom Territory. Skip around into an area that has a lot of immigrants from Europe or South America and Anteaters rule. If you are a sedentary female who doesn't travel a lot, doesn't live in a very culturally diverse area or don't sleep around a bit, chances are that you are familiar with one kind of penis.

Here's a secret for all you ladies fearing an Anteater: Because the head of the uncut man's penis is nicely protected by its special hood, it's so much more sensitive than the penis that just dangles around all day, blowing in the breeze, getting all desensitized due to excess stimulation. What I'm saying here is that sex becomes less work for you and more pleasure for you both. Have you ever given the blow job that just doesn't seem like it's going to end? Try yourself an Anteater and watch out; three words: Two Pump Chump.

Ladies, consider something. If you had just given birth to a beautiful baby girl, and the doctor came to you and said all cheery and chuckling: "Congratulations on having a daughter. We're just about ready to take her in to have part of her clitoris clipped off. Not too much though, just enough so that it will be even harder to find." I'm assuming you would freak the fuck out. Hello, what's the point? Won't that affect her sexual health in the future? Don't they consider that genital mutilation in "those other countries?" Uh yeah...So give our hooded boys a chance.

Ignorance is keeping people from experiencing the pleasures that Anteaters bring to our lives. Ignorance leads to discrimination. And what better way to end such things? That's right, kids: EDUCATION! And what's my favorite way to spread awareness and educate people? T-SHIRTS, BUTTONS AND BUMPER STICKERS!!!

So, Ziggy, I dedicate these slogan ideas to you and all of the other Anteaters out there.

I'm starting a revolution-a campaign for equality. I think I may have found my platform in life. My mother was an English teacher, (one of Ziggy's in fact) and always taught me that education was power.

"Anteaters need love, too"

"Proud to be an Anteater"

"Anteater por Vida" (for the Spanish speakers)

"Straight out da hood, yo" (for the urban anteaters)

"Eat more Anteaters" (Chic-Fil-A rip; regional, of course)

"Anteaters, We Shall Overcum"

"Anteaters do it in a Hoodie"

"From the Hood with Love"

"My Anteater could kick your Mushroom's ass." (girls' baby tee's)

"I Heart My Anteater"

"I'm with the Anteater"

"Anteaters offer a little something extra"

"I'm not overly sensitive. I'm an Anteater."

"Will the Anteaters please stand up?" (for those seeking only the uncut)

"I break for Anteaters"

Ahhhh...My mom is going to be so proud...

As you were.

Friday July 21, 2006
Reality Snap in 109

So here is the simple fact: My roommate is a paranoid schizophrenic.

Did I know this before I moved in with him? Yes.

Why did I move in with him in that case? He's not violent or harmful to anyone. He's just a little odd. Frankly, if I wasn't his roommate, I might find his behavior amusing-antics performed by the absurd, really. I needed a place to move into quickly, and it was the most reasonable choice at the time.

What is causing me to face his issues? Well, they are becoming a part of my daily life. Duh, we live in the same apartment.

What have I witnessed? Good Lord, get your popcorn:

Sunday night: My roommate, who usually goes to sleep no later than 10:00 pm was up stomping around, opening and closing drawers, huffing and puffing on the phone, irate about something. I found out the next day that he was convinced his sister had intentionally given him a birthday card to upset him. The card said: "You're getting to the age where trying to be hip could cause you to break one." His old roommate had both of his hips replaced a few years ago, and my roommate got it in his head that she was making fun of him. He got so upset he wrote her a long letter and tore it up before calling and reading it to her on her answering machine. He even called the old roommate and told him what his sister did. The old roommate spent about an hour telling him that he was reading into it way too much. The whole time he was telling me this story, I was standing at his bedroom door, listening to him recount his woes while trying not to see his cock ring and ginormous bottle of lube on his nightstand. DID I MENTION THAT HE NEVER CLOSES HIS BEDROOM DOOR!?!   ::shudder::

Monday night: I was out running some errands with The Object Of My Affection, and my phone started blowing up. It was my roommate, and I didn't answer because lately he's been pretty clingy towards me, almost like a little brother who wants to spend time with his big sister. I'm not his sister. His sister is a lesbian who broke his arm three different times as a child. I'm his roommate. We split the bills. Anyhow, I listened to the messages, and frantically he stated that he had slammed the sliding glass door and it had shattered. I didn't find this too odd as it was old and didn't slide well, yet I couldn't help but remember how flustered he was the night before.

Tuesday night: I was heading out to have dinner with a friend. As I was getting ready in my room I could hear my roommate talking, but couldn't understand what he was saying. When I walked past his room, I could hear what sounded like a child singing. I looked in and there he was in boxers, jumping up and down, singing and clapping like a child with a bicycle light on his head. When he saw me, he continued to jump and giggled and said, "You gotta' make some noise so I know you're coming." I just said, "Or you could shut the door."

Wednesday night: Oh, this one's good...You'll love it. I was again on my way out to meet some friends in from out of town, and as I was walking to the door, I heard some odd noise coming from the kitchen. Passing by, I looked in, and there was my roommate, giggling like a child with his boxers pulled down, spanking his own bare ass with a wooden spoon. I asked, "What are you doing?" Still spanking and giggling he said, "I'm just trying to remember what it used to feel like when my mother used to whip me with one of these as a child." Oddly, nothing came to mind, so I just told him I would see him later and left. Upon my return around midnight as I opened the door, I heard (in his high pitched squeal like something out of *The Shining*) "There she is!" He came bounding down the hall, threw his arms around me and kissed me on the cheek. Uhhh... whoa. Ok. Goodnight.

I've never seen him like this. I've seen him really bad, like when he used to lurk around outside late at night with his sunglasses on thinking that someone was trying to kill him, but never in this goofy, childlike state.

So on Thursday I called his doctor and basically said, "What the fuck, dude?" He said, "I know he's not taking his medication. He's only taking Valium. What you need to do is tell him that he needs to call me." Hmmm...Great. Not taking his meds. That's just wonderful. So I called his former roommate and told him what was going on. He said that he would come over in the evening to discuss the matter with him. Sadly, he wasn't able to make it. I talked to a couple of friends. The common consensus was, "Robin, this isn't your cross to carry. You've done your time at the asylum, and you are free to go at any time." All I know is that I don't need to deal with this. No one is going to declare me a saint over this for fuck's sake.

THE BIG PICTURE:

You know you're really living in LA when you quit your stable job, cash in your 401k, live without health insurance, reside with a schizo, dabble in the industry, get turned down for every job you apply for because you are too over-qualified or just not the right fit, yet manage to travel and stay in cute clothes because you're cashing nice unemployment checks, and you really couldn't be happier and couldn't imagine living anywhere else.

Who, the fuck, have I become?

Shit, maybe I need to go see my roommate's psychiatrist.

Stay tuned...Even I can't wait to see what happens next. Hell, I'm going to TIVO myself!

As you were.

Friday July 21, 2006
18 Inches of Total Bullshit

About a month ago my friend Tracy and I went to get some ice cream at Coldstone in Atwater Village. I was craving that cake batter flavor, and Tracy had a hankering for something that looked like it had the kitchen sink in it. We arrived about 4:45 pm and the meters aren't free until 6:00 pm, but (much to my good fortune) the available one was out of order. SWEET!

After discussing my move to Chicago and enjoying our treats, we headed to the car. Staring me in the face was the torrid red and white envelope that holds any driver's nemesis, The Parking Ticket. At first, I was livid. The meter was out of fucking order!!! Everybody knows that it's a freebie!!! I read the ticket. Yelling, I said, "Tracy, they gave me a ticket for parking more than eighteen inches away from the curb, those bastards!!!" Then a calm came over me. As I ripped it into pieces and put it in my purse, I smugly looked at Tracy and said, "What does it matter, I'm selling my car and moving to Chicago in a month anyway."

Suddenly, Steppenwolf blared in the background, and smoke came off my tires as we peeled out in our tight leather outfits, our big hair billowing in the wind, looking for the next adventure, whatever was coming our way...

Fast forward...I'm still in Los Angeles. I still needed to pay my parking ticket. My mother was so worried that I would go to jail if I didn't that she sent me money to pay for it. Wondering how I was going to make good on my debt to the community with an envelope in pieces but still ticked off, I decided: tape. I taped the envelope back together, and shredded the ticket. I wrote out the check for the amount of $35 and in memo line I printed in thick black letters: TOTAL BULLSHIT. I put the ticket confetti and the check in the envelope and then taped it as if I was five year-old so that they surely had to cut into it. Into the mail it went.

Yesterday I was checking my bank account balance online and was tickled pink to see my check image there on the screen. Some poor schmuck actually took the time to break into that envelope. I bet it made his day to read my memo. I'm sure he could relate. They got their money, and I got my frustration out. There's just something rewarding about seeing your own handwriting up on the big computer screen...

What can I say? I guess I was just born to be wild...

As you were.

Tuesday July 25, 2006
Hey Man....You're Like an Office Genius

Once again, I'm amused by a job posting I found on Craigslist.com for a job LA:

"I need an office genius, an experienced assistant to interact with clients, handle appointments, travel and correspondence. Must have excellent communication/administrative skills. Must be highly organized, self-motivated, detail-oriented, versatile, cool-headed, and a problem solver. Mac/PC proficiency required. Photoshop, Website Excel, Quikbooks.
This will be a hectic/laid back home office. If your attitude and work ethic is like that of a PA - you will thrive.
"personal duties":
- walk the dog
- run errands
- help me plan my wedding
- etc etc
"office":
- this will eventually be your office - make it efficient and productive.
- everything it takes to get us a killer launch of the product this Winter.

Starting Salary : Partime 3-4 days a week (however I forsee fulltime very soon)
12$ per hour
(oh and you must be 420 friendly)
I am looking to train someone to take over for me as I am starting 2 new businesses.
This position is great for someone who does not mind working hard to get to the top.
You MUST be eco conscious - VIP
Job location is Hollywood Hills
Compensation: 12 per hour"

::sigh::

Where do I begin?

First of all, what in the hell is this business? What is the product that is to be launched? Why would anyone respond to ads where they have no information regarding the nature of the business? Save yourself some time in making that phone call to the penis ice cube tray factory, people!

I love how this is supposed to be a part-time job, yet the person posting the ad thinks that it is possible to do all of these things and make an office run efficiently and create a "killer launch" by winter, three or four days a week. Winter is not that far away.

Obviously this person does need help of some sort, as she (I am assuming) is planning a wedding. I must ask-do you want an office manager or a wedding coordinator? They should not be the same person. I bet she doesn't realize how many shades of white there really are. Wait...How do I just know that this wedding will be described as "non-traditional"?

Hmm...Going to start two new businesses, while building one product part-time, while planning a wedding, while being high? This person must be high to think that all of this can just happen through hard work three to four days a week for $12 an hour. What is it with people wanting you to run their lives and make them a shit-ton of money for less than $50,000 a year? I mean, really.

Who flat-out states in a job posting that they do drugs? That's a given in this town. You don't have to flaunt it. Idiot.

And what's this "must be eco-friendly" crap? Does this mean I have to make sure your cans of organic soda, foil and broken bongs are put in special containers by the road each week in the middle of all the other duties?

Plan my wedding, run my business, walk my dog while I get high and as I give you barely enough money to cover your rent and bills, DON'T YOU DARE FORGET TO RECYCLE!

Ummmm...Fuck you?

What this person needed was someone to write their ad for them. Who am I kidding? They deserve the type of person who *would* respond to an ad like this. I wonder if it ever crossed the mind of this moron that the pot might be inhibiting her ability to do all of the things she needs to do to be successful and keep her business costs low? I doubt it.

:)

As you were.

Monday July 31, 2006
The Power of 1

I'll lay it out straight for you. I'm pretty far down in the dumps. The past week was tough.

I had three interviews set up and not one of them went well. Being able to land interviews in LA is no easy task. It's purely a numbers game. I would say that for every five people/places I contact, I land one interview.

During the first interview, I dealt with a woman who stated she was incredibly busy, but goofed off on her instant messenger during my interview while mindlessly asking me questions that were plainly stated on my application and resume. She also kept my driver's license by accident and then tried to convince me that she had given it back to me. Oh, my God. I wanted to push my fingers into her eye sockets.

A French woman was my next interviewer. During our discussion she explained to me that her office was quiet and soothing because she suffers from an inner ear disorder in which small noises, say, the clicking of a pen, sound incredibly loud and painful to hear. The people in the office were all wearing either foam flip-flops or soft-soled shoes. There were no radios on or speakers attached to the computers. Let's face it. Despite the fact that I would have loved attempting that job, I wouldn't fit there at all. It's no secret that I'm noisy, express myself quite audibly and adore cute little heels that clippity-clop as I swish around, looking authoritative. Yet, I was still a little hurt when I got the, "you're just not the right fit," phone call. I honestly can't imagine living with such disorder but, I'm not going to lie-I just want to call and snap my fingers into the phone to see if she would pass out in anguish. Did I mention that she was French?

The third was just awash. The uppity-up I was supposed to have a simple phone conference with didn't even bother to keep our appointment or call to cancel. "Oh, I'm just far too busy this week. Call me next week," is what she told me. Thank you for giving me the power, but what the fuck? I love it when people in high places are so busy that they can't keep up with their appointments. *I wonder if calling to leave her a message thanking her for causing me to lose my apartment and my car would make her realize her lack of professionalism. Doubtful.

On top of all of this, I have been dead to the bed with the worst sinus infection and chest cold I've had in the past five years. There's nothing more frustrating than being sick as a dog with nothing to do but think, medicate yourself and try to breathe in bed when your world is crashing around you. I think this is where despair came for a visit. There was a point when I finally got in a position where air was flowing through one of my nostrils and I was so comfortable. Ahhhh...Yes...relaxation and then...what? Oh Lord...snot was running out of the other nostril and onto my face and the pillow. There was no way in hell I was moving to blow my nose. I just reached around, found a dirty t-shirt at the foot of the bed and put it under my face and the let the shit drip right onto the shirt. It was going in the washing machine anyhow. Finally, I was in control of something.

When I was awake I entertained myself with good movies filmed in Texas: *Terms of Endearment, Urban Cowboy* and *The Battle of Mary Kay.* There's nothing that makes a weak transplant feel her roots like seeing shots of her hometown peppered with Jack Nicholson, Shirley McClaine, a girl who can ride a mechanical bull in a Pasadena Honky-Tonk and a female business owner who operated a multi-million dollar corporation on The Golden Rule.

Post tears, nasal drip and caustic hack, I got back on the bull today and started making calls again. I set up three new appointments for this week and next. Looking into my closet, I realized that I need a new power suit for interviews. I decided to hit the mall and find a pantsuit. No luck. Bummer. I walked into a store I normally don't shop in: Arden B. I looked around and saw a nice black pencil skirt with some sassy, but classy tops. I thought...Mary Kay always believed that women should wear nice dresses and skirts to not only show their professionalism, but to keep their femininity while they do it. I looked through the skirts and found sizes: 1, 6, and 12. Umm...anybody see a 4? I looked at the 1 and thought, "There's no way, but what the hell, try it on. What's one more stab at your pride these days?" Much to my surprise, it was a perfect fit. A size 1? I haven't been a size 1 since like the sixth grade! I'm sure it's just their sizing, but who cares? It's not a suit, but it feels pretty damn powerful, I say. Thank you, Arden B. And special thanks go out to The Three S's: sex, stress and sickness, as they are my new diet and exercise plan. The last two will kill you, but the first helps fix them so they are a perfect triumvirate.

Here's to another week in Hell-A!

*As an aside for those who love a good connection, I lived in the neighborhood where *Terms of Endearment* was filmed during my nanny days. When I was five, I rode the bull at Gilley's Honky-Tonk in Pasadena, Texas where *Urban Cowboy* was filmed before the place burned to the ground (ok, I just sat on it). Later in life, I worked with Mickey Gilley's granddaughter Jennifer at The Firm. And most importantly, I got my best business polishing from being an Independent Beauty Consultant for Mary Kay. I sure wish more places invoked her business practices. I feel like I'm in the middle of my own battle: "*The Battle for Robin Kilgore*...How one woman was determined to find and generate goodness, honesty and integrity through a city with none..."

And I must say-the love and support from my friends and family lately has been amazing. What would I do without them all? I shudder to imagine...

As you were.

Tuesday August 1, 2006
Excuse Me, You Are In My Underwear

While watching *The Hills Have Eyes* with The Object Of My Affection at his apartment the other night, I decided I needed to take a break from the gore (which I find just over the top and boring, yet he craves it like a man in the desert craves water). I stepped into the library, also known as the bathroom.

The bathroom? Yes. It's the room in his apartment where I can shut the door and just be alone for a bit. (Predominantly, only child habits die hard.) Not only did I have to whiz, I also enjoy reading his magazines. He's got a stack of them by the can that could keep me occupied for hours. "Blender," "Stuff," "FHM," etc. I have yet to find any true smut or porn, and for the record, those would probably keep me occupied just as long. I find magazines for men helpful for both men and women. They are full of articles about etiquette, fashion, new electronic gadgets, news, events, sports stuff and of course, pictures of pretty ladies all shiny, airbrushed, half-necked with that open mouthed/bedroom eyes/come hither look (a look which I am convinced you are either born being able to do or not. I've practiced it in the mirror before, and I just looked like I had malaria or something).

Anywho...So I was sitting in the library perusing the periodicals when I came across an article about this DROP-DEAD GORGEOUS European girl with a set of the most delicious E-sized natural breasts I've ever seen. I read the article...She was nineteen!!!! Good Lord!!! I can't imagine looking like that at nineteen. Hell, at nineteen, I was still wearing Dexter loafers and acrylic fingernails, hoping that my big hair would balance out my wide hips. I turned the page, still perplexed by her layout and then I'm stopped cold. In one of her full page shots, I realized that she was wearing a bra and panty set that I HAVE. It took me a second to recognize it as it looks nothing like that on me, but yep, those were mine...

Hmmm...so I did the appropriately incorrect thing to do. I walked out into the living area, magazine in hand and said to The Object Of My Affection, "What do you notice about this picture?" (I'm great at set-ups.) He said blankly, "Nothing." I laughed and said, "Look closely." He shook his head, smiling, and shrugged. "Don't you recognize these?" I prodded. "Babe, I'm trying to watch a movie. What are you talking about?" he asked. "She's wearing one of my bra and panty sets. Funny how we look totally different in the same ensemble, huh? Her breasts are real, too," I jabbered. He looked at me and said, "Didn't you read what she said about her body? She said that she knows her breasts are attractive, but she really wishes she had more of a butt, and we both know you've got the backside that would make her react the same way about you as you are about her."

That's right ladies, not only is he brilliantly well-read, but he can passionately make you relate to the material he reads. He's a literary God, I tell you. (And I'm not saying that because I'm biased. ;))

As you were.

Tuesday August 1, 2006
Maryjane and I Just Don't Get Along

For all of you who keep asking me to smoke pot or wonder why I won't do it, this is for you...

As I think back over my little lifetime, I cannot remember the first time I was around marijuana. One day, sometime in high school, I guess, it just became a natural part of a lot people's lives around me. Hell, my mother is an old hippie at heart and still day-dreams of "the days when pot was safe."

Still, at the age of twenty-six, I get a lot of amusing peer pressure and have had many a humorous discussion about why I don't partake of the toke. One of the main reasons I don't smoke pot is that it's illegal, and I don't need it to function. I'm not against the use of pot at all, though I do see that it makes most people quite useless when enjoyed in excess, just like most things. *This is coming from a girl who at one time in her life could drink enough gin that she could hallucinate and shit actual juniper berries while still getting up in time to go to work. (It was the only way I could stand that office.)

The other main reason I don't smoke pot is because, once, I actually smoked it. Amazingly, I lived to tell about it. The story goes a little something like this...

Picture it, Houston, 2003 (or was it 2004...the memory gets fuzzy), Memorial Day weekend. It was Sunday night, and I was on the couch preparing to stay in when the phone rang. It was my partner in crime, the ever lovely, fun and voluptuous, Alba. "Amy and Tracy (yes, a male named Tracy) got married today and the people who were supposed to share their adjoining Bridal Suite at The Hotel Icon had a fight and they asked me if we wanted it." Before I could get the words "Fuck yeah" out of my mouth, I was getting dressed.

Alba was at my door in about five minutes, and about seven minutes later we were valet parking at the hotel and proceeding to traipse around downtown, hitting up our favorite bars. We knew one of the bartenders at a bar (which no longer has the same name or the same bartender) and began soaking up vodka tonics. Now, this is a little-known fact about me, but I have the ability to attract older men like bees to honey. I don't know why, but if he's got on a tacky rayon print shirt, a head of steel wool hair and a propensity for little assertive chicks, he will attach himself to me in a heartbeat. Soon enough, we were both trashed, and an out of place older man in a watermelon print shirt and I were salsa dancing (I'm pretty sure there was no salsa music playing, FYI). My alter ego was emerging (Oh yes, also a lesser known fact about me, I have a drunk alter ego...), and when he asked what my name was I said rolling my r's, "Rrrrraquel." He smiled and asked if he could have my phone number. "Rrrrraquel does not give out her phone number," I sassed back with a Spanish accent. About a foot away from me, Alba was yelling: "Robin...Robin...Robin!!! Do you want another drink?" I turned to her and smiled a wicked grin and yelled, "Alba, my name is not Robin. It's Rrrrraquel." In her drunk hazy voice she yelled back, "Awww hell no...If you get to use a fake name, I get to use a fake name." "Fine. What do you want your name to be then?" I asked. She paused and got the pondering look on her face, then said with uncertainty, "Priscilla?" I turned back to the man who was still standing with his body pressed up against me and said in all seriousness, "I'd like to introduce you to my best friend, Priscilla."

::snap::

The next memory I have of the evening is suddenly being in the hotel room with the newlyweds and Alba. The couple was enjoying party favors (*ahem) and packing a pipe. Just as it was being passed to me, Alba said, "Wait. Make sure she wants to do it first. Robin, do you wanna get high?" Drunk and goofy already, I said, "Yeah."

::snap::

The next thing I recall is the couple saying, "We're going out after hours dancing, but we made you guys a bubble bath. That tub is amazing and shouldn't go to waste." (The Hotel Icon does have amazing bathrooms!) We stumble-floated into the bathroom, and like two little kids, we ripped off our clothes and dove into about two inches of scalding hot water and fifteen inches of bubbles. I have no idea how long it took to regulate the water level and temp, but it seemed like we instantly needed more pot. Amazingly (and with zero coordination), I volunteered to go get it, and we smoked that pipe until it was dead. There is a blur of trying to keep each other from drowning and checking "just one more time" to make sure there was no more pot left in the pipe which suddenly was followed by me running my hand through her hair, and leaning in very close Alba. "Don't move. I'll be right back." I proceeded to get out of the tub and vomit my guts up. I could hear Alba laughing, saying, "I can see your naked white ass."

::snap::

I woke up in the most comfortable bed, and I was wrapped in a warm, soft bath-robe. I was in a different room than the one I was in the night before. I heard Alba on the phone in the other bed, laughing and talking quietly: "Robin did the gateway drug last night...The best was when she started crying and said that she couldn't do this ever again because Mary Kay was going to call her to run the company, and she wouldn't be able to pass the pee test." In a raspy, throaty Southern voice I said, "I'm awake and I hear you Goddamn it." Thunderous laughter erupted from us both. The Groom knocked on the door and brought in my clothes, which I had left in the couple's bathroom. I went into the bathroom and was horrified by what I saw. Weed resin was smeared on my face like war paint. I looked like about ten miles of bad Texas road. Not too long after that, I began to hurl my guts up...for hours. I crawled to the bathroom several times and then finally just laid on the tile floor next to the toilet like a sick, hot, dog, breathing all shallow and sweating. Upon our exit from the hotel, I proceeded to toss my cookies in a vase in the lobby. Ahhh...yes...pure class. I spent the rest of the day trying piece the night together. I honestly didn't feel normal again until about 5:00 pm the next day. It's safe to say that was my last dance with Maryjane...

Many people have heard this story and have tried to give me multiple reasons for why I got sick and how I need to just smoke pot all by itself and all sorts of shit...But really, I do fine with a glass of wine or a cocktail here and there. More than anything though, I get more comments on the lack of steamy sex I didn't have with my hot best friend in the sexy bathtub scene.

I don't get high. I don't have wild sex in hotel rooms with my girlfriends. What can I say? I'll never make it on "Girls Gone Wild." I guess I'm every guy's fantasy letdown. You know, I'm ok with that.

As you were.

Friday August 11, 2006
More Like A Job UnFair

My dear friend Sarah Cole in Nashville gave me a burst of employment inspiration last week. "Have you ever thought of doing pharmaceutical sales?" she asked. I told her that it had crossed my mind, but the pursuit had never been actualized. While we were chatting, I started searching online for companies, etc. Suddenly, I could see myself walking into doctor's offices with a rolling cart full of pill samples. Shit, why not? Drugs are the only one of the three recession proof industries that I haven't been a part of. *They are alcohol, cosmetics and drugs. In the hardest times, people always want them, no matter what...

Anyhow, I put on my super professional thinking cap and decided to call in a consultant for my resume. My dear friend, Shannon L., has been asking to see a copy of my resume for a while. I sent it to her and told her that I was looking into pharmaceutical sales. When it returned to me, it landed in my inbox looking like it had been on one of those Extreme Makeover Reality shows. Damn. Every word of it is true, but it makes me sound like a different person. A bionic person...

Armed with my new, printable version of me, I pulled out the business suit, the good heels, the nice purse, and the corporate jewelry. With "Eye of the Tiger" blaring in my head, I stepped out Wednesday morning to meet the faces of Big Pharma.

Five pharmaceutical companies were scheduled to be in attendance at a Job Fair I found during my Internet search. Great. That's five chances to make a great first impression.

The first challenge: driving to the Fair. One-and-a-half hours in traffic. Feeling ten feet tall and bullet proof, I walked into the hotel and found it to be about ninety degrees inside and so crowded that I could barely walk. (Keep in mind that I'm really only five feet tall and because of this my life is pits and tits. In a hot crowded room, trust me, I can tell if you're "Sure" whether you are raising your hands or not.) I headed to the registration desk. I filled out the paperwork and asked where the pharmaceutical companies were and was told, "Only two showed up. One you can meet with, but unless you filled out the pre-screening survey online before arriving, you can't meet with the other." Umm...How would one know about the pre-screening survey, exactly?

"Fuck it," I thought. "I'm here-I might as well just meet with the one and get as much useful information as possible."

I turned the corner. There was a line forty people deep, all hot and in competition with each other. I couldn't wait to go chat that line up. And I did for an hour-and-a-half. Yep. I waited for an hour-and-a-half to have one moment with the rep. I might as well have been in line for "American Idol"...

Finally, the door opened and a tall, former jock, nerdy-looking woman in a bad outfit poked her head out and said, "Next," which meant me. I walked in with a smile on my face, feeling great, and introduced myself. The woman moved like a robot and only said, "Please sit down. Because there are so many people here, I'm just going to quickly read your resume and then ask you a few questions."

She lowered her glasses on her nose and began to skim. Then after reading all about me she raised her head and said, "So, tell me a little about yourself." What? You just read about the biggest chunk of my professional life and now I have to tell you a little more? Ummm...ok...So I told her why I was looking into pharmaceutical sales. Blah... Blah...Blah...She smiled and said, "Do you have sales experience?" Ummm yeah...You just read that I did on my resume...

She asked me if I had any questions for her. I had a ton. I wanted to know everything about her job, the integrity of her work, the amount of hours she put in, how she felt about her products. I threw in a bunch of information about the company and told her that I felt like I related to the company. She gave me the most stock answers I've ever heard. I could have sworn she was reading from cue cards over my shoulder. It was horrible. "We look for people from all types of diverse backgrounds as we believe in building teams with strengths in all areas. I like my job because the company is well respected, and I'm very competitive." I noticed that her skin seemed a lot like plastic and that she really wasn't blinking very much...She was a fucking puppet!

She concluded by telling me that she would forward my resume to the rep for the Los Angeles area and that I should also apply online. What? That's it? No fucking way. She didn't have business cards to hand out or company literature...nothing. She was just there to pick up resumes!!!

I walked out thinking that I wasted my time, but I was wrong. I also wasted money. When I got to my car, I found a parking ticket on my windshield. I drove the hour-and-a-half home thinking about how I just paid $45 to sweat in my nice suit and be told that I should use my own resources at home by a big, nameless puppet. I think the steam is still coming out of my ears.

106

At least I got a hot new resume out of the deal...

Grr...

As you were.

Saturday August 12, 2006
Pretend You're Camping

A friend of mine went on a camping trip. I was surprised that he was going. He just doesn't seem like the kind of guy who would enjoy "the elements" and lack of modern conveniences. "Oh God-I hate camping," I told him before he left.

After our conversation, I started thinking about why I hate camping. I've only been camping once. My parents rented a camper trailer. We hauled it out to a state park and sat around in it for a few days. I remember hating lake water because it was so murky. Our boat motor sputtered out and I had to swim to shore while my legs brushed against treetops in the water (I still grit my teeth and get the chills thinking about it). I never felt clean the entire time. And the bugs. I remember walking through an area with standing water and inhaling gnats-millions of gnats. *The only cool part about that trip was coming home and playing in the camper like it was a clubhouse. My friends wanted to play "house," but I wanted to play "movie." I said things like: "If you need me, I'll be in my trailer." ::shrug::

But there's more to it. I realized that there's a psychological connection to not liking camping as well. Growing up, my mother used to use the phrase, "pretend you're camping" in times when something was lacking and a lesser substitute would have to suffice.

Here are some examples:

Out of toilet paper: "Pretend you're camping. Drip-dry just this once."

Power outage: "Pretend you're camping. Use a flashlight."

Dropping your toothbrush in the toilet: "Pretend you're camping. Scrub your teeth with a washcloth."

And the one I loathe the most:

Having to pee during a long car trip with no gas station in sight: "Pretend you're camping. You're peeing on the side of the road."

When my friend returned from his trip, he talked about how nice all of the facilities were and how great it was to cook out on the grill and listen to music and all this stuff that I just don't associate with being out in the wilderness. It seems like camping just means getting away from work, the neighborhood, the norm and sleeping near something natural and more quiet.

Hmmm...If that's the definition of camping, I've been camping for over a year now. All I've done is goof off, travel around finding quiet places to relax and get away. Living out of a suitcase, sleeping in strange beds and having to share a bathroom with friends and relatives are all just the same as camping. Come to think of it, I never want to stop camping! Send me on a camping trip anytime!

As you were.

While eating dinner the other night, a friend and I started talking about how children misinterpret concepts. I looked down at my plate and laughed because I had a perfect example.

Growing up my mother used to tell me: "Robin Amber, do not go to other people's houses and ask for food."

I took this as, "When you go to other people's houses, don't eat."

This caused a lot of anxiety for me. In a neighborhood with about twenty kids, there was always a mother handing out fruit roll-ups, granola bars or popsicles. I would never take them. The worst was being at someone's house around dinner time. I would panic because I was afraid I was going to get into trouble if I ate. At the same time, I was afraid that I would get in trouble for not following the rules by not eating with the other kids when food was served. Often times I would just say that I didn't feel good to get out of eating.

This problem manifested and grew and carried over to school and in public places as well. Do you remember all of those art projects you could eat in kindergarten? I'll never forget creating these stupid Rudolph the Red Nosed Reindeer out of half a peanut butter sandwich, pretzels and Redhots. We were sitting in a circle creating away, and I was dreading the point where Mrs. Kerbow was going to say, "Ok, kindergartners, eat up!" Suddenly, there was a fire drill. While the other kids were shrieking about having to leave their treat, I was tossing that bitch in the trash can and walking out the door on the already learned "Fire Drill Escape Route." Whew...Saved by the bell...

Unless my mother was there, I wasn't eating out at a restaurant either. I actually got so nervous at Mr. Gatti's pizza once that I threw up in the dining area. My grandmother didn't know why I was such a food spazz and simply started ordering my food to go.

As you can see, there was a reason why I weighed only forty-five pounds in the fourth grade...

Sometime in High School, I just got over it and grew out of the anxiety, but it wasn't until recently that my mother and I were sitting around talking and the truth came out. She said, "I remember the days where we didn't have two nickels to rub together. All the neighborhood kids would come over to play and would ask for snacks that I couldn't afford to give them everyday. Money was tight. That's why I used to tell you not to go to other people's houses and ask for food."

I got a cold chill and said, "Oh my God...I thought you told me not to eat at other people's houses. I used to have so much anxiety about it. It wasn't until, like, junior high or high school that I got over it."

"Well, I'm so glad you've presented me with another way that I have ruined a huge portion of your life, Robin Amber. Goddamn it. Can I do anything right?" she grumbled.

As we all know, I have recovered quite well and will eat at anytime of the day or night if allowed to. It's what happens to starvation victims. We overeat and hoard food in fear that we will starve again. ::sniff sniff::

My advice: repeat instructions to your children and make sure they understand your intentions. It will save them Twelve Step Programs later in life.

As you were.

Saturday August 12, 2006
It Was A Graveyard Smash

Last Saturday a group of friends and I combined two festive occasions together into one. My friend/cousin Sarah P. was celebrating her twenty-ninth birthday. As it was a summer Saturday night, The Hollywood Forever Cemetery was having its weekly screenings of movies in the cemetery.

What? You read correctly. The cemetery hosts movie screenings on the lawn, projected onto the big mausoleum. The cemetery is amazing. It's been renovated and is more like a park than a creepy Hollywood graveyard. For $10 a person you get to head in before the sun goes down and set up a picnic with your buds, while enjoying the sounds of a DJ spinning songs and beats while a pictorial slide show of art, old Hollywood photos, etc. flips by. Around 9:00 pm, the feature starts and the crowd snuggles in; it gets pretty chilly and dewy in the cemetery late at night. After the show, the DJ starts again and while the people are filing out, you have some time to dance off your chill and your buzz.

Last Saturday was so much fun. Sarah P. had a huge group of friends there, and the feature film was none other than *Pee-Wee's Big Adventure!* There were soooo many people there that they were turning people away at the gate. Luckily, we made it in early and had plenty of room to spread out. Before the movie started, Sarah's Graveyard Party got an extra treat. Paul Reubens and a great number of the cast members were actually there and got up to introduce the movie and address the crowd.

I think the best part of the night was during the Alamo scene. You know the one. Pee-Wee calls his girlfriend, Dottie, and tells her that he's at the Alamo. She doesn't believe him. He tells her, "No, really, listen," and steps out of the phone booth and sings, "The stars at night are big and bright," and not only did the people in the movie respond, but so did every Texan in the crowd! "Clap. Clap. Clap. Clap. - Deep in the heart of Texas!" Hollywood Forever didn't know what hit it. The Texan force was strong! As people were leaving a girl came up to our group and said, "Bye, Texas." That cracked me up! Texans never stand alone. We are one Lone Star...

So, let's review...Sarah P. had a birthday gathering at a celebrity-studded, trendy Hollywood hotspot event, filled with friends who serenaded her with "Happy Birthday" at sunset before a screening of a cult film classic. It doesn't get anymore LA than that! And no, Large Marge wasn't in attendance...or was she??? Bwah ha ha ha ha ha ha...

As you were.

Monday August 14, 2006
14 Hours In The Desert With A Jewish Cowboy

On the way to a "Cowboy and Indians" themed birthday party for my friend, Tim C., I made the comment to my friend Ryan (a Jewish former investment banker from Pittsburgh turned comedian/actor whom I met on the set of *The Holiday*): "I want to go to Vegas. I haven't been since I spent eight days there for Thanksgiving."

"I want a Green Tea Vitamin Water," he replied.

And so naturally, after spending time visiting with the birthday boy at his shindig, we drove to Vegas looking for Green Tea Vitamin water. Hmm...Going into the desert for water. We're both very bright, don't you agree?

I was able to grab a few things as we headed out, but all he had was his cowboy outfit, some cash and some deodorant. I jokingly made a rule that anything he needed further could be purchased at Rite-Aid. He surprisingly agreed.

As we drove we stated our further intentions. "All I want is to drink my favorite Lemon Drop Martinis which are made at The Seahorse in Caesar's Palace. They have the best sweet/tart sugar around the rim," I declared. "I want to go bungee jumping at Circus Circus," Ryan said.

There's nothing like driving into Vegas at night. The dark desert is suddenly lit up. Just imagine the opening scenes of the movie *Casino*. It's stunning. We rolled into town around two in the morning, hoping to grab my best friend, Alba, but she was already in bed. She recently moved to Vegas and is currently the Food and Beverage Manager for Circus Circus so she wasn't able to play. (Oh boo...)

Vegas is under a ton of construction, and somehow I got diverted into the backside of a Caesar's Palace parking structure. Now on foot, happy to be out of the car and a little turned around, we somehow stumbled into the closed pool area of Caesar's Palace. If you've never been in there, it's quite opulent. It's got huge, unique pools, private bungalows, huge spas, (truly looks like a Roman bath with marble columns and the works). Naturally we began acting like fools and taking goofy pictures. Ryan looked at me and said, "We have to come back here during the day. I'm going to have to get some shorts." "Rite Aid," I said with a smile.

After we had conquered the pool area, we slipped in through an open door. It was near The Seahorse, so we moseyed right up to the bar. I told the bartender that we had driven all the way from LA for some of those lovely Lemon Drops and before I could say, "please," they were in front of us. He also left the martini shaker two-thirds full, sitting with out glasses. Nice. Six drinks for the price of two. Feeling the Citron Vodka, we paid out and got up to leave. Passed out and slumped over was a really sunburned old man just screaming "Fuck with me, please!" So, just as I leaned in for a photo-op, which the crowd thought was hysterical, he kinda' woke up. I stepped back, watched him fall back over and then made my move, only to be barked at by a cop (who I swear was from *Super Troopers)* who was on his way to come get him. "Now that is just cold-blooded," he said. I impishly laughed, and we headed out onto The Strip.

It was hot! Like most people, when we decided to make a random trip to Vegas, we didn't consider that it's August in the desert and going to be ninety-five degrees at 2:00 am. The Strip was crowded with hideous creatures. Ghetto fabulous thugs and thugettes were everywhere. People were dirty, falling down drunk, passing out in places and throwing up here and there. Despite the ugliness we were determined to play. We went in and out of a few hotels and wandered around, watching people play at the tables. I was VERY tempted to take all of the money in my purse and put it on RED at the roulette table. I had some visions of red on the table while driving. I have knack for calling the numbers at the tables. * I couldn't do it even though I saw red come up two times in a row at the first table.

Things after that get a little fuzzy. Lemon drops...

Next I did something that I know I regret. In my drunken state, I initiated something really dirty with Ryan. At 4:00 am, I asked to eat at McDonalds. I haven't eaten a McDonald's hamburger since I read the book, *Fast Food Nation*, in 2003. I'm still ashamed and fasting today. Despite it all, I made friends with some unfortunate women who had just come from "Thunder Down Under." They were so excited to show me their pictures with the men. Mmm...Just what I like, steroid-infused, gay men who dance together. While I shoveled those deep-fried starchy, sticks of cellulite down my throat, Ryan directed my attention to the table behind us where all of the guys had ENORMOUS suck marks on their necks! I'm talking about some serious bruises here, people. Those hickeys were out of control! After seeing that, I was done. (Actually, I was done after seeing several large women in white pants come plodding through the door, but I just couldn't stop myself...I lust after those fries.)

We wound up at a Walgreens (an exception to the Rite Aid Rule) where Ryan began looking for some shoes. His boots were killing him! All I remember about stopping there was finding this bin of rubber Elvis head pieces. When you put one on, it gives you Elvis glasses and hair...we goofed around with those for a while and then got in line to check out. My eyes became fixated on these ghetto hoodrat hoochie mamas in front of me. They were dressed like super ho's with short dresses, chunky heels and bad weaves. I couldn't stop staring at the shoulder of one of them. Amidst some of her cheap, tacky tattoos of baby-daddy names was a huge bite mark. Not just the front teeth, but the whole grill...Somebody truly staked out his territory on her...Come to think of it, maybe it was one of the guys from McDonald's...

Retracing our steps to the car, we naturally had to go back through the Caesar's Palace Pool! I remember just suddenly deciding that it was a good idea to jump into one of the huge empty "Towel Drops." Don't you jump into big painted clay pots in the middle of the night? Somehow I managed to hurt myself and called out in rather loud Southern drawl, "I have busted my ass at Caesar's Palace!" Being intoxicated and unaware of your own volume is neat. I limped my way back to the car.

We arrived at Alba's around 5:00 am. I know we all sat and visited for a bit. I cannot tell you about what. Ryan passed out on the couch, and I fell into this slowly deflating air mattress and curled up with Alba's roommate's dog, Floto. I woke up in a canyon in the air mattress to the sound of Ryan on the phone. I couldn't wait to get up and brush the sweaters off of my teeth and wash my feet.

Ryan was raring to get out the door. He had decided that we must return to the scene of the crime. We must go back the pool. "Oh Jeez," I thought. Without changing clothes or washing my face, we were back out on The Strip. My head was pounding. This time we went into CVS so that Ryan could purchase the rest of his ensemble. He settled on an amazing t-shirt. It said, "Country till the day I die," on it...It came equipped with a ridiculous accent that he was able to slip in and out of all day. Wow...He really was taking this costume party theme seriously. Now armed with a t-shirt, sandals, and some aerosol sun block (which made me glisten like a boxer about to fight according to Ryan), we were ready for the pool area. Just like the night before, we slipped in again through a side door and found a place to lounge. We ordered food, relaxed and had lunch at Snackus Maximus next to the Neptune Pool. Ryan still hadn't had his Vegas wish of bungee jumping fulfilled. After lounging for a while, we visited with the concierge. No bungee jumping anymore, anywhere in Vegas. (I can't imagine why that would be the activity they would discontinue...) I offered to spot him if he wanted to jump off a railing somewhere, but he declined. Oh well, I had my martinis...just trying to help...

Ryan played some 21 at The Bellagio, and I watched. The table he was playing was LAME! The dealer, Kyung, was a very stern, older Asian woman with serious dislikes of Jewish cowboys. She just kept giving Ryan the most blank death stares. I secretly think she was remembering her days as a Geisha and was trying to seduce him with one look...but it just wasn't working. Ryan won a hundred bucks and we goofed around a bit longer, stopping to chat with tourists and watch fools get arrested for selling water. Only idiots sell water...Don't they know it's drugs that people want in Vegas?

By then it was nearing 4:00 pm. Ryan had to work Monday, so after chatting with Alba for a while, we decided that it was time to head home. Upon our departure we realized that we had only been in Vegas for about fourteen fucking hours. How could we be this tired? The car ride home was pretty brutal. It wound up taking five hours. There's nothing more exhausting than sitting in traffic in the Mojave Desert after eating and drinking badly, not sleeping enough and having to stare into the setting sun. *New rule: Never leave Vegas on a Sunday if driving.

Poor Ryan; despite winning a hundred bucks, he never got to bungee jump. It's been debated as to whether or not he even stopped to pee during the whole excursion. We never did find his Green Tea Vitamin Water.

Guess we'll just have to go back...

This type of story is why I love living in Los Angeles.

As you were.

Thursday August 17, 2006
Netflix Return and Sex Date Tonight

Oh wow.

Oh dear.

Ok...

Yesterday, I received an email from my roommate entitled, "Netflix Return and Sex Date Tonight." It was two simple paragraphs:

"Hi Sweetie, I was wondering if you would be able to drop off the Netflix I left on the DVD player or somewhere in the kitchen in the mail for me...I forgot to do that on my way out this morning. If not, no worries as it has low priority.

Also, I have a sex-date tonight around 8 or 9pm and I'll be discrete when passing him through. His name is Robert and he's very nice (personally and physically). I just wanted to give you a heads up just in case you see a stranger in the house loosely clothed (just kidding). We'll be very discrete and private in my boudoir."

You see...My roommate doesn't have people over, and he doesn't get involved in serious relationships. He's far too sweet and overly accommodating to a fault. If he feels the slightest bit under appreciated, his feelings get super hurt. So...no relationships-just sex dates he procures from the Internet. Anyhow, whatever...I really don't have to be told about it. As long as the people coming into the house are not going to hurt anyone, steal anything or defecate on stuff, hey, have all the sex dates you can afford and handle.

I responded to his email:

"I'll get the DVD in the mail for you.

Thanks for the heads up on the sex date.

Speaking of a heads up, my mother is going to be coming for a visit August 26th - August 31st."

I figured since he is prone to having slightly random visitors, he should know in advance when staple goods like dear ol' mom are going to be here for a solid amount of time.

To this he responded:

"Oh cool - and like I said before, I'd be happy to give up my bed for her as I have a futon I can sleep on and set it up in the living room. I hope that would be OK and you and I can share your bathroom so's not to disturb her in the morning, and I'll get my clothing ready the night before. Honestly, it would be my pleasure to share my room."

As those words processed through my eyes and into my brain, I had a vision of my mother standing in his bedroom doorway with her purse on her arm and her sunglasses down on her nose with her famous tightjawed expression: "Robin Amber, you gotta' be fuckin' kidding me," in full force as she gazes at the heavily-shrouded, mystical "boudoir," complete with lube and cock ring by the bed for her viewing pleasure.

It's amazing how he just jumped from gettin' wicked between the sheets in one email to offering them to my mother in the next. Now, let's be serious. We all get wicked when we can on our sheets, but I can tell you right now that my mother has little interest in sleeping in my bed, much less the bed of my very unique roommate.

So... I called my mother and told her about the initial email and how funny I thought it was. She guffawed at his odd way of just throwing the sex date in an email as if it was a part of the daily errands. Then I explained that my response included the alert of her arrival. She laughed and said, "I'm no sex date, but I'll be discreet." Then I shared the good news that she didn't have to sleep on the couch but wass going to sleep in my roommates room. There was a sudden chilly silence on the other end of the phone. "Pardon me?" she finally said. "My roommate has offered his room to you. Isn't that nice of hm?" I goaded her, knowing she was going to burst. "I don't even fucking think so," she unloaded. "Why can't I sleep on the futon in the living room? I'm not sleepin' in the room where he does the hoo-doo with whoever. Can I at least have a bed roll on your bedroom floor? Tell him that I am very particular about where I sleep and that I just love your couch or something. Jesus God, Robin Amber," she puffed. I just laughed and told her that I had diffused the offer with kind regards, even though I knew he will shove it in her face when she arrives. "You better, Robin Amber or I'll go stay at a hotel," she demanded. Hmmm, not a bad idea, regardless...

My mother... I guess it's apparent as to where I got my bawdy, colorful mouth. I can't wait to have her here with my roommate for a week. He's already planning some tasty soy meat dishes that she's just going to love. He just knows it. This is going to be good...

As you were.

Thursday August 17, 2006
Herve "Tattoo" Villechaize's Widow Found in The San Fernando Valley

The other day my friend Tracy and I combined forces to tackle the days' errands together. The list of stops included:

-Smog check for Tracy's car. (Yes, in LA there is so much smog that they check to make sure you have your required amount.)

-Pick out Tracy's bridesmaid dress for friend's November wedding at David's Bridal (Remind me never to go in there ever again.)

-Storm retail stores selling LORAC Cosmetics. Do field research on the brand for Robin's upcoming interview. (This one was a big stretch for two make-up artists, let me tell you.)

-Eat.

All tasks were accomplished with usual wastes of time thrown in like stopping for gelato and trying all the lotions at Bath and Body Works. However, there was one moment that is still on my mind and will not go away.

After goofing off at the Smog Check place doing my best "Grease Lightening" dance in the gas station's garage, we hopped in the car, proud that it passed the inspection, and as we were turning right on Victory, something caught my attention in the side mirror.

Standing at the corner, (I assume) waiting for a bus, was an older, chubby midget lady with bright, red-orange Bozo the Clown 'fro'd out hair wearing a Hawaiian floral print moo-moo and tan orthopedic nursing shoes. This was a visual stunner folks. I looked over my shoulder and out the window, hands and face pressed up against the glass.

114

Despite her short stature, she was so much to take in. I begged Tracy to turn around so we could get a better look at her, but my request was denied, even though Tracy was equally impressed with her presence.

As we got a few blocks away her image quickly shrank and disappeared into the distance, but as I rolled down the window, I swear I could hear her saying in a pinched voice: "De bus...De bus..."

As you were.

Friday August 18, 2006
Testicle Elbow

I'm not sure what I have done to my elbow, but it is injured. I'm suffering from a sneaky ailment that only makes itself known occasionally, of course, when I'm not expecting it. The slightest touch to the skin when Venus is in House of the Seventh Sun or some shit sends a sharp pain pulsating about my elbow. It's not in the joint. It's in the skin. Wow, is it tender.

I've been told that a man's testicles are similar in that they hang around all day long, doing what they do, but if they are slightly grazed the wrong way, the pain can be nauseating. My elbow is the same way.

I'm suffering from a wretched case of testicle elbow.

I wonder if I could get someone to suck on my elbow...or just hum on it. I wonder if someone could fit my entire elbow in their mouth. Maybe that would help.

Wow. That actually made me laugh out loud.

As you were.

Sunday August 20, 2006
Gumma On A Plane

The only good thing that will probably come from Samuel L. Jackson's new movie, *Snakes On A Plane,* is the conversation I had with my grandmother (Gumma....pronounced Gum-maw) this afternoon.

Me: I went to see a movie last night.

Gumma: (Giggling) Was it about snakes on a plane? [Even my seventy-five year-old grandmother thinks this movie is a joke, and she doesn't actually GO to the movies anymore.]

Me: No. It was...(Gumma cuts Robin off)

Gumma: What would you do if you were on a plane and some snakes got loose?

Me: Probably just sit in my chair and keep my hands and feet tucked close to me? I don't know why anyone would travel with a snake. I really don't like it when people travel with animals anyway. I was a witness to a small dog peeing on a woman in the seat next to me recently. Even though I was polite to her about her dog, I just kept thinking, "Why is it really necessary to cart this little dog with you on trips?"

Gumma: You mean the dog wasn't wearing a diaper????

Me: [I could feel her soapbox building.] Ummm, no. Most animals don't wear diapers in public.

Gumma: Well, they damn sure should. If people are going to treat these silly damn little pets as children then they should go all the way with it.

Me: You mean college funds and everything?

Gumma: (Ignoring me) You remember my cousin Dot, right?

Me: Sure do.

Gumma: Years ago she told me that when she dies she wants to come back as a dog, because it's a dogs life. (Starting to giggle again) You know what I told her I want to come back as?

Me: I don't know, what?

Gumma: A snake! You wanna know why? (paper crinkling can be heard) I made a list:

#1. No lips...no lipstick.

#2. No eyelashes...no mascara.

#3. No hair...no haircuts.

#4. No boobs...no bra.

#5. I would only have to change clothes once a year.

But even though those are great, I only have one reservation.

Me: What's that? (smiling)

Gumma: If I get a sore throat, where will it end?

Ain't she a riot? No wonder her 2006 V8 Mustang has a Cobra embroidered on the headrest and reads, "Venom."

I had this vision of my grandmother as a snake getting loose on a plane, only she wouldn't attack anyone. She would casually slither by, offering her thoughts and advice to the passengers about sugar intake, the length of their hair, the type of shoes they're wearing (wear only shoes that are good for your feet), etc., etc., etc., etc...

I had to laugh, regardless of realizing how different she and I are. The idea of not having the traits that make me feminine are depressing, but she could care less. I got all of that from the other grandmother. I'm surely glad that I got my sense of humor from this one, though.

I never would have thought in my whole life that Samuel L. Jackson would be the springboard to a conversation with my grandmother...and especially over this type of movie. Will wonders never cease?

As you were.

Friday August 25, 2006
She Really Was In My Underwear...

As I prepare for my mother's visit, I am reminded of her last visit to Los Angeles. Actually, I'm reminded of what happened after her departure from her last visit.

First of all, my mother must have unpacked and repacked her suitcase a million times while she was at my apartment. I don't know why, but if she wasn't in the living room, chances were that she was ass end up on the floor, diggin' in her damn bag.

After I got back from the airport, I noticed that ol' Cinderella had left behind one of her Sketcher's Slippers, a typical mother move to make sure that she had a reason to come back or call.

A few days went by, and the phone calls for the shoe began. I'm lazy at times. And I know that my mother has an entire closet completely devoted to shoes. I knew she wasn't missing it, and the true need for me to make a special trip to the post office (though I love the post office) wasn't necessary.

One afternoon, I was getting dressed and began looking for one of my favorite black bras. It fits well and it's one of the lesser worn-out articles of intimate apparel that I own. I remembered the last time I wore it. It was when mother was in town, and we went to dinner at Louise's Trattatoria. When I came home I took it off and draped it over the hamper, as I had only worn it for about three hours. Where could it be? I looked and look and looked, tore apart the bottom of the closet, looked in the bathroom, the drawers, inside my shirt just in case I actually had it on...

And then it dawned on me that my mother's suitcase was sitting in front of my closet while she was here. Was it possible that it fell on the floor and, with all of her packing and unpacking, she picked it up?

I dialed my mother up on the ol' telephone and caught her in her hotel room before going out to dinner with her friend Phyllis. They were visiting Austin together and had been out and about all day. I asked my mother, "Mom, did you happen to pick up a black bra from my room on accident? It's a Victoria's Secret Satin Demi looking thing..." She got very quiet and then said, "I'll be Goddamned. Is that why this bra is so fuckin' tight? I think I'm wearing it. I told Phyllis earlier that I must have gained five pounds on my trip to see you because my bra is too tight now. I think it's giving me a headache." She rambled on and on in a choppy manner as she promptly ripped the "damn thing" off and tossed it into her bag. She then followed her grumblings with, "I'll send you your bra when you send me my shoe."

Crap. She had me cornered. I was going to have to make a special trip to the post office for a shoe I knew she wouldn't wear for months if ever again. So a few weeks later, my roommate (at the time) took the shoe to work and sent it to her via FedEx.

I waited for the arrival of my bra. I waited and waited. I wound up having to buy one on a random trip to Vegas, as I needed one to go under a black dress.

Damn it. I had been tricked. She knew what she was doing all along. She didn't leave the shoe behind so she could come back; she took my bra so I would come home! The shoe was nothing but bait.

And shortly thereafter, I did in fact go home for a visit. She handed me my bra with a smug, motherly grin on her face.

This time when she leaves I will be sure to treat her like TSA and search her bags thoroughly. If I don't find anything in her bags, there will be a cavity search. Let that be a warning to the rest of you.

As you were.

Friday August 25, 2006
MoneyGrams

Right now $100 to me is more than a lot of money. I'm nearing the end of my unemployment funding and am still being turned down for jobs left and right. As stressful as this is and as much as I walk around wondering what in the hell I'm going to do come the end of September, I seem to keep making it.

A dear friend of mine, Peter Garcia, recently said to me on the phone, "Money will come into your life and will go out of your life. All that matters is that you are living right."

With that, I continue on living right. Last Friday night The Object Of My Affection and I were invited to go see Earth, Wind and Fire perform a concert with two other couples. We were having an OK time. (One of the wives is a really insecure cunt-drip and was being incredibly rude. I wanted to stand on her throat until she quit breathing, but I was informed that was not allowed. Hmph.) Anyhow, we got in line to get a beer for The Object Of My Affection and he nudged me. "Look down," he whispered to me. I looked to the ground and between the feet of the large, sloth-like drunkass loudmouth in front of us were some twenty dollar bills. The Object Of My Affection began to whisper instructions on how to pick it up. It was too late though. I was already in the zone. My heart was racing so fast. I looked to the left, then to the right and I quickly bent over, reached between his feet and picked up the cash. It was one of the most exhilarating feelings of my life. I handed The Object Of My Affection one of the twenty dollar bills to cover his beer and shoved the rest of the cash in my pocket. The Object Of My Affection was as thrilled as I was until I told him he already got his cut of the cash and was about to drink it. I pulled the cash out of my pocket and counted it. Including the twenty I handed him, I was holding a hundred dollars in cash in my hand. I almost cried. My little brother's birthday is next week, and I have to send him something. Rent is due...you name it. Every time I turn around the city of Los Angeles is taking another bite out of me for some ridiculous parking violation. So, to answer your question before you ask it, no, I don't think I should have asked the man in front of me if it was his money. Not this time. *It sure made up for having to be treated poorly by the insecure cunt-drip and for losing $100 to Mr. Level-well almost.

118

A few days later, while searching for a business card in an old purse at the top of my closet, I saw a folded piece of paper in between some of the business cards. "No way," I thought. Sure enough, it was a twenty-dollar bill, crisp as it could be. When I put my hands on it, I got a little chill and had one of those deja vu, kinda' feelings. I remembered how my Grandma Sue used to purposefully tuck a little cash away in her purses when changing them out and putting them away in the top of the closet. "Thataway, I've always got at least some collection plate or gas money in my purse in case I forget to drop my billfold in it," she told me. *Needless to say, I always loved to dig in her purses when playing dress-up at her house.

I got this funny feeling while standing in my room that maybe my Grandma Sue, who is now deceased, is trying to help me out. I know it might sound silly or hokey, but she always told me that she wished she could help me out more in a financial way. Wouldn't it be awesome if she was somehow channeling me money from The Great Beyond? MoneyGrams...Get it? Money-Grams...Grandma, Gram...

Hmm...I also randomly bought a lottery ticket this week. I have never bought a California State Lottery ticket before and only did once or twice in Texas. The California Jackpot is up to $51 million. Now, if I win any amount of that, I will fully believe that Grandma Sue's MoneyGrams are flowing...

Come on Gram...Om...Om...Om...(This is me channeling her...)...Om...Om...Om...

As you were.

Friday September 1, 2006
Just Putt It Away

One of my dreams/goals in life is to travel, teach and train either product knowledge or cosmetic application for a cosmetic company. I have come to believe that I could become a brain surgeon, the President or a fucking piece of bread with more ease than trying to permeate my way into a cosmetic company.

The majority of these companies are no longer privately owned. The way to get in is to start at the make-up counter and work your way up for years. Had someone told me this when I was in college, my weekend/part-time job would have been spent smearing seasonal colors on people's faces instead of being a nanny. I don't regret my choices in the least, but interviews for counter jobs at my age with my decent resume don't go very well. "I don't believe you really want to retail cosmetics," they say. "Fuck you," I think. Part of my background as a Mary Kay consultant taught me that I should be able to do both retail and training, etc. Women at these counters don't know that secret and certainly aren't going to promote the idea.

Anyhow, I was recently given what I believe to be a golden opportunity. I was able to get an interview to be a product development assistant for the privately owned, LORAC Cosmetics. I was out-of-my-mind ecstatic about this interview. I did more preparation for that interview than I did for any test I've ever taken in school, for any date I've ever had and for anything I've ever cared about. If you know me, you know that's just past the point of obsession level. I did tons of online research. I memorized product names, ingredients and went to retailers that sell the product and performed in-store analysis of product placement and employee knowledge of the product. I watched the consumers' attraction to the displays and got messy with the product with a friend, taking notes on both of our professional make-up artist opinions. I did a total SWAT analysis of the company.

The first interview went well. I was interviewed by the Marketing Assistant and the Director of Finances. I thought this was odd until I realized that the company is tiny. I was asked to come back for a second interview the following week. It was a panel interview with the same two ladies, the business' attorney and the owners. I was once again ecstatic. My roommate was ecstatic. He helped me pick out my outfit and helped me prepare for interview questions.

My brother-in-law, Sean, gave me great advice and helped focus my interview questions for them about their company. I reviewed all of my notes. Before I left the house I talked to myself in the mirror like Dirk Diggler did in *Boogie Nights*. "You're a STAR!" I was pumped. The interview went very well. I got the tour of the facilities, made the panel laugh, looked hot and even did a hair flip at the business consultant. I wanted that job in a passionate way. This was the "IN."

The day after the interview, my phone rang. The two ladies who interviewed me initially called and in the cheeriest voices ever said, "We want to thank you so much for coming out twice to interview with us, but we've decided to go with another candidate. We just didn't think you were the right fit." The room went dark. All I could see was a tunnel of light in front of me. A piece of my being died. I couldn't think straight. I couldn't breathe. I just had to feel the piece of death consume a part of my system and watch it float into the light. When I hung up the phone, I cried. I've been turned down for plenty of jobs lately and none of them killed me quite like this. The rejection was disappointing, sure, but those weren't on my list of dream jobs. I cried like I had just been disqualified from The Olympics.

What in the Holy Fuck are these people looking for??? This isn't cancer research. This isn't running a mission in Liberia. This isn't a government think-tank. It's a cosmetic company! They are like the fucking Mafia!

So, armed with the advice of my brother-in-law, Sean, (who listened to me completely breakdown on the phone, God bless him) "Get back in the game," I said, "You know what? You're exactly right." When my friend Stephen asked me to play Putt-Putt Golf, I agreed in a heartbeat. There's nothing like getting out on the ol' AstroTurf, sharing good consulting time with a good friend and getting a grip on things as you send a little purple ball sailing straight through the mouth of a giant clown or into a bubbling pond filled with water colored a mysterious "Blue No. 5" while Top 40's music blares over the sounds of screaming, sticky-fingered children. Not only did I feel better about myself after beating Stephen by one stroke, but I also got a hole-in-one on the first hole. Things progressively got worse until about the ninth hole where I started to get more control. Story of my life in Putt-Putt...Started out amazing, hit a few snags, sunk myself, had to dry out and have finally started to bring it back around...

Putt-Putt-the answer to all of life's problems. Wait, no it's not. It just makes for a good afternoon of not sitting alone at home, crying in the fetal position...and getting the fuck over yourself.

*I won't lie-I did have visions of wandering around the house in my bathrobe like Steve Martin in *The Jerk*, bawling and gathering all the things I really need in this world, like a ping-pong paddle, a book of matches and a stapler. Then I realized that I do that all the time anyway and went to play Putt-Putt. I still think I should have hit the green in my bathrobe though...

As you were.

Friday September 1, 2006
Missing A Step

I love my mother dearly.

She's a woman of passion, and strength, with an amazing personality, a warm heart. She's also a great teacher with the ability to give and follow instructions.

That last attribute should have been my reminder when she told me she was flying into LAX.

M: Where are you going to pick me up?

R: I will pick you up curbside at the baggage claim area outside the Southwest Airlines exit.

M: I may not check a bag, though.

R: It doesn't matter. You're still going to exit the airport from that area. Just stand in front of the Southwest Airlines area and don't move around, so that I can find you.

M: Sounds like a plan to me.

Airport day arrived, and I got to the airport earlier than expected. If you've never been to LAX to pick someone up, you're missing out on the chance to drive around in a circle like you're cruising a gay bar. Everyone is looking in every direction except the one in front of them. Everyone is going at different speeds. At every terminal, there's always someone who just has to zip across at the last minute from the far left to the far right lane. It's just unnerving. If you park, you pay a high price. If you idle you get a ticket from the police who are like hawks, just waiting for you to slow down long enough. I called Mom and left her a message letting her know I was there. So I was cruising around...and around...and around. Thankfully there was an interview on NPR with David Sedaris, the author of *Me Talk Pretty One Day* (among other books). I was entertained, as I always love hearing the voice of the authors. Pretty soon the interview was ending, and I was starting to wonder where the hell my mother was. The trouble with LAX is that there are two sets of loops to circle. The inner loop is right up against the curb, which you use when your traveler has arrived. You exit the outer loop and swoop in to grab them up. There are lots of cars at a stop, loading and unloading, etc. The outer loop is for buses, taxies and cruisers awaiting arriving travelers.

Around and around and around...Around and around and around...I think my car was getting dizzy.

It was near thirty-five minutes later than her expected arrival time. It was possible that the flight could be delayed...Hmmm...

From the outer loop, I slowed some and realized that she was standing on the curb with her suitcase. I made one more loop around, zipped over from the far left to the far right and called her on her cell phone again. She answered:

M: (in her busy, terse voice) Hello.

R: Hey. How long have you been waiting?

M: I've been waiting a while. Where are you?

R: I've been driving around here for about thirty minutes. Why didn't you call me?

M: You didn't tell me to call you. You just told me to stand out by the curb, not to move and to wait for you.

Oh, Holy Christ. It's not like I'm waiting for her at a bus stop in the desert. This is LAX! A zillion people come through every hour of every day of the year!

I calmly said, "Sorry, Mom. I guess I missed a step," as I helped get her bag into the trunk and gave her a big hug.

It was so good to hug my mother.

As you were.

Friday, September 1, 2006
"It's George!"

I'm not sure if my family will ever understand or be completely comfortable with the fact that I moved to LA. (Hell, there are some days I wonder why I ever left the womb...)

The day my mother arrived for her visit, we headed straight to Trader Joe's from the airport so that she could experience the shopping wonder that it is. On the way back we passed by a house around the corner from my apartment. The yard was peppered with police officers, and several neighbors were being questioned. No one seemed too frantic, yet sorrow, confusion and concern could be read in their faces. It took me a second to catch the word "coroner" on the side of one of the cruisers, and when I did, I knew my mother wouldn't be pleased. Scenes like this do not help concerned parents with children who live in far away places. There wasn't any police tape or men in trench coats taking notes on little note pads, so we are left to believe that whoever went to meet The Lo-ard, did so quietly and on their own.

Thankfully we stumbled upon a scene that does help concerned parents who have children in far away places while my mother was here. We decided to go see a movie at the Arclight Theatre on Sunset. Tickets to movies are $11, you get assigned seating and a pimple-faced teenager with a crackling voice comes out and welcomes you to the show, giving you a little warm up and preview. La-dee-dah. Anyhow, we walked in and as we were approaching the counter, I noticed a guy and said, "Hey mom, I think that guy's an actor, but I can't think of his name..." She looked over and then looked back at me with this wonderful, "kid on Christmas morning" expression. "It's George!" she exclaimed with her eyes wide. As I looked back I realized that she was right. It was

T.R. Knight who plays George on "Grey's Anatomy." He was standing with a tall girl and when they turned around, I realized it was Katie Heigl, who plays Izzy on the show. How cute. They hang out together outside of work...

Mom was grinning ear to ear and saying how much she just loved George's character. They looked so approachable, so I said, "Hang on, I'm going to go get them." She looked at me like I was nuts as I walked away.

I walked up with a smile on my face and said, "I normally wouldn't bother actors, but my mom is visiting from out of town, and it would make her trip if she got to go home telling everybody that she met two celebrities." They were more than happy to do it. When she turned around and saw them walking towards her with me, the classic star struck expression spread across her face.

The conversation is kind of a blur, but I recall Katie asking my mother what her name was. With pride my mother said, "Penny Buenger," as if she was the Countess of a small European country. Katie complimented her strong name. There was discussion of movies and well wishes on her vacation and then they were gone.

It was the cutest I'd ever seen my mother act. When they were gone she kept saying things like, "They are such good people," "That was so nice of them to talk to me," "Did you see how pretty and fresh Izzy looked?" "And George...He's just George." Off and on throughout the evening during a quiet moment she would say, "I met George from "Grey's Anatomy," you know." Then she started in on the things she wished she would have told them, "I'm a retired English and Theatre Arts teacher, you know," was one and the other was, "I should have told them that you are an out of work make-up artist and asked them if either of them needed a personal make-up assistant or if they could get you into the Union." I think I would have grabbed her by the throat if she had done that...and I thanked her for not. Oh dear God...

For one brief second, I think my mother finally got it. She understands why I (and so many people) love living here. Sure, it's got its big city problems that hit close to home, yet because of Tinseltown's entertainment magic, we are able to forget about the problems in our backyards when we can get lost in the moment meeting the people responsible for helping us suspend our disbelief.

As you were.

Saturday September 2, 2006
How Alarming

Good fucking God...Nothing can go normally for me, EVER. There always has to be a hitch in the get up. I had an interview yesterday morning that just proves my point perfectly.

I am registered with a placement agency here in LA, and was scheduled to interview with a legal research consulting firm in The World Trade Center downtown to be an administrative assistant. I truly cringe at the idea and fear for my life going into an office again, but I've gotten myself into a pickle, and I've got to get myself out.

So I was up early, dressed up, got directions to the office and headed out. The music was great on "Morning Becomes Eclectic," and the traffic was light. Seemed pretty dreamy so far.

Things started to get a little off course when the directions I was given turned out to be wrong. Luckily, I have a half-assed amount of downtown navigation skill and was able to quickly find a new path that got me to the building's parking structure with relative ease. I squeezed into the tiniest parking space I've ever seen and proceeded into the building. The sounds of my heels on the parking garage floor, the transfer elevators, the look of the office...They were giving me a small panic attack as it reminded me of how I used to feel going to work at my old job each morning. I just kept breathing and telling myself that everything was going to be fine.

There was hardly anyone in the office. I could hear some voices down the hall but, there was no one at the reception desk. I sat for about five minutes and then a lady, dressed in jeans and a t-shirt, came around the corner, saw me and asked if I had been helped. I told her who I was there to see, and she went to get my interviewer.

A lady with a smile came out of an office down the hall and came to shake my hand. "Hi. It's nice to meet you, but you're not supposed to be here until three this afternoon," she said.

I checked my planner again and saw that it said 10:00 am, and apologized for the misunderstanding. I asked her if I should leave and come back later that afternoon or if there was time to interview now. It was then explained to me that the reason she had wanted me to come in later in the day was due to a routine fire drill that the building was going to be having at some point within the next two hours, and if I was there I would have to participate in the drill.

After hemming and hawing back and forth about it, we agreed that we should just go ahead and start the interview. If she didn't like me in the first five minutes she could let me go. We got past the first five minutes and really started getting into the interview when sure enough, because, that's just how bizarre and surreal my life is, an ear piercing WHOOP WHOOP began to sound off. She jumped up and told me to get in the hall and wait for her. The people who were tucked away in their offices were now filing out and heading into a stairwell. My interviewer came flying around the corner armed with a clipboard, paperwork and a truly unflattering plastic orange vest that she must wear to show that she is the fire marshall for her office.

Before I knew it, I was trying to hustle my overdressed ass down what seemed like endless flights of stairs. It was casual Friday so most people were in flats and running shoes. But me? I was in heels, praying to God that my blind ass didn't miss a step, or twist an ankle and injure myself.

We finally got to the street level and were instructed to line up behind some guy who had the great job of holding up a big red sign that designated the area for people working on certain floors. And there, as I stood out of breath, sweating and being stared at by the entire staff, a woman in a plastic orange vest continued to interview me about whether or not I could type and handle a busy desk.

I thought, "Lady, I just ran I don't know how many flights of stairs, probably ruined a shirt, am dirty, now need another shower and did it all with a smile on my face. I think I am adaptable and work well under pressure."

I'm not certain yet if I will make it to the next round of interviews, but if I do, I have an extra edge to discuss with the partners. Not only am I comfortable with jargon that they will be using around me due to my legal background, but I'm already skilled in the emergency evacuation procedures of their office. Can the other applicants top that? I doubt it.

What doesn't kill you makes you stronger? No kidding. My thighs are killing me today! Ain't nothin' easy in this world...

As you were.

Monday September 4, 2006
Busted His Ass

Ok everyone, gather around! It's time to add another person to the Fucktard List!!!

For the past three months I have been dating a man I met right at the time I had decided to move to Chicago. We met on a commercial shoot in El Segundo on the beach. I was doing make-up, and he was the key grip. It was obvious that we were instantly attracted to each other, but it wasn't until I saw the look on his face when I first pulled down my sunglasses so that he could look into my eyes that I really considered keeping in touch with him. It was one of those frozen, stunned looks where he lost his train of thought. As we were wrapping, I slipped my card into his truck.

A few days later I received a text message from him stating that he would like to take me to dinner. What the fuck? What thirty-five year-old man asks a girl out on a date via text message? That should have been the end, but instead I thought it was sweet that he was a little nervous to ask me out. I am quite a strong force to deal with.

We started getting to know each other, and up front he informed me that he has, oh let's just say, a delinquent past. He grew up in East LA and lived a thug's life, doing some time for some pretty bad behavior. I respected his honesty and his reform. He was from then on, however, known only as Cholo in conversation.

Keep in mind that at that time there was still a strong possibility I was going to be moving to Chicago. Cholo had other plans. He stayed at my apartment several nights a week. He planted a toothbrush in my bathroom without invitation in the first two weeks. Within the first month of our dating he was asking me to move in with him, telling me that he wanted me to be the mother of his children, telling me that he would pay my bills, and the list of things goes on. He kept telling me that I had walls up and that I wasn't letting him in...blah blah blah. I kept telling him that we needed to move slowly as I've known plenty of guys who get what they want from women only leave them crying to their girlfriends because they got their hearts broken. Who gets that close with someone they've only known for a month? I kept a little distance being that I'm not the type of girl who takes advantage of situations of this sort. Sure, it would have been great to dump my bills on someone, but that's just not me. And as we all know, I decided to move in with my next-door neighbor instead.

The second month of dating was pretty nice. I was officially committed to staying in LA to look for work. I let him get a little closer. He became The Object Of My Affection. Things were really good. I was introduced to his dearest friends. There were some snags, but that's natural, right? He worked like a dog; I got really sick; we had some bad communication. I put my foot down on some issues about what I wanted out of the relationship. Strain occurred. He quit coming over to my apartment, and I was staying at his apartment all the time. It didn't bother me as he was working crazy, long hours and I was not, but his apartment was filthy and it's a small studio. Not a place for two people to be living. Despite the moderate strain, I did all sorts of nice things like super-clean his apartment and make sure things were in order for him. I stepped up the attention like sweet notes and text messages, etc. Sadly, I started to notice that he didn't seem to give a shit. I dismissed it as him being overworked.

Month number three was a blur. I actually was only around him for the first half. I noticed that our communication was lessening, but when it occurred it was still good. The film he was working on was super busy, and he said he needed some space. I respected that and gave it to him. This is where I look like a dumbass. Instead of just cutting him loose, I kept thinking of all of the good things about him. Stupid, generous, kind-hearted girl...

But tonight is where the tables turned.

He had basically stopped calling me for about a week. My mother was in town, and he explained that he was going to be too busy to meet her. That's a load of shit. He chose not to meet her. When I hadn't talked to him for five days, I called. We had an unpleasant conversation. When I asked why he was being so distant, he said that he really felt like he was too busy for a relationship. Once again a choice, but I stupidly said, "Oh, now come on. You know I'm committed to this relationship, and we can get past this stressful time. You are part of the reason I didn't move away." He then gutted a small portion of me by saying, "If you stayed here it was for other reasons. Don't use me as an excuse. If you think it's because of me then you better call Chicago and get going." Stunned and ticked, I kindly reminded him of all the things he said to me and he replied, "Those were things I said, and you listened." I'm taking that to mean that fucktard was admitting he was a liar. The conversation ended with him saying that he wouldn't have time to sit and talk to me until Monday.

Ummm...no.... My heart and head were spinning. I couldn't believe what I was hearing. Could it be that I was just simply being disposed of? I did everything I could to do to keep from being crushed. I was thankful that I hadn't let him get too close to my heart. However, he was close enough for me to feel so sick that I couldn't eat or sleep. I can't stand being put off and ignored. If he wanted to break-up, fine. I hate break-ups. Who doesn't? My feelings were hurt. Here I was on my end, thinking of all the ways to make things better, and he was on his end, not giving a shit and putting me off. Way to keep a promise of always working things out, Cholo.

At two in the morning, I decided it was time for him to hear my side. I did the one thing girls are not supposed to do. I drove over to his apartment. And what did I find? A girl's car parked next to his truck. How did I know it was a girl's car, you wonder? I'm assuming that most guys don't drive Ford Focuses with fuzzy princess seat covers

and license plate covers that read, "This princess needs no training." I was livid. "Oh...
Hell no, you motherfucker," I fumed as I started walking to the door.

Yes, that's right. I busted his ass. No one walks on me and disrespects me like that. I
walked right up to the door and rang the door bell for, oh, I don't know...three to five
minutes. It's no normal doorbell. It's like a fucking fire alarm. I knew he was there.
There were lights on, and the windows were open. When he opened the door he tried
to act all gansta' hard, asking me what I was doing there when less than a month ago he
was trying to get me to live there.

To his question I responded, "I want my things out of your apartment." He got all
puffed up and said, "What things?" "Oh, I don't know my tables, my clothes and my
toiletries," I responded. "You can't get them now. It's two in the morning," he said.
"Why not? Do you have a girl in there?" I asked. (I knew he did, duh.) He said "Yes. I
do." "How dare you do this to me? Is this what I get for putting up with your requests,
being there for you and being so understanding? It was less than month ago that you
were asking me to move in here!" I was getting heated. (I was making sure to be extra
audible so the poor girl inside could hear the whole thing. I wanted to make sure she
knew what she was getting into with him. Aren't I nice? Tee-hee.) "Well, we're done
and you need to go. Our relationship has been done and you know it. You have no right
coming to my house at two in the morning," he barked. (No, shit, we're done.) "And
you have no right to treat me like shit. Just how long were you going to wait to tell me
that you are already fucking someone else, while I sit and worry over how we could
make our relationship better and ease the tensions we have? You ought to be ashamed
of yourself. You just lost one of the greatest women you could have ever had!" I hissed.
And with that I was walking away.

Had I waited until Monday to talk to him I would have been that pathetic girl trying to
figure out a way to work things out. Instead, I put on my "nobody fucks with me and
the world doesn't revolve around him" suit and went with my gut and found him in just
the way I needed to see him. It was so liberating to tell him off. He had told me on
several occasions about situations with the fellas who cheat on their wives and mistreat
their girlfriends...and there he was getting busted, acting just like them.

I dedicate this to my mother because she once said to me, "Every now and then I get
tired of being the bigger person. Sometimes I just want to be the shitty little person
who gets to really let someone have it."

Tonight I was the shitty little person, and it felt so good! Though I was in shock, I had
never felt stronger or taller.

Tisk, tisk, tisk...Once a cholo, always a cholo.

When I said that no one was going to walk on me anymore in this town, I meant NO
ONE.

As you were.

Saturday September 9, 2006
Rumble In Ol' Milwaukee

While cleaning out an old wallet the other day, I noticed that there was a slip of paper in one of the teeny tiny mystery pockets. Hoping it was money, I quickly pulled it out only to find that it was a flimsy hotel identification card from the Hilton Milwaukee from October of 2002. I couldn't believe I still had it, and it made me instantly chuckle as the memory of my time there came rushing back.

At that time, I was a budding paralegal at THE hot-shot, big-balls-in-cow-town law firm of America and had been put on a case that no one appreciated or wanted to work on. Being of the overachiever, people-pleasing mentality, I took on the stepchild challenge and began working like a dog on this case alongside the few other trial team members we had at the time. I did a lot of travel and took on many tasks.

The first solo trip I took was to Milwaukee. No one wanted to go to such a glamorous place and our lead partner, Michael Lee, sent me alone. I had to work with co-counsel and meet with clients for a day. It sounds like your typical business trip. No big deal, right? Not even close.

After a long day of working with some of the nicest attorneys I'd ever met, one of the partners came in and said, "Robin, we would love to take you out to dinner but our wives probably wouldn't approve." (I was a pretty, perky, metropolitan, fresh-faced recent college grad, completely unjaded by the woes of the corporate working world at the time. Middle-aged married men who wanted to keep their wives knew better than to take me out on the town.) "However, we do have an unmarried associate, Randy, who has volunteered to take you to dinner," he followed.

Randy came into the office where I was working, and we chatted about the legal field (yawn) and nothing too spectacular (bigger yawn.) Dinner was seeming like less and less of a good idea, but I figured I'd better go to be nice. I could always go hang out at the hotel. There was an indoor water park in it for Christ's sake!

Randy wound up taking me to some really neat bars-fun, eclectic places where we slowly gathered some of his friends. After a few bars and a few glasses of wine, we made it to a really nice wine and cigar bar. The group we were with was lively and friendly. They were having so much fun with the fact that I was from Texas and decided that no matter what I said, it sounded pleasant due to my slight southern drawl (which becomes less and less slight when I take in a little alcohol.) All was going great as we gathered around a big table with tall stools.

And then, enter Asshole. Asshole was about 6'2", portly, bald and loud. And where did Asshole sit? Right next to me, of course. The first thing he said to me was, "So, who are you fucking tonight?" "Oh Jesus, so this is how business trips turn ugly," I thought.

More wine made Asshole louder and things a little more blurry. Before I knew it we were all smoking cigars and singing stupid songs at the top of our lungs. I excused myself from the table and went to the ladies room. Upon my return to the table, I stupidly reached for my glass before hoisting my tiny self up onto the bar stool. I wound up spilling my wine on myself and Asshole.

By his reaction you would have thought I threw bleach in his eyes. He was yelling and cussing, "Look what you did to my tie! Fuck. Fuck. Fuck." I started laughing because it wasn't that big of deal. I told him I would pay for his dry cleaning and that I was so sorry. He leaned in so close to my face that his nose almost touched mine and said, gritting his teeth, "You can't help it. You're just a simple, tipsy BITCH." Stunned, I looked for Randy, who was already on his feet, heading to the bar to get his tab. I got to my feet and began to walk away, but Asshole grabbed me by the arm and tried to hold me back.

I don't know what came over me, but all I remember is yelling at him to "let go of my fucking arm." I pushed him as hard as I could, and then out of nowhere, I reached for my cigar with my free hand and promptly began to put it out on the side of his head yelling, "Don't mess with Texas!" He grabbed the side of his head and began calling me all sorts of nasty things. I looked at the table of people I was with. They either sat frozen, jaw-dropped or were laughing hysterically. I took off out the front door with Randy not far behind. He was dumbfounded and extremely apologetic. My adrenaline was pumping and things were fuzzy. Needless to say the evening was over, and I was graciously dropped off at my hotel.

After the initial shock of the event wore off, all I could think about was facing the office in Houston when I got home. I could just see myself losing my job over something so stupid. I sat with Michael and slowly explained everything. When I was done, he looked at me and said, "I'm so proud of you. Here I was feeling guilty all day that I had turned you loose alone and you took care of business. That's the way you earn your stripes around here. I'm going to start sending you alone more often." In the next few days, I got random high fives and winks from some of the attorneys around the office. I couldn't believe it.

*I later learned from Randy that Asshole was newly divorced and had just taken a job with a law firm in Chicago the Monday after my departure. When his new co-workers asked what happened to his head, he told them he was stung by a mosquito and it had gotten infected. Ha ha ha ha ha...Have you ever seen a Texas sized mosquito? They are friggin' huge...about five feet tall and around a hundred and ten pounds...

As you were.

Monday September 11, 2006
Fit For Compliance

With a great sense of relief and a greater sense of exhaustion, (and a dash of pride) I can finally say that I have a JOB! I'm not sure that it has sunk in yet. I still wake up each morning with a lump of coal smoldering in my stomach, thinking about searching for work.

I'm still having a hard time wrapping my brain around the last few months. The ups and downs have been so new and unique. I feel like Rocky after the fight and am skittish like an abused animal. Though triumphant in my pursuit, I have wounds that will take a while to heal.

I have always been a firm believer that all things happen for a reason and am entering my new employment endeavor with an open mind. Somehow by the grace of a good recruiter, a person who sees themselves in me and some excellent coaching and mental grooming from friends and family, I am taking on a job at a web-based equities trading firm in the compliance department. The company is young, growing, very casual and eager to have me. I keep waiting for the call that there has been some mistake and that they really don't want me or that they've found "a better fit."

I have concerns that I might not do well with this position as it's something I have zero experience with. However, a call from my mother this morning reminded me that maybe a job in compliance is right up my alley after all. She told me that my grandmother was cleaning out a drawer and found some old art projects and things I had written when I was little. The item she was most tickled with was a three-page handwritten memo I had prepared for my grandfather when he was going to be taking care of my childhood dog, Cupcake, while we were out of town.

That's right; at the age of probably nine I was already developing plans of action and lists of rules for people to execute and follow in order to achieve results. The memo said things like, "Be sure to arrive promptly at 6:30 am to let Cupcake out to pee…If she is good, she is allowed one dog biscuit," and expounded such things as "Exceptions to these rules are not allowed." I believe the closing statement read: "Your attention to these instructions is appreciated in advance." I wonder what Grandpa's reward was for doing all of this? *Looking back, I would have loved to have been there to hear my very stern grandfather standing at the door having to yell out, "Come here, Cupcake." That would have been a riot.

Good God, all I've ever wanted was peace, balance and people to do what they are supposed to. It makes me nutty when people don't keep their word and can't follow a system. How fucking hard is it to do what you're supposed to do? This just might be a good place for me…And working around people who know how to invest money is not a bad idea either.

Now, with a year of whirlwind whimsy and strife under my belt, I look into my closet and prepare to pick out an outfit suitable for the first day back to the grind. I can wear jeans, yet I need something that still shows authority…Hmmm…Perhaps dark, slim-fit jeans, a shirt with some flair and a collar…certainly some snappy heels so that I am heard as I walk through the office. Oh, and a whip because I'M IN THE COMPLIANCE DEPARTMENT, BITCH! (Ok…That sounds lame, but whatever.)

Oh, I can't wait to start hating getting up early and driving to the same place everyday only to long for Fridays and dread Sunday nights…

As you were.

Monday September 11, 2006
Unexpected Friends

I'm a lucky person. When I moved to Los Angeles, I had a good handful of friends living here who had already made the journey in their covered wagons, leaving their land in the wild Texas plains, cattle and tumbleweeds behind.

One of my dear friends from high school wound up being my closest neighbor, living one trendy neighborhood away. Jason is quite unique. My mother was actually one of his teachers in junior high. She was his speech teacher and was always amazed at his smooth speaking voice. Jason went on to be a master debator in high school and college. Somewhere on the road of life, he wound up moving to Los Angeles with another dear friend, Roel. Roel headed back to Texas to save our hometown from utter destruction and left Jason behind. Jason is, well, a very private person and often hides from us for months on end. He's got a huge heart, a great wit and a lust for women who are... well, not worth his true time. Since Roel's departure, Jason has become "so LA." He works for a beauty supply distributor, bought a car (he used to refuse and only rode the bus), aspires to be a writer and recently had a bout with over-the-counter sleeping pills. Jason rarely calls. He is a hermit for the most part, but as he is practically family, I let him get away with this behavior and enjoy his company when he decides to be social.

When he randomly called the other night and said he wanted to take me to dinner, I thought something must be wrong. He might call to say hello, but calling to initiate dinner, no, that wouldn't happen. I asked if he was ok and he said, "I know that you're going through a hard time, and I just want to take you to dinner." I got quiet and then said, "I'm not interested in ever having sex with you, you realize." He laughed and we agreed to head out around eight for dinner.

Right on time, Jason arrived. When I came out to the car, he stepped out, nicely dressed and proceeded to give me a huge, warm hug and opened my car door for me. At this point I was thinking that Jason must be nearing death from an odd disease or truly losing his mind and trying to hit on me.

As we drove away and approach the intersection ahead, I saw a man crossing the street. I noticed that his profile looked very familiar. My brain went into super scan mode and, despite the darkness of night, I deduced that he looks like our other dear friend from high school, David, who now lives in Florida. David is off conquering the marina expansion world, utilizing his degree in How to Make a Ton of Money, and we don't get to see him that often, though he loves coming to LA. I had just talked to him two weeks prior and he made no mention of coming to LA anytime soon. I said, "Jason, that guy reminds me of David." Just then the guy turned and looked at us. I was studying him so intently that he gave me a look and I started whacking Jason telling him to stop to look at the guy. "Look at that guy. He looks so much like David. Stop. Stop!"

I threw open the passenger door and called out to the guy, "Wait. Come here." He turned around and started slowly walking towards the car. It was David!!! Jason was starting to back up and was slowly rolling as I was trying to jump out of the car. It suddenly hit me that they had set up this little moment as a surprise and a pick-me-up for me. We shared a good laugh, and Jason made fun of me for being obviously freaked-out by his random actions. I was actually quite impressed by their scheme. I would have never expected that from them.

What an awesome treat! We went to Good, a tasty Silverlake microbrewery and grill where we tackled all of the important issues of our lives while making fun of each other, just like we did in high school.

There's nothing like good friends who care enough to trick you into letting them buy you dinner.

As you were.

Saturday September 16, 2006
New Job Drivel

My New Place of Employment: Software Based Institutional Brokerage Firm

My Department: Compliance

My New Title: Compliance Administrator

My thoughts throughout my first week:

-Hmm...Everyone is genuinely nice and seems to keep to themselves.

-I love being fingerprinted. I guess this means I can't steal office supplies.

-My ID badge photo looks great! It almost looks as good as my driver's license.

-Wow. A corner office with a view of the mountains overlooking downtown Burbank...
Who cares if I can hear people peeing in the bathroom on the other side of my wall?

-What do you mean the elevator shuts down after 4:00 pm and I HAVE to use the stairs?

-I hate Excel.

-I hate Excel.

- (question from new boss) "How are you at using Excel? We want your new spreadsheets to be done in Excel." (balderdash response) "Oh, I can do anything if I put my
mind to it. I'll just have to dust off the files in the back of my mind and whip out those
Excel skills." (translation) "Awww fuck, I hate computer program bullshit. I'm going
to have to call the IT department where I used to work. They'll help me."

-(later staring at Excel) "I hate you."

-Thank God I get to wear jeans and my Chucks everyday while listening to music and
talking on my cell phone. If I'm going to be trapped at my desk, I might as well enjoy
it.

-(out loud) "No. I didn't work on any big blockbuster movies that you would recognize." (internally) "No, stupid, I didn't work on any blockbuster movies you would
recognize. If I did, do you think I would be HERE?"

-Wow. Note to self: Never suggest that the color of the Soft Dollar Invoice Folder
should ever change.

-Oh, look, I hate the fax machine as well.

-That man never washes his hands after he uses the bathroom. *Don't shake his hand.

-Am I seriously in an office again?

-This is a great place to be if I'm in an office again.

-I'm going to get a paycheck soon!

132

-Insurance benefits aren't far behind!

-I wish I was at home writing.

-God, there is not one hot person in the entire office.

-Why am I so tired? I don't feel like I did anything all week.

-Getting up at the same time everyday blows.

-I have forty-two paperclips in my paperclip holder.

-I'm going to poke myself with a needle every time I even think about eating any of that free junk food.

-I haven't got a clue as to what in the hell these people are talking about.

-Great. HBO is filming on the street below my window for a month starting Monday. That's super. I can't wait to watch the make-up people scurry around down there. If these windows opened I swear to God, I would shoot things at them with rubber bands.

-I love leaving the office at 4:30.

-Did I just take a nap at my desk?

-I don't think they noticed that I wore the same pair of jeans all week.

-Where are my PENS??? The only things I ordered were my pens. I only like to write with UNI-BALL VISION FINE INK PENS!!!

-Why would I decorate my office? You don't pay me to decorate my office. You pay me to stare at Excel.

-I hate Excel.

-Loafers with tassels and the stench of cheap cologne. I am back in an office.

-I'm trying so hard to find this industry interesting.

-"Will somebody please make sure my seeing eye dog is kept clean when I go blind from staring at all of these scanned contracts? It will be hard to tell if he's clean if I'm blind and all."

-This is truly a place where I cannot admit that I've never seen *Star Wars* or *Star Trek*.

-This office needs house music, stat.

-I hate Excel.

As you were.

Sunday September 17, 2006
Bowl Full of Characters

Last Friday I treated myself to one of my favorite events of the year: a Willie Nelson concert. The timing of his annual arrival to my town was impeccable; I had just been offered the position at my new job and am recovering from a train-wreck break-up. It was high time for me to experience some pure joy in the form of my all-time favorite living music legend.

*Willie Nelson has more talent in one of his braids than most people have in their entire fucking family. He's published over twenty-five-hundred songs, has released over three-hundred-fifty albums; six are coming out THIS year, and he even pays his taxes now. He does amazing duets with many of YOUR favorite artists.

I digress.

I was thrilled to see that he was playing at The Hollywood Bowl. I had never been there and couldn't wait! The Hollywood Bowl is another amazing spot in LA that somehow seats a trillion people, yet is nestled just so into a canyon of sorts that unless you know where it is, you speed past it not realizing its enormity as you maneuver to get out of Hollywood Proper and onto the 101. The Bowl is home to the Los Angeles Philharmonic and hosts a myriad of others throughout the year. The outdoor venue allows you to bring in your own picnic food and booze, which is fantastic since you probably paid a pretty penny to park, though tickets range in price. There truly isn't a bad seat in the house.

My partner in crime for the evening was none other than The Jewish Cowboy. During our fourteen hour excursion in the desert, he revealed that he would love to see a Willie Show. He was so excited that he called me a few days before the show to tell me what he was wearing. *He's not gay. He has a sassy cute girlfriend, I swear.

In preparation for the show, I looked to see who was opening for him. It turns out that, well, being the bad ass that he is, Willie was opening for HIMSELF with The Los Angeles Philharmonic!

Now, let's focus on something here. Willie Nelson is playing in Hollywood with The Los Angeles Philharmonic. Wow. I couldn't help but wonder what kind of crowd would be drawn to this show as it's a unique mix of worlds. Willie always draws a pretty exciting and sometimes rowdy, good ol' boy kinda' crowd. That's not exactly The Philharmonic crowd, right?

As The JC and I made our way up Highland and into the underground tunnel to The Bowl, we ran across the first character of the night: The Emphatic Anti-Bush Grass-roots Movement Pamphlet Freak. Good Lord. There is a reason why Republicans stick to the word conservative. Nothing good comes from a woman in a big floppy hat, hobo clothing and a blinking, seizure-causing novelty necklace, chanting, "George Bush is ruining America." I'm not a George Bush supporter, but really, can't we find better representation of the Left side?

Next on our path came a treat-a man singin' the gathering crowds some gospel music. He was an older handicapped black man in a wheelchair, croonin' away. He had something special about him that really drew in the tips, a gimmick in the form of a puppet. As he belted out hymns with his Madonna-style headset in tact, he held up a dog puppet who was supposed to be the one singing. So I guess that made him more of ventriloquist. At least that's what I think we were supposed to believe; he covered his mouth with his fist so you couldn't see his lips moving while the dog danced and sang.

Dude, gimmicks sell. If it weren't for that fuckin' mutt you know he would just be that annoying old guy in the wheelchair who's all preachy.

Willie had already dropped the Texas Flag (which signals the beginning of every show) by the time we got to our seats. Willie was on stage in a nice suit jacket, not his typical tank top and bandanna. We were experiencing Smooth Willie. (Say it with me like Barry White...Smooooooth Willie.) It was wonderful to hear his music played so beautifully by The Philharmonic. I couldn't help but get tears in my eyes hearing the orchestral version of "Crazy." There was a full moon, and the evening was nice and cool. The crisscrossed spotlights created a force field in the smoky-looking cloud cover above, giving the venue the feeling of being in one of those dioramas often built by junior high kids. After their fourth song, Willie leaned into the mike and said, "We're really rockin' and rollin' now." Seventy-something years old and still a funny motherfucker.

To our left was a crowd of young, drunk goobers. They were smokin' weed and were a tad loud. The JC somehow wound up talking to them a bit and it came to light that they were from Pittsburgh near the same area where The JC grew up. Hmmm...People from Pittsburgh are drawn to Willie and The Philharmonic. *We didn't talk to them anymore after the exchange of information on residential history.

To our left and down a few rows was a trio of very nerdy intellectual white women who were super excited to be there, like they had just been let out of a cage or had never been to a concert before. They were chatty, doing the white girl, no-rhythm dance and snapping photos on their disposable camera all night.

Directly in front of The JC and me was a real wild pair. The man on the left had the personality of Ross from "Friends" and resembled him slightly. He was obviously peeved at the chatty chicks and the rowdy people from Pittsburgh. His mere body movements were snippy. He just looked like the type of guy who had to write "have fun today" in his Franklin Covey. His date seemed way too cool to be with him until she turned to the left, and I realized that she was actually a HE who looked a lot like Johnny Ramone. At intermission the pissy duo gathered their wine, cheese and murses (man purses) and stomped away to find other seats away from the mere mortal noisy crowd.

Sometime during Willie's performance, (yes, he changed into his normal concert apparel and probably smoked a fatty) an old white couple settled next to me and The JC. Why? I'm not quite sure. There was PLENTY of room elsewhere, yet nearly pressing up against The JC was where they wanted to be. It was rather chilly. Perhaps they were hoping for warmth. The woman perched herself on some cushions and when she rose to go to the bathroom, they sprung up and smacked The JC as if a prank can of peanut brittle had been opened and those springy snakes popped out. Bizarre. She then began slurping on a peach for a while and then later decided that nothing follows a good piece of fruit like a bottle of Miller Lite. Gross. Fruit with a beer chaser. Why didn't she just drink a Lambic Peche Ale? People are perplexing.

And then there was us. I was so happy to be there. I just kinda' sat singing along with those wonderful, familiar and comfortable songs through most of the show while The JC spent most of his time text messaging his girlfriend and recording snippets of the set on his cell phone, trying to avoid the woman on his right. Suddenly, it hit me during "Angel Flying Too Close To The Ground" that I wasn't going to have to move. I had very stressfully fought to stay in Los Angeles and won. I was two pants sizes smaller, yet my skin is two layers thicker and I was enjoying a Willie Nelson show at an amazing venue with a dear friend. FUCK YEAH! Willie moved into "I Saw the Light" and the whole crowd was on its feet. The spirit moved through me and as I reveled in my triumph and joy, I looked over at The JC who was still seated. He was looking around and said, "So, do you think I'm the only Jew here?"

After the show we bought unauthorized concert t-shirts for $10 a piece from some ghetto thugs surely straight out of Compton. I guess they caught wind of the *Milk Cow Blues* album. The shirts they were selling were the shiznit, by the by.

A motley crew was drawn to Willie at The Hollywood Bowl last Friday night, and I was proud to participate in a familiar Texas tradition in my home away from home.

As you were.

Tuesday September 19, 2006
Promiscuous Boy At The Dresden

While driving home from work I was surprised to hear that Robert Siegel was doing a story on NPR about that stupid song, "Promiscuous," by Nelly Furtado and Timbaland. When I turn on NPR I'm expecting to hear about more pertinent topics such as the economy, debates on upcoming elections, gas prices and things of that nature. Evidently, since gas prices have fallen we can now move on to the deeper issues like the effect of "Promiscuous" on the youth of our society.

Some other public radio station had a student debate about the lyrics, which I'm not going to get into, but the general points from the students were:

*Yes, this song is very true. Guys and girls do approach each other in a very forward way. Chivalry is dead.

*This song will not make you go out and have sex unless you are already sexually active.

*You can't blame this song for the way young people act.

After a hearty chuckle at the subject matter puffing out of my radio, I tucked the story away as I proceeded to go out for the evening.

My friend Tracy and I decided to have dinner and grab a drink. After some crap-ass Italian food at il Capricio on Vermont in Los Feliz, we headed across the street to The Dresden. Yes, yes...THE Dresden, home to the famous Marty and Elayne-lounge singer extraordinaires, made famous in the movie, *Swingers*. If you come for a visit I will gladly take you there so you can put your tushie in the same booth where Vince Vaughn had his in the film.

Blah, blah, blah...So, we were sipping our Blood and Sands (it's the house drink) piano-side and out of nowhere appeared a guy on my right, eager to perch. "Is this seat taken?" he asked. "No, dude. It's yours," I said and went back to my conversation.

Instantly, so did he. "So do you come here often?" he inquired as I bust out laughing. Who asks that in all seriousness??? I saw that he was serious and continued to laugh. After that it was just typical small talk gone wrong. It was hard to tell if he was on something or trying to sober up as he was pretty retarded and only drinking soda. "So how tall are you? Wow. Five feet tall? Stand up," he blabbed. "No," I said, sending him the "furrowed brow-go away" face. He then responded, "Well that's almost regular, I guess."

At that point, I didn't even want to be casual eye contact bar buddies with him ever again much less anything else. But he wasn't finished. He had to go all the way. With obvious "scram" tension in the air, he got up from the table and said he would be back after he had a cigarette outside. He asked if we would still be there when he got back. We both said, "Sure," and proceeded to move to the bar while he was gone.

"Ding" went the bell for Round Two, and the idiot was back, smoke stench clinging to him as strong as he wanted to cling to me. And that is just what he did. Seeing that we had moved, he decided to get as close to me as he could without actually touching me, yet causing me to lean at almost a forty-five degree angle towards Tracy. He smelled so offensively, and with every word I wanted to spit in his face like he was belching cigarette breath at me. I just reached in my purse and handed him a piece of gum and said, "Chew this. You stink." And like the idiot he is, he did.

There were a few more minutes of him asking stupid questions followed by longer stretches of time where I completely turned my back to him, only to have him lean in a little closer to say one more stupid thing. Just before I was about to get rude, he said to me, "Look, I gotta' go meet up with some friends, but can I get your number so we can hook up later tonight?"

I'm sure the horrified look on my face was enough, but I couldn't resist saying, "Umm NO! Are you kidding me? What on Earth would make you think that I have any interest in sleeping with you after the interaction we have had in the last fifteen minutes? Dude, get lost."

He then tried to reason with me and asked, "Why not?" I followed with placating language: "I'm sure you are a great guy and that there is nothing wrong with you (total lie), but I just don't give my number out in bars (half lie). No thanks (dead serious)." Even after that he said, "Well you should try giving your number out in bars sometime. You might like it."

And then my Death Stare set in: Jaw clenched, lips pursed, head tilted to the right, eyes narrow and piercing. I folded my hands on the bar and focused my gaze on the center of his forehead channeling my powers of spontaneous combustion, and before you know it... ::POOF:: ...He was gone.

I turned to Tracy and said, "That fucking song, 'Promiscuous,' is ruining society! I heard all about it on NPR today..."

Never question NPR, and don't fuck with me.

As you were.

Wednesday September 20, 2006
Now That's Just Cheesy

Yesterday at work, I had one of those days where nothing I planned on saying or doing actually happened at the time I hoped it would. I spent the day doing all sorts of things that I have never done, swore in college I would never need, and things I am not convinced I will ever truly be interested in.

It was a "Hey, guess what; you're not leaving your desk until 3:00 pm" kinda' day. Somewhere in all of the madness, I managed to eat one of my favorite feta cheese, spinach and sun dried tomato pizzas at my desk.

Afterwards, I had to make a run to the bank and head into a couple of meetings. Surprisingly everything seemed to go pretty well and smoothed out as the afternoon slowed down considerably.

As I was closing down my office for the night, I pulled my lip gloss palette out of my purse to freshen up before my departure, and I saw that I had something on my face. I had a pencil eraser-sized piece of lightly toasted feta cheese stuck on my face near my chin.

I brushed it off, but then suddenly did a quick rewind of how long that piece of cheese must have been stuck on my face...since about noon...It was 4:30! I did another calculation of how many people I interacted with at close range and realized that between the number crunching, the bank run and the meetings, I had come in contact with about FIFTEEN FUCKING people! Hello! Help a sister out! Do I not have any friends in this world?

It dawned on me that they probably thought it was a huge zit. It was a slightly golden, puffy whitish blob on my face. Sitting at my desk, I imagined how serious I must have looked discussing facts and figures and forecasting break-even points and commissions with the compliance team. I wonder if they even heard a word I said...I'm sure they were trying not to look at my blemish! Oh! How I laughed at myself!

I'm actually pretty happy I found that little cheesy morsel on my face. I had been working hard all day and was starting to stress. That feta friend reminded me not to take things so seriously and to just brush the small stuff away at the end of the day before leaving the office.

And that's just what I did.

As you were.

Thursday September 21, 2006
Miss Kilgore, Your Biological Clock Is Holding On Line 3

Let's review: I'm single. I'm going to be twenty-seven years old in less than a month. I live with The 38 Year-old, Gay Schizophrenic Male. I'm only two weeks into being able to scratch unemployed off of the list. I have no reasons to believe I will be getting married or producing offspring anytime soon. People keep telling me that I will become infertile and wish that I had children in my early twenties and that if I'm not married soon, no one will want me. Usually I tell these people to lick my balls or remind them that no one wants me now, and that's part of the reason why I'm not married and have no children, aside from the fact that those things aren't of serious interest to me at this time.

But, this past week I have been creeped out by something incredibly strange at work. Each morning when I get to my desk, I have a voicemail from a baby; ok maybe a toddler. Yes. That's what I said. I'm not kidding. Press play and you hear the sounds of a small child making noises and a television in the background. I call him Phantom Baby. The calls come between 9:00 pm and 12:00 am. Every morning, there's my message. It's fucking scary!

While at my desk this afternoon my phone rang, and I noticed that the number was local. I answered and I'll be damned, it was Phantom Baby calling me direct, telling me to settle down, give up all this LA bullshit and start droppin' pups. I made note of the number with the intention of calling back in hopes that an adult would answer that I could chew the fuck out of for being so negligent of their child. And if Phantom Baby answered I would tell that lil' shit to suck a tit and leave me the hell alone or else I'd hunt him down and smother him with a shit-filled diaper. *Who am I kidding? If Phantom Baby answered, I'd wet my pants.

Before I could do that I spoke with my dear friend, Don, who is on vacation this week. When I told him about the APB that my ovaries must be sending out into the cosmos, he told me that I was on crack and that I should search "reverse phone number look up" on the Internet and find out who the number belongs to.

I had never heard of such a thing. So, I did as suggested and damn was I shocked that having a simple telephone number, I could find not only the person's name and address, but the value of the home they live in and the average annual income of their neighborhood as well. Before making one of my famous Julia Sugarbaker Soapbox Speeches into the ear of some unsuspecting individual on the phone, I decided to mention Phantom Baby to my co-workers. The first person I mentioned it to said, "Oh yeah, I meant to tell you about that. We get those a lot." I said in return, "Whew. Here I was thinking that my biological clock was calling." She turned to me and said, "Oh girl, please. You're what, twenty-two? You have plenty of time before that starts happening." "Actually, I'm about to be twenty-seven," I responded with a big smile on my face. Her face dropped and with her brows raised she said, "You're almost twenty-seven and you ain't got a man? Girl, you better get busy."

Please see paragraph one, sentence seven, words seven through nine for my response to her, now that I know I'm clear of Phantom Baby.

I still plan on calling this household back and giving them a piece of my mind. It would be my luck that the person is some special needs person who has no other form of entertainment or interaction with others. Oh well, just because they have special needs doesn't mean they can bother me at work. Get a support group.

As you were.

Sunday September 24, 2006
She Will Save Him

What I'm about to say is pure crap. Yet, when you live in LA, it's just what crosses the mind.

I saw the cover of *Vanity Fair* for this month, and who did I see? None other than Tom Cruise, Katie Holmes and their lovechild, Suri. Ugh...My eyes rolled back in my head.

Hollywood has been buzzing about this damn trio for, what, a year now? Their whole relationship has been plastered all over EVERYTHING. Nothing is private even when they try or pretend to make it so.

All year Cruise has been making headlines, causing a stir everywhere he goes with a glassy, nearly neurotic gleam in his eyes, insulting interviewers, jumping on couches and generally making a spectacle of himself. The fans started to notice, and box office sales PLUMMETED. *Have no fear, Tom, in several decades they will make a movie about you, your Scientology, your wives, your children, your rise and your demise. You've done just what this town wants you to do!

Alas, he does have something that could keep him in the limelight. Baby Suri! She is his ticket to testimonial fame. I envision a commercial that starts out with "Old Time Rock and Roll" by Bob Seger as Baby Suri comes sliding across a hardwood floor in a diaper, a tank top, dark sunglasses and socks while the lyrics, "Just take those old records off the shelf..." belt out. Then there will be action shots of Suri doing sorta' dangerous baby shit, like climbing on things and running out into the street, and stealing candy from other babies. All the while her diaper keeps her dry and doesn't leak!

At the end of the montage, Cruise will sweep her up and save her from harm and say something like, "Let's face it, not keeping your baby in Luvs is risky business."

Oh wow...or there could be a whole *Mission Impossible-* themed one as well...Then she could do a *Top Gun*-themed spot...and when she's old enough she could do a whole *Eyes Wide Shut* one for cable...Endless revenue...

Cruise lovers who just won't let go will cheer and diaper their children in Luvs and his fan base will be even more solidified, even though they would secretly see him as a "has been."

Yep. That's what crossed my mind this morning at the grocery store check-out line staring at a magazine cover. What happens to you?

As you were.

Monday September 25, 2006
Not My Typical Walk In The Park

Saturday morning was sunny and cool here in The Happy Village. I woke up early, and as I felt the crisp air dance across my face, I decided it was most certainly a morning for a hike through Griffith Park.

I threw on some sunblock, a hat and clothing appropriate for sweating in and took off up into the park. I felt like I was out pretty early, yet the park area was buzzing with people. People everywhere means cars everywhere which means vehicle exhaust everywhere...not what I was hoping on inhaling during my trek upwards.

I got through the neighborhood and past The Greek Theatre, and I saw a whole slew of school buses. High Schoolers were out in full force, decked out in their track uniforms. There was obviously going to be a cross country track meet in the park. How cool is that? What an amazing place to train.

I headed on up into the area where I like to huff around and noticed adults with walkie-talkies spread about at different points along the winding trail. Hmmm...Perhaps this was going to be a part of their route. No one said anything to me as I trotted past them until about midway on my journey. A man with a badge around his neck and a big floppy sun hat said, "There are going to be some runners coming through here soon." "I should be off this part of the trail shortly," I responded. I waved and continued on my way.

In the distance behind me I heard a voice blare out over a bull horn, "Runners, take your marks!" I turned around to see a large group of young athletes taking off and beginning to run their hearts out. From across the canyon they looked so tiny; all of their multi-colored uniforms were mere streaks against the sandy hillside. I just continued on.

Then out of nowhere I heard the sound of loose dirt scattering about behind me. I looked over my right shoulder to see a handful of runners already on my heels! How in the fuck did those kids make it through the trail so fast???? They stormed past me as if I wasn't even there!

I heard more loose dirt again and turned to see a steady flow of these teenettes getting closer and closer. I headed to the inside of the trail nearest the hillside to get out of their way and a group of them seemed to clip me as they passed by. So I moved to the outside of the trail, which overlooks a huge canyon below, full of trees, brush and whatever has been thrown over the edge to die year after year.

Suddenly, I was bowled over. My feet were sliding; those little powerhouse monsters were taking me out! I felt one foot touch the edge, and I thought I was a goner. Perhaps divine presence or just mere luck gave me some extra inches of trail on the outside of my right foot. I planted that foot and turned sideways, making myself as thin as possible. I figured if I fell over the edge backward, perhaps my face wouldn't get too beaten up, and I would still have a chance at looking somewhat pleasant in my coffin. I let the herd blow past me. I felt like Billy Crystal in *City Slickers* realizing that I was out of place. I focused on my low center of gravity and hoped it would root me!

When they were gone I caught my breath, felt my body for missing parts and stepped away from the edge. About fifty feet in front of me was another adult yelling, "You better run!" I laughed and said, "Maybe fifteen years ago!" He narrowed his eyes at me over his sunglasses, looking down at my clothes and said, "I thought you were one of the girls."

I was wearing a solid-colored orange shirt and black running shorts. I did kinda' look like I was in an issued uniform. He said, "I was wondering how you got away with wearing a hat in the race..." I smiled, waved and carried on. There was no way I was going to stand there chatting it up, waiting for the next wave of teen spirit to come whip me around.

As I watched the pack of determined she-beasts forge ahead and around the next turn I thought, "If you ever stop running, little ladies, I can't wait for you guys to discover sex, drinking, drugs, the freshman fifteen and the day when your asses all fall down, never to rise again." But then I remembered where I live and edited my thought: "If you can ever stop running your anorexic bodies into the ground you might stop drinking, enjoy discovering healthy sex, and the joys of food and watching your ass fall down, never to rise again. I'm sure two thirds of you already do drugs as is..." I'd have given anything for a BB gun to pelt their asses with...

Oh, I'm thankful I'm not a teenager anymore. It's good to be a woman nearing her late twenties who gets confused with teenagers, though. Well, sorta'...

*Mental note: No jaunts in the park on mornings when school buses are present.

As you were.

Saturday September 30, 2006
What Did We Do?

Friday was a slow day at work. There was a point when I had practically nothing to do but wait until the clock in the corner of my computer screen said 4:30 pm so I could run out of there as if the school bell had just rung.

And what did I do with all of my free time? I did what every other person in my office was doing; I was surfing the net. As I bounced from site to site it dawned on me that I have never worked in an office that didn't have the Internet. The World Wide Web became a household staple when I was in high school. I have no clue what it must have been like to not be able to jump into the cyber world whenever I felt like it during the day.

What did we do before the net gave us the ability to browse for products, information, housing and love? I looked toward the older generation for the answer and here is what I found:

Periodicals: People actually took time to sit and read hard copy versions of newspapers and magazines during downtime at work.

Books: In offices now, the idea is to look as busy as possible all the time. I would fall over if I saw someone at their desk with their feet propped up and their nose in a romance novel.

The Water Cooler: Employees once actually gathered to socialize around the bubbler, but now with instant messaging services, we don't have to leave our desks or speak to each other face to face, for that matter. The water cooler is a lonely island.

Quick Fixes: Like clockwork, people still take those coffee and cigarette breaks. They look like ravaged monsters until they imbibe another cup of joe and suck down all that comes with a stick of cancer. Can you imagine the days when people smoked in their offices? Fucking gross.

Meals: What ever happened to the "three martini lunch?" People used to go out for lunch and take an hour to do so. Often times now, it's so common to shove some semblance of nourishment into the face while sitting at the desk. Nothing healthy about that.

Office Affairs: With nothing else to do but tempt each other, people who now search online for affection used to spend downtime boinking co-workers. I can't imagine that at all actually. I've never dated or slept with anyone I have worked with...(oh shit, wait...but that doesn't really count...that was college and so cliche looking back.)

Waited: That's right. People waited on things. Emails didn't exist. Fast responses weren't possible. When there was something to be said, it got typed and passed around by hand. Times were slower and that's when the office affairs would happen...while someone was passing out the memos.

WE WORKED LESS FUCKING HOURS: We all know the Dolly Parton song, "Workin' 9 to 5." If Dolly was really working nine to five, she was probably only working seven-and-half-hours a day and a whopping, thirty-seven-and-a-half hours per week. That is quite rare to find these days and let's face it, we all wind up working more than thirty-seven-and-a-half or forty hours a week when we add in the commute, the time spent getting ready for work, the time attached to electronic communication devices, etc.

I look at those things and think, HOW FUCKING BORING! I'm barely office material as is; I wonder what I would have done in those times...

I wonder if my office would mind me bringing back the "three martini lunch?" I wonder if they will notice when I do? *Nothin' like day drinkin' to cut the edge off the afternoon!

Hmmm...

As you were.

Saturday September 30, 2006
Pink Cheeks, Heart Attacks And Busted Ear Drums

The hardest part about working in an office is that I'm separated from the world. My experiences are very limited. My interaction with the world is cut off. The feeling of living slides into mere existence. It's a suffocating feeling that I must defeat.

Having said that, it's well known that I am prone to either being witness to or having some of the most ridiculous things happen to me. When I cannot be on the front lines, my friends are but a phone call away to share the wacky world with me.

A friend of mine told me that she was going to have a bikini wax at an establishment called Pink Cheeks. That alone cracked me up. Naturally, I had to find out about this place. Stuck in the office, all I could do was look them up on the Internet. Much to my surprise, (wow...oh wow) they give the different styles of waxing funny names like, "The Playboy" and "The Thumbprint." My favorite part about the descriptions was the use of the term, "in the butt," which means they are ripping the hair right out of your ass crack. Wow. And I thought I was living life. Aside from doing waxing, they do a service that I never knew I might need in life. Anal bleaching. What in the hell is wrong with the color of my anus skin? What's wrong with yours? Who decided that asshole skin should be a certain color? And for the love of God, who can handle having bleach put on their ass skin? Isn't it sensitive enough? Just using the wrong toilet paper has me down for the count...Fuck...

*I'm highly considering going in for a waxing just so I can have a fuller knowledge of the "in the butt" term. I for one have never associated the term "in the butt" with myself in the slightest.

Late last night, while at a concert at The Roxy on Sunset, (the part of the story I will get to in a moment), my phone rang and my friend who had just had "The Normal Bikini" wax was now drunk at the County Fair. As if hearing that LA has a County Fair wasn't big enough news, she was calling to tell me about the most disgusting food item she has ever seen. At the booth where you can get all things deep fried and on a stick, the newest, hottest item is...now prepare yourself...get a defibrillator ready...a battered and fried chicken breast with a slice of Swiss cheese between two Krispie Kreme doughnuts with a side of honey for dipping. Is that not the grossest thing you've ever heard of? I thought Roscoe's Chicken and Waffles was crazy, but this is just fucking stupid. I looked at my acquaintances and told them what my friend was about to eat, and they all looked petrified. I haven't heard from her today. I hope she's ok.

Oh, The Roxy on Sunset. It's one of those venues where old bands made their name and got their start. It's a part of The Strip in LA near The Viper Room and The Whiskey-a-Go-Go...tons of history and still a place to catch up-and-coming artists. Last night I went with The 38 Year-old, Gay, Schizophrenic Male to see Mojave 3, a band I knew nothing about and after seeing them, care even less about. I find this to be music to slit your wrists to, really mellow, barely a beat, each song pretty much the same as the next and the last. The whole crowd looked like it needed a bath and a pulse-check. My roommate, however, took on the role of making sure the crowd was alive. The hermit came out of his shell in a way I never would have expected. In an indoor venue no larger than a gas station parking lot, my roommate drank about six bud lights and began shrieking out things like, "Fuck yeah," "No fucking way," "I want to fuck him!" at the TOP of his little femme lungs. He would scream into my head at the end of every song so shrilly that my natural reaction was to slap the fuck out of him. People were staring, and he was making a total scene. This crowd was the kind of crowd that sits around barefoot and holds hands while talking about granola, yurts and peace...and there bellowed my gay, schizo roommate like a woman being raped, "Ooooooooooooooooowwwwwwwwwwwhoooooooooooooooooo...Yeaaaaaaaaaaaaaaaaaah..." It went on for the whole concert. I thought I was going to have to leave him there. The sad part was that he was so happy and didn't realize how ridiculous he was. I just sat there waiting patiently for the whole awful experience to be over.

Hmmm...maybe being separated from the world in the office isn't so bad after all...

As you were.

Monday October 2, 2006
My Kind of Grill

My mother is so excited because she's having a huge BBQ pit built for her. She loves to grill food more than any woman I know. Her retirement has brought her a lot of time to perfect her skills. She is even looking into doing some grilling for events where she can make a buck or two. I think that's awesome! She needs to get her ass to LA to show these fools out here what a grill is really for.

Speaking of that...

During my lunch hour I escaped from the office to take a brisk walk through the shopping area around my building. As I passed by a record shop, a poster taped to the store window caught my attention. The poster wasn't for music or movies or stereo equipment. It was for grills!

I know most of you are thinking, "What on earth would a record store be doing selling BBQ equipment?" Kids, I'm not talking about the kind of grills that use propane; I'm talking about the kind that rappers want you to show them. *grill: a term used to describe a metal decoration that covers all of the front teeth.

Completely fascinated, I had to go inside to see if the poster was simply something you could purchase to hang on your own wall so that you could dream of a grill of your very own, or if it was an advertisement for grills you could actually buy. Much to my excitement, I found a showcase of grills mounted in all of their mouth-decorating glory in pretty, velvet jewelry boxes.

Rows and rows of them sat there gleaming, each one a little different from the next. Some were very plain, the standard faux gold and platinum. Others were jeweled; some were very flashy with lots of texture and inlaid rhinestones.

But then I saw the one I must have...In a super shiny pretend platinum setting was the word "TEXAS" spelled out in ice...*ice: a term used to describe diamonds. Nothing says National Republic of Texas pride like a mouth full of diamonds and platinum. It just might be my birthday present to myself.

*I always thought the accessory motif for Texas was denim and diamonds, but I guess putting denim in your mouth would be rather strange.

::shrug::

At least these precious metals won't soak up a lot of saliva and cause you to drool like denim, and they might pick just up a radio station or two...

It always amazes me how much like my mother I am becoming.

As you were.

Thursday October 5, 2006
Pissed at Pickwick

In an attempt to break up the work week monotony, my friend Stephen and I decided to go bowling last night. Bowling is not really my thing, but it's a cheap form of entertainment, so I was game.

I found a place in Burbank (close to both my work and his apartment) called Pickwick Gardens. The facility houses a bowling alley, an ice rink and a place for wedding receptions. Woo-hoo...???? Nope.

I will never go there again. The entire staff is on my Fucktard List.

I arrived at 4:45 pm since I had never been there before and thought I should get a lane as soon as I could in case there was an after work rush or something. The place was packed! Only one lane was open. I paid for our first game, got the fungus-filled shoes and proceeded to wait for Stephen.

Creed was blaring out of the sound system. The cleaning guy was oiling our lane with this loud machine, and, much to my surprise, all of the other bowlers were special needs adults. Only a hit of acid could have made this scene any more surreal.

About fifteen minutes later, the girl who sold me the games came up to me and told me that I would have to leave in the next ten minutes because the league bowlers were coming and they would be taking up all of the lanes. I asked her why she didn't tell me that when I bought the first two games, and she said that she thought I would be gone by the time the league bowlers got there. Uhhh...No, stupid sixteen year-old dipstick...I wouldn't be done with an evening of bowling in half an hour.

She further disappointed me when her response to my pleasant, "Oh, well, I'll just take a refund and be on my way," was, "Yeah, see, we don't give refunds." To this I sternly inquired, "You mean to tell me you don't refund money on services not rendered?" She looked at me blankly and said, "Yeah, see, we don't give refunds." Fuck...I was in The Valley after all...

Poof, be gone. And she was.

The Twerpy "Manager" appeared before me looking less than interested in my situation. "So, what's your story?" he asked as if I was causing a stir. I explained that I wasn't informed that league bowlers were coming in to take up all of the lanes, and I wanted my money back. "She tried to page you, but you didn't respond," Twerpy snarled. Between the music, the oiling machine, the hollerin' tards, and the video arcade, I could barely hear him, much less a dipstick valley girl paging me. Did she even know my name? Come on!

Then Twerpy proceeded to say, "Yeah, see, we don't give refunds. They're really strict about it." Very nicely I said, "Fine. How about some passes for some free bowling? That's fair." He looked very perplexed and then said, "Fine," and walked away to return with two pieces of yellow paper. He scribbled on them and handed them to me. The voucher said, "Free bowling when lanes are available, not valid on Friday or Saturday night" and they expire in one month. I asked him when the lanes are available. "The best time to come in is during the week day. Leagues take up the lanes weeknights and weekend days."

What the fuck? Do you really think I'm going to take a day off from work to go bowling? Who am I, Roseanne Conner from Landford, IL? I don't think so. I decided

146

against asking him who could fire him, took my vouchers and headed for the door to call Stephen and share the news.

What bothers me more than anything is that the manager didn't even try to utilize the ol' "the customer is always right" motto to win my affection for the place. He could have given two shits as to whether or not I came back or bad-mouthed his business. And that's what I plan to do. Fuck Pickwick Gardens!

I also plan to go back and borrow a bowling ball. I think that's only fair. I'm going to walk in, take a ball and walk out and take a picture with the ball in front of their sign. They don't care about my business, and I don't care about their balls. I'm then going to write the owners. The letter will go a little something like this:

"Dear Sir:

I recently was asked to forgo my bowling experience at your amazing establishment due to a misunderstanding about what time league bowlers take over the alley on weeknights. Upset that I was unable to receive a refund, the manager said that I could have one of the bowling balls from Pickwick and two vouchers for free games. He said it's what he does when customers don't understand your stupid No Refund Policy. He agreed with me that it was essentially stealing from the public when you can't get your money back for services you didn't receive. Anyhow, here's a picture with me and my new bowling ball, courtesy of your fine manager. You should give that man a raise for giving the best customer service ever.

Fuck you sincerely,

Robin Kilgore"

Ahhhhh...Now there's your stir, Twerpy.

As you were.

Wednesday October 4, 2006
Gumma On The Phone

I checked my voicemail after returning from a hike in the hills, and I had a message from my Gumma that said, giggling:

"Hey, it's Gumma. I finally got it right. I was able to leave you a message when I finally stopped trying to call you from the TV remote control."

When I called her back I tried to joke with her that, as she repeatedly dialed my number from the TV remote, she had actually been changing the channel on the television in my living room. At first she didn't believe me, but then she started giggling again and said, "Technology is something else. I hope you liked the programs I chose for you this afternoon. I want to make sure you're keeping it G-rated." We both laughed and then she said, "Do you remember when you were four and we were playing Hungry Hungry Hippos on the kitchen floor?" I said that I did, remembering this story very well already. She continued, "Do you remember what you said to me when I beat you at the game?" "I think so," I said. "You got so dern mad at me and said, "Old people aren't

147

supposed to win!" And that I did say. She finished, "I would like you to know that whether you believe it or not, I am still winning." And that she is. That she is.

Yikes! Calling me from the TV remote...I wonder what other appliances she gets confused with each other!

Growing old with grace and humor, that's my Gumma.

As you were.

Monday October 9, 2006
No Playboy Party For Me

::sigh::

I had a fantastic weekend packed full of awesome people and new and fun experiences. The big events included attending a bi-annual art walk at the old Pabst Blue Ribbon Brewery turned-artist community downtown, droppin' it like it was hot (and trust me; it was) at a hip-hop show in Santa Monica and discovering everything I never knew I needed at a Flea Market on Fairfax and Melrose.

But the one event I didn't get to attend was a celebrity poker tournament/fundraiser at The Playboy Mansion. Yes, that's exactly what I said, The Playboy Mansion. And why would I be able to say that with such authority, you wonder??? Because one of my closest friends here in LA (a person to which I'm technically a cousin) did actually have the opportunity to attend.

I called Sarah P. to see if she wanted to go to the art show as she is in fact a photographer and has talked of looking for artist housing in the recent past. An event like that was right up her alley. When she turned me down because she had to be back to her house by a certain time to get all gussied up to go to Hef's house, I nearly fainted. What makes this so funny is that she's not the type of person (like my ridiculous self) who would get super excited about an event like this. She actually turned down the offer to go originally. Thankfully, another friend, Sara S., prodded her for a few days and got her to go. Sara S. (and rightfully so) is the person who got to be her partner in crime for the night.

Completely baffled that I couldn't just join the party, I began bargaining to get to go... These were my points, all of which made no difference:

1) I'm your cousin! (in a round-about way)

2) It's my birthday month!

3) Pretty girls do not travel in pairs, they travel in packs. You are an up-and-coming actress. You need an entourage.

4) I have five formal gowns!

5) I have my own set of bunny ears that have been waiting for an experience like this.

6) These functions are iconic. We should all have a Playboy party in our LA story collection.

7) I respect the idea of the possibility of a swimming pool filled with THC infused Jell-O and naked women, really...

Alas, nothing.

My dear friend Don said he was extremely disappointed in me in that I wasn't just showing up at her house, decked out and ready to go, telling her, "When I said I wanted to go, it meant that I am going." He also suggested that I show up at the function early and tell the person running the guest list that I was HER! Now that's just too far. I wanted to go WITH my friends! That's the whole point! Don's a little more wicked than me...

The message I left Sarah P. the following day went something like this, "Hey there. The art walk was ok; nothing to rave about. You have to call me and tell me all of the details of the party. I don't care if you were horrified and hated every minute of it, you must make something up to make me feel justified in all of my jealousy."

The message I got in return went something like this, "Hey. It's Sarah. The party was pretty cool, but it was still weird, cuz' it was the Playboy Mansion. I really wish I could have gone to the art show. Nobody wanted to go with me today, though..."

Well no screamin' shit! They wanted to go with you LAST NIGHT! LOL!

Ho-hum. Of course, I'm over it. If dudes like Ryan Seacrest, Andy Dick and Mario Lopez are still getting invitations to that place, mine is not far off...::shrug::

::sigh:: I guess I'll just have to put these bunny ears back in the box...

As you were.

Wednesday October 11, 2006
Horrifyingly Retched

When you have read this, you will say out loud, "Who DOES that?!?

The Jewish Cowboy called me all in a stir, retelling a series of events from his previous night out that certainly made me shout out, "Who DOES that?!?"

The JC and his boys were out getting dirty and wild on the mean streets of Hollywood in celebration of one of their birthdays. After a long night of D&Wness, the boys came fumbling home.

The JC rose the next morning to find a scene that ranks as one of the grossest things on the planet in his kitchen.

One of his boys couldn't hold his liquor and wound up unloading his digestor into his own knapsack. Instead of just tossing it out on the porch, the "friend" decided to pour out his purge into the sink, a sink full of The JC's household dishes, and proceeded to leave his knapsack in the sink as well. And by leave it there I don't mean until he woke up, I mean left it as a calling card so The JC didn't have to wonder who did it! No note, no pathetic attempt at an apology, just a sink full of semi-dry vomit on someone else's dishes and an empty nest of blankets on the couch.

Yeah...go ahead...Expound it now, "Who DOES that?!? *I couldn't wait any longer either, and I've already thought about this several times today...

Ugh! The JC was far too nice in my opinion. He simply soaked and re-soaked the dishes, and washed them himself. *Nope, no dishwasher to sanitize them in. He did throw the knapsack into the dumpster. (which is funny because the party puke deserter had some smoking paraphernalia in the bag...He puked on his own weed! LOL! Wow...What a tool!)

If this had been my friend who left me with a scene like that involving my dishes, oh, oh God save me from my own evil thoughts...I swear I would have gotten on a pair of rubber gloves, put all of those dishes in a plastic sack and driven over to his house and dumped them out on his doorstep or tried to get in and put them on his bed. In my house, you don't leave any body excrement on anything and just walk away. Say something; make some attempt so that I'm not left concocting ideas of how to make you re-consume what you tossed onto a plate. I don't care if it is your own goddamned birthday.

People never cease to amaze and disappoint me. Wow...A man I don't even know has made my Fucktard List.

Oh, say it again...You know you're thinking it:

"Who DOES that?"

::eye roll::

As you were.

Saturday October 14, 2006
Paper Clips

Last weekend I experienced something I have heard about, but never experienced first-hand: the racism some black women project against white women who are paired with black men.

I was out with a black friend, Sol, dancing at a club in Santa Monica where I was one of the only white people in the whole place. I only really noticed when my friend and I were dancing, and right in front of me, two young black girls were looking at me like I smelled as if I stepped in dog shit and began to make comments like, "Who does that white bitch think she is, bein' up in here wit him," and "Look at her tryin' to front like she knows this music." Wow. Normally, I would have said something back, but instead opted to ignore it as I wanted to continue having a fun evening. I fumed internally as I couldn't believe how stupid they were being. It's 2006, and we were in Santa Monica, California!

Later in the week I received a DVD from Netflix called *Paper Clips*. It was a documentary I had ordered a while back and forgotten about. I put it in as I was going to bed. After it was over I was a puddle in a mess of used tissues in my bed. Why? It's one of the best stories about diversity education I've ever seen.

The film tells the story of Whitwell Junior High in Whitwell, Tennessee and the world-wide attention they received when their school principal decided they needed to do a project that would teach Whitwell's students (and community) about people different from themselves.

They chose to teach about the Holocaust. When it was taught that over six million people were exterminated, one of the students asked, "What does six million look like?" A project began to emerge. They decided to try to collect six million of something to get a visual of the size of such a loss. After researching the Holocaust further, they chose paper clips, as they were a symbol against Hitler during that time. The children began a campaign to collect paper clips. They wrote letters to famous people, newspapers, The Whitehouse and scores of others. Over time people caught wind of the project and just like any amazing idea, it started getting attention and visits from Holocaust survivors, the media and people from other countries. By the time their project was complete they had collected over twenty four million paper clips and erected one of the most unique and touching Holocaust memorials I've ever heard of. For something like this to occur in a low income, completely Protestant, tiny Southern town with only a few blacks, Hispanics and no Jews at all is more than remarkable.

And it all started with a few paper clips...

As the credits rolled, I thought about the young girls at the club in Santa Monica who just couldn't stand me because I was a white girl dancing with a black man. I really wished I would have seen this documentary before going out. I would have been armed with paper clips to silently and kindly slip over those ignorant girls' flappin' lips...

As you were.

Saturday October 14, 2006
Calculated Showdown at High Noon

Thursday at work I was given the assignment of "running some numbers" for the big boss man. Ugh. I took on the challenge because I had to and began to throw all of these fun figures into an (::shudder::) Excel spreadsheet.

I hate Excel.

I sent the three pages of pretty numerical data to the big boss man in a pretty professional email to get some flack in return. I had not presented him with what he wanted. I sent him an email that said, "I am so sorry for my mathematical shortcomings, but unless you tell me specifically what to change in some of these requests, I wouldn't know to do so. What is it that you want me to do?"

I was given a clear response and went back to crunching, thinking the whole time that I couldn't believe this was a part of MY job! I could hear my high school algebra teacher, Mr. Robinson, saying to me again, "You just aren't going to get this, are you?" I pushed him out of my head and calculated on.

Again I sent the data in its pretty form to the big boss man. Again I got an email...not just a negative one but one that sent the sensation of SOUR directly to my gut. It simply said, "We will discuss the mathematical calculations of this at noon."

Eww...It was like receiving a note from your doctor saying that it was time for a booster shot or pap smear. In the long run the procedure will be good for you, but the anticipation of the event is filled with nothing but pure dread.

Why am I not just a whiz with math and spreadsheets???

And then I could hear Dean Ho in my mind. He was my upper level economics professor for two semesters at The University of St. Thomas. What an amazing man complete with one of those super "coming to America for the American Dream" success stories. His Chinese accent was incredibly thick, and he was trying to teach econ...It all sounded like Greek! I was struggling with my assignments and went to visit with him in his office. He made me explain my work and the theories to him. I could do that with no problem. He looked at me and said with great passion in his elongated English, "You veree veree smot, but you a-fraid mathmatics. Iiiit is yooor tooooll. If yoooor a-fraid yoooor hamma, you hit yoooor hand wit iiiit!"

Full of pride, I sent the big boss man a one line email that said, "My thumb hurts."

And at noon, dressed in solid white, I went downstairs for my showdown with The Evil Mathematics. Decked out in all black my nemesis stood before me. On the count of three we drew our weapons and began to duel. It wasn't pretty, but I was the one who walked away; wounded only slightly.

I left The Evil Mathematics in the dirt.

Remember, despite my shortcomings, I'm veree, veree smot.

*Oh, I still hate Excel. Thank you.

As you were.

Thursday October 19, 2006
Into The Oblivion

Recently, a very smart gaggle of gals I went to college with and I got together and created a Tuesday Night Goal Setting Conference Call. I'm very excited to be a part of it and have set some valuable goals in place in my life. One of them, which I think is crucial for my personality type is to stop getting into toxic relationships with men. Since God refuses to just put Mr. Yuck stickers on bad guys, I realized that I'm just going to have to take matters into my own hands. To avoid Fucktards, I know I need to take things very slowly, listen better, not get attached and not let someone else's life overrun my own.

Since this intention was set in place, I put it to the test and agreed to meet up with a guy who I had met on MySpace and had been chatting with via email. Through the written word, I found him quick-witted, smart, interesting and kind. In person I found him to be very confident, yet still rather reserved in an innocent, sweet way. He was handsome, well-educated, courteous, rather charming and laid back. We were off to a good start. We went on two short, very casual mini-dates. I didn't think too much of them, but certainly found him worthy of getting to know further.

This morning I opened my email, and this is the exact message I received from him:

152

"dude, i like, totally haven't written back to you. truth be told, i have no excuse. you are fun, cute, and smart and very well spoken and i had fun hanging out, but I don't feel a lot of spark on the romance front and i wanted to tell you upfront rather than just ignore you into oblivion."

I actually started laughing when I read this. I had a feeling he wasn't that interested in me, but seeing as we had only been around each other for three whole hours in our entire lives, I decided not to worry about it. What's most astonishing about this to me is that I went against a big part of my nature and didn't pursue him like I normally would a guy I was thinking of exclusively dating. I let him call. I let him pick what we did when we went out. I was just plain ol' me, and it got me NOWHERE! My intentions of simple dates backfired! What the fuck was he hoping for in three hours; me to throw myself at him? A girl who wouldn't stop calling? A mustache ride??? I mean, really.

I emailed him back and told him that I appreciated his honesty and that if he wanted to be friends with me, I wouldn't be opposed. No sense in wasting a good human, ya' know? I hate being disposable and don't treat people that way.

Now I have to get a little bitchy here. He did this the day before my birthday. That's not cool. He could have done it as soon as he felt it, but no. Grrrr...That was pretty tactless. Good thing I only care enough to notice the fact.

The amusing part about his email is the way that it's written. He's from Boston, but as you see, it reads like a Valley Girl wrote the opening sentence. He hasn't lived in LA THAT long!

Hmmm...Am I to assume that, as I have received this email alert, he is now going to commence ignoring me into oblivion? Probably so.

And if life is as it seems to be in my world, I'm sure I will run into him and his new girlfriend or fiancé in a month or so.

I guess if you can't get a hold of me for a while that's where I'll be...Out in The Oblivion somewhere...

Wow, dating blows.

Way to stick to my goals, though...According to my goal-setting class I think that means I'm entitled to a "pink dot privilege", which is a treat to myself...::yawn/eye roll combo::...

As you were

Saturday October 21, 2006
No Muss. No Fuss. Just US!

Birthdays.

They are benchmark days. Every year on your birthday you find yourself reflecting about where you were the year before, what you were doing, who you did it with and where the last twelve months have taken you. Right? I know I do.

As yesterday was my twenty-seventh birthday, I thought about the events around my

153

previous one. Last year I celebrated my birthday in LA for the first time. I had just come out of make-up school and was adjusting to life as a poor, freelance make-up artist. I was in a nebulous, pseudo-relationship with a guy who works for a gun store. There really wasn't anything that I wanted to do for my birthday, but Gun Store Guy wanted to take me out. We wound up going to the 4100 Bar on Sunset Boulevard. I hadn't eaten anything. I got a little more drunk than I expected, and we wound up having some stupid (and bad) sex in his truck in the parking lot. Yep. That was me with my big ol' white ass pressed up against the windshield for all to see. Yikes. So not me and so not a good idea. Birthday sex can be highly overrated. (Don't you hate it when you do a stupid thing on a benchmark day? Ugh. You can't ever escape the memory!)

To avoid another tragic LA birthday memory and to keep my tushie out of tourists' photos, I declared the theme of this year's birthday to be, "No muss. No fuss. Just US!"

After a surprisingly delightful day at the office where I was showered with kindness and birthday attention, I headed home to find that The 38 Year-old, Gay, Schizophrenic Male had surprised me with a cake and a "Melt Away Your Ex-Boyfriend" candle. *He's nutty, but he's funny. Frankly, there just aren't enough of those candles...

In accordance with my theme, I had declared that I was going to have a Girls Only Evening. We were going to go to a play called "Tender" in North Hollywood and out for dinner and some cocktails. And that is just what Sarah P., Chelan and I set out to do.

The evening was chilly, the play was thought-provoking and cocktails were calling our names. As we walked to the car chatting about where to go, I, with the power of MoneyGrams on my side, (*see previous blog entitled such) found a crisp ten dollar bill on the ground. Parking money! We headed into Hollywood.

Hunger motivated us to try Hollywood and Vine, a restaurant on The Boulevard where the drinks and much laughter began to flow. Frankly, I could have stopped drinking and gone home directly afterwards, but...ehhh...well, I wanted more booze. I was thirsty for some action.

*The following is only told to the best of my recollection.

Two decent lemon drop martinis deep, I took the girls into The Frolic Room. There's never a dull crowd there! And like most nights it was full of interesting characters. The first guy to try to perch on our trio was a little man originally from Miami, Florida who was a writer. We convinced him it was my thirty-fourth birthday and talked circles around him to the point where he went out for a smoke and never came back! Oh wait...Nope. I still haven't shed a tear. The only thing I can remember about the second suitor was that he was originally from Fort Worth, Texas, and he had an extra really tiny front tooth in the middle of his two front teeth. While he was trying to do whatever it was he was trying to do a fight broke out, and after escaping the sandwich I got shoved into for safety, I decided I should break it up. Suddenly, I became the soothing voice of reason and found myself sweetly caressing the shoulders and neck of a very angry man, telling him, "He didn't mean to hurt you. Let it go. You're much too smart to get into trouble over something so silly." Where the fuck that came from, I don't know. He melted in my half-embrace like warm wax. "You're an angel," he said as I smiled and walked away. ::shrug:: I didn't correct him. Somebody should still think so. Deciding that I should soak up as much free alcohol as I could, I went back to the bar and smiled at a man in those all too familiar black and white striped pants. I can pick out a chef a mile away. It turned out the he was the Executive Chef of Hollywood and Vine. Needless to say, the girls and I were invited for an entirely free meal and bar tab whenever we want it. I have always had a way with the culinary artists...

As the night was winding down, I said my goodbyes to Ruben and Joel behind the bar. Ruben motioned me to the end of the bar and proceeded to sing me "Happy Birthday" in Spanish and spank me while trying to kiss on my neck. Holy SHIT! I wasn't expecting that at all! After about a minute of this seedy, out-of-the-blue birthday bar lovin', I scampered away with Sarah P. and Chelan into the night.

About thirty seconds before being stumbling drunk, I was dropped off at my door, full of food, fun and a great LA birthday to my name. There was no muss; I still had on a full set of perfectly painted lips and lids. There was only a little fuss which I helped diffuse. And it was just us. I fell into my bed, happily alone...That is after having a "forgotten until this morning" photo shoot all by myself in the foyer of my apartment building. *Digital cameras are the devil. Those photos have since been deleted. Oh, shut-up. You know you do it, too!

Incidentally, Gun Store Guy actually called me on my birthday. We keep in touch; after all, we were once really close friends. He was the first new friend I made here. He made my transition to LA seamless. I will always be very appreciative to him for that. Toward the end of the conversation, I realized he didn't remember that it was my birthday. He asked what I was doing this weekend and I said, "Well, it's my birthday so I'm going out with some friends." He responded, "I didn't know it was your birthday." I had to laugh. Either he has tried to forget the scene at the 4100 Bar as well or he must have a lot of sex in bar parking lots with girls.

Here's to still having THREE MORE FULL YEARS in my fabulous roaring twenties...

::sigh:: Good God, help me...

As you were.

Friday October 27, 2006
Is This Thing On?

Remember being in school and sitting in an assembly in the auditorium or perhaps sitting in a classroom among peers and listening to a lecture or presentation? Remember how at the end they would ask, "Are there any questions?" How often did people have tons of questions? Rarely, right?

It's my conclusion that not much changes in the big kid world of Corporate America.

This past week I had to give a very short presentation three times to three different groups of people at work. I was a little nervous as I don't know my co-workers well and am still settling in to my role (and all of the new information that's being shoved down my throat daily).

All three times at the conclusion of my little show, all I heard were crickets. These people just sat there. Grown, educated adults, just blankly stared at me as if they were trippin', and I was a fiber-optic flower, twinkling before them.

155

And let's be real, here. I put on a great show no matter if I'm talking about new company regulations, my weekend or the smell of an armpit. I'm pretty fuckin' entertaining and to stand in front of a bunch of mannequins who offer no response is just, well, lame.

"Hello! Is this thing on?" I wanted to scream. Why bother doing a live presentation? I could have just as easily sent out a presentation via the web for them to pretend to read.

I did get some feedback from the receptionist. As I walked past her desk when my last presentation was over she said to me, "You should work for Disney. I can totally see you as one of the Princess characters. You have so much energy and are so animated."

All I could say to her was, "You're probably right," as I had a vision of the people who just sat before me at Disneyland with their children, acting overly interested in hopes of making their child's visit there the most magical event of their lives.

I guess that's what I need to keep in mind for my next presentation; dress up like some character and do something to make this the most magical event of their lives. Hmmm...Perhaps I wasn't so far off with that comment about them being high. Maybe I'll just moonwalk for them while speaking, or do the whole presentation with a flashlight under my chin, telling it ghost-story style...What about doing the whole presentation in sign language? Now that would be fun. Oh! I know. I'd give them each a slip of paper with a paragraph of my presentation on it to stand and read out loud. Then I wouldn't have to do a fucking thing, and I could just sit and stare at them!

::shrug::

What can I say? I'm just a Disney Princess, after all...

As you were.

Friday October 27, 2006
Don't Get Snippy With Me!

A very dear friend of mine, Mark V., told me, "I've known you since we were sixteen, and I'm still trying to figure you out. You're so multifaceted. I feel like I should sell Cliff's Notes to boys who might want to date you to help them out, but I don't think it would be enough."

This crossed my mind as an old boyfriend (we'll just call him Mr. Snips) called to tell me how surprised he was that I had sex in a parking lot. I sorta' felt like saying, "What, are you jealous? Are you judging me? Maybe you should try it." Instead I said, "I'm sure you've done some things you aren't proud of." He followed that with, "Well, I've never had sex in a parking lot." ::insert my eye roll here::

And then I instantly remembered (and reminded him) that Mr. Snips may not have had sex in a parking lot, but he once almost cut his penis off in hopes of getting more oral sex.

We were in the shower, and I think I was shaving my legs and grooming myself. Somehow we got on the topic of his pubic hair. I said that it wouldn't be a bad idea if he mowed the lawn a little as the long ones tend to get caught in the back of the throat.

::insert the sound of cat trying to dislodge a hair ball::

With lightening speed he got out of the shower and grabbed some tiny scissors and began to go at himself like Edward Scissorhands. Just when I swore he was about to create a swan he let out a yelp. He had cut a chunk out of his own penis. Now, Mr. Snips is a six-foot-tall former football player. When he began to freak out and bound around the bathroom, it was truly a sight.

Pause. Think about it.

The men are squirming.

The women are laughing. We bleed once a month from our loins, and it can hurt like a bitch. The justice card is being called out here!

Proceed to roll around in laughter as I did in the shower while he pouted, "This isn't funny, Robin." *Mr. Snips has always been wound a little tight. He nearly killed me when he found out that I told my mother. I remember thinking at the time, "It's not like you cut the whole thing off and sent it to me in a box...No...That would have been romantic!" So it wasn't sex in a parking lot, but it was an attempt at sexual gratification. Put away your stones, Mr. Snips.

So to my dear friend who is keeping notes on me: In fits of frustration, Robin will act out and do things that seem wild and out of character, yet if the right guy can really get to her heart she won't have to act out randomly, but only with him, all the time.

Get it?

As you were.

Friday October 27, 2006
Dogg Treat

Let's review: (I like to do this)

I'm a twenty-seven year-old straight, single Caucasian female of Czech/Polish/Scots/Irish decent who grew up in Houston, Texas in an area that was predominantly populated by Mexicans.

I know what you're thinking, and you're right. Robin must love gangsta rap!

Wednesday was supposed to be a hiking day. The goal was to take my friend Sol up through Griffith Park as we take turns sharing our favorite activities with each other. When he called me Wednesday afternoon and said he had to flake out, I could feel the heat rising in my neck. I hate flakes! When he said he wanted to make it up to me by taking me to a show where his brother was playing, my interest was piqued. Sol's brother is Kamasi Washington, a very accomplished jazz musician. (Go. Google him.) I asked where he was playing, and he said that he was playing at The Greek Theatre with Snoop Dogg.

Fuck, I almost fell out of my chair at the office. Hike? I dropped that hike like it was hot! What hike? I'm going to go see Snoop Dogg. What a treat! The show was great.

I'd never seen anything quite like it. When he came out on stage he wasn't alone. The stage was full of his fellas. There were over twenty-five people just hangin', being cool with Snoop while he did his thing.

The show was actually a benefit for the Snoop Youth Football League. The team he coaches was there in their jerseys. They were so excited! I'm not sure that a bunch of eleven year-olds need to be at a gangsta rap show at 10:00 pm on a school night, but well, if it's for a good cause that will keep them out of trouble and teach them good sportsmanship, why not?

I was surprised at how many songs I knew almost all the words to. I never realized how infiltrated my life has been by his (and a lot of other) rap music. I may not run out and buy new cd's, but I bet you also know all the words to "Gin n' Juice." I still remember where I was the first time I heard it. I was making out with my very first boyfriend, uhhh...we'll just call him El Primero. EP was just as white as me, yet did his best to pull off the jersey and Air Jordan look. I remember thinking, "Are they talking about... drugs??" EP seemed quite ok with the lyrics and the message it sent across. I almost wonder what happened to him...Ehh...Not really. Good lord...I've come a long way.

And speaking of weed, Snoop's microphone was diamond encrusted, and I do believe it had a diamond marijuana leaf on it the size of a dinner platter. The evening was a tad humid, so the ample amount of weed haze hung in the air like a film over the incredibly diverse crowd. It really didn't bother me at all. The weed issue wasn't left behind at the show. Snoop was arrested the following day at the Burbank Airport for possession of it (or possession of something).

::shrug::

When are the authorities going to give up and realize that the Snoop D-O-Double G and the original outlaw, Willie Nelson, are always going to have weed on them? It's just what they do...Ain't nothin' but a g-thang, baby...

It's Friday, and I'm still trying to recover from the show actually. And by recover I mean deprogram myself from responding naturally when someone calls me a "bitch" or a "ho"...

*Actually, I got my hike. As the show was near my house, I made Sol park and walk uphill to the venue...he he he...NOBODY FLAKES ON ME!!

'Til the next episode...Fo shizzle...

As you were, my nizzles.

Thursday November 2, 2006
Single Female Deviled Egg On The Run

Tuesday was Halloween.

I didn't dress up, and more than a few people were shocked. I had several people make a trip up to my office to see if I was decked out in some way. The Fairy Godmother of the firm poked her head into my office, and I actually saw the glimmer in her eyes fade when she saw me in my everyday street clothes. It's almost as if she was hoping that "the make-up artist" would break the mundane atmosphere of the office and show up in a full face of prosthetics. I joked with her that Halloween was just an excuse for women to let out their inner slut and dress up as hookers disguised as "the sexy nurse," "the sexy fire fighter," or "the sexy dead girl." And who besides necrophiliacs find anything sexy about a dead girl? ::shrug::

I wasn't going to waste perfectly good make-up to sit in my office all day...Uhhh, no. LA is a BANGIN' place to be on Halloween, but I couldn't even begin to think about fighting the traffic and parking nightmare in West Hollywood on a weeknight. I wasn't being a Halloween Humbug; I just don't find it a priority to dress up for this holiday. ::sniff sniff:: Do you smell that? I smell an adult! Whew...damn...somebody, light a match...

Now don't get me wrong. I still participated in Halloween in my own way this year. After work, I helped two of my gay guy friends get into drag make-up so THEY could go fight the crowds in WeHo.

In all seriousness, Halloween is a very special and kind of private day for me. This Halloween marks the two year anniversary of the day I decided to move to Los Angeles. Yep. Lots of people ask why I moved here, and I could go on all day about every emotion that catapulted me West, but I'm going to narrow it down to just a few moments.

Trying to defeat the "sexy _____" girl costume motif, I went for something more original for Halloween 2004. I dressed up as a Deviled Egg. Go ahead. Take a minute. Picture a soft foam egg that covered my head and body with holes for my face, arms and legs. Throw on some yellow felt on the stomach for the yoke and a set of red horns and a tail and you have a Deviled Egg. Ha ha ha ha! Right? I customized it by Velcroing a handmade sign to the costume that read, "Single Female Deviled Egg Seeking A Nice Strip of Bacon to Smother With Love." Oh, the sparkling wit! The night started out fun. I went to a party and then headed into downtown. I took the Light Rail. And somewhere between my slight buzz and a homeless man staring at me, I had some sort of breakdown, or rather, a breakthrough. (Omit about five years worth of back story) Waves of thought poured over me.

"I hate my job. It has eaten my soul."

"The people I'm about to hang out with aren't really my friends."

"I'm tired of being drunk several nights a week."

"I don't fit in this town anymore."

"I'm fucking twenty-five years old and this is my life; a confusing blur."

"All of the values I once had for myself are gone."

"I have a personals ad adhered to my chest disguised as a Halloween costume. I'm no different than "the sexy _____ chick." I've just spelled it out in peel and stick letters!"

"None of this is me!!!!"

And with that, I began to cry. Oh yeah. Big crocodile tears...a little blubbering as well...maybe even a whimper. I cried sitting alone-a giant lonely ovum on Houston's premiere mode of transportation. If you know anything about that ridiculous contraption, you know it doesn't take you anywhere or very far. "How fitting," I thought.

When the Light Rail came to my stop, I took a deep breath, got off the train and found my friend Michelle M. She was working the door for extra cash at a bar where her friend was DJ'ing for the night. Michelle M. had mentioned that she was moving to LA and needed a roommate. I walked right up to her, and as seriously as I could be taken dressed as I was, told her that I was moving with her.

And three months later I found myself nestling in to Los Feliz Village, in Los Angeles, CA. And the rest has been not history, but the beginning of me taking back MY life.

Not everything about being an adult stinks like rotten eggs...

***Comments I heard dressed as Deviled Egg:

"I call Bacon!"

"I'd rather have you over easy."

"You're making me hard-boiled."

"If you let me hold you, Egg, I'll let you hold mine."

"You are Eggcellent."

"What would it take to get under your shell?"

I still had a lot of fun. It was a breakthrough, after all.

As you were.

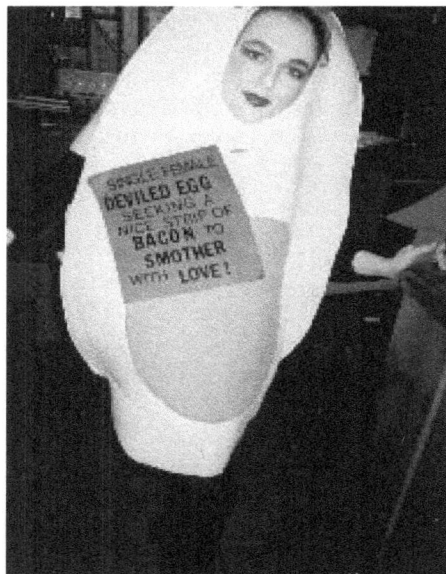

See? Told ya'.

Saturday November 4, 2006
He Saw Me Naked And Married My Roommate Instead

In an effort to dig myself out of the debt I have created this past year, I am grounded! Impulse buying is a thing of the past. The word budget and I are best friends. If it is to be dry-cleaned, I don't wear it. I only allow myself to eat out once a week. All of these things really don't bother me, yet there is one item that I greatly miss just slapping on my credit card: airline tickets. Oh, how I miss just deciding to go to Chicago, New York, or Hawaii at a moments notice.

I'm feeling this yearn in a very strong way today because I should be in Houston at a wedding. My greatest college roommate, The Angel, is marrying her college sweetheart and our former dorm mate, Newspaper Man. (He works for a newspaper and she is in fact, an angel.)

When I talked with The Angel about me not being able to be there, she said, "I'm really bummed that you aren't going to be able to make it. You are a big part of the reason that we are together in the first place. Don't you remember how you used to tell me that Newspaper Man and I just needed to do it because of all of the tension between us?"

I cracked up when she said that because it reminded me of how we all became friends. Newspaper Man and I had a philosophy class together at 9:00 am Tuesdays and Thursdays. We began to study together often, and I found out that one of his hobbies was photography. I think I convinced him that he needed to take some nude photos of me for his portfolio somehow. Yeah...It was my idea. What can I say? I decided that I probably wasn't ever going to look any better than I did then and wanted to have something to remember my youth by...And NO, nothing happened between us. It was as professional as amateur photography in a dorm room could be.

Anyhow, jump forward a semester, and The Angel and I moved in together. Newspaper Man and I still hung out a lot. I noticed, however, that he wasn't coming by to see me as often. He was coming to see The Angel. Weeks and weeks of this 1920's style courtship had gone by and nothing. The tension was intense. I do recall telling my roomie that she and Newspaper Man just needed to do it! I think that was in 1999. Almost what, seven years later, they finally are! Getting married, that is. (God, I hope they've already done it...and I mean IT!)

I told The Angel that it's probably best that I am not attending the wedding. I would be that old roommate of hers who Newspaper Man used to take naked photos of in the dorms who would be walking around telling everyone so. There I would be in the buffet line and Newspaper Man's seventy year-old aunt would say, "So how do you know our sweet Newspaper Boy?" And I would say... "Oh we used to live together in the dorms. I posed nude for his photography portfolio..." And then an ambulance would have to come to take her to the hospital. It would just be too much, ya' know?

While going through a box yesterday, I actually ran across those nude photos. I'm proud to say that I think I actually look better now than I did then which makes me believe that I'm doing something right. I also thought about framing one and sending it to them as a wedding present. Come on, without those photos, chances are they wouldn't be together.

161

Imagining the look on The Angel's face when she opened that gift is priceless enough without having to make it a reality. Hey, a gift like that would be more sentimental than a stupid set of steak knifes and much more of a conversation piece, don't you think?

They are great people a part, and an amazing couple. I truly wish them the best!

As you were.

Saturday November 4, 2006
Psychic Syrup?

The 38 Year-old, Gay, Schizophrenic Male is out of town, so in between farting out loud in the living room and dancing around naked, I decided to make some strawberry pancakes this gorgeous LA Saturday morning. Mmmm...Nothing like my big, thick Bisquick pancakes with fresh fruit tucked inside, smothered in butter and drippin' with syrup.

As I reached for the Aunt Jemima syrup, I noticed that Aunt Jemima doesn't look quite the same. That bitch has had some work done! The look of the packaging has had a face lift. Now, I know that companies like to move with the times and try to keep up with society and its trends. KFC made the Colonel some goofy, animated, dancing dude in a white suit. Strawberry Shortcake reappeared on the scene lookin' like some anorexic fashionista. Yet, I'm perplexed about good ol' Aunt Jemima. She used to look more like Mammie, and now I'm seriously thinkin' she looks like Dionne Warwick. I can understand the movement to drop the "I don't know nuthin' bout birthin' no babies" persona, but shouldn't they be gearing their progressive strong black woman to re-semble someone more along the lines of, say, Rosa Parks or Coretta Scott King or heck, Oprah? I'm not sure that a singer who developed the "Psychic Friends Network" is really the role model I want on the breakfast table with children.

I suppose I should be careful what I think about this. Then again, I guess it's too late. That bottle in the fridge is probably a channeling device that sends Dionne messages. I think I've figured out how she stays connected with the universe. She already knows that I think her new scheme of flexing her psychic skills is stupid.

::shrug::

Oh come on, if you believe she's psychic, you would believe she could channel you through a breakfast condiment.

Silly consumers.

As you were.

Tuesday November 6, 2006
Plotting The Demise Of A Woman I Don't Even Know

As one of my six month goals is to move into another apartment, preferably on my own, I was ecstatic to learn that Karm, my Indian neighbor across the hall, was mov-ing out this past weekend. The emotion only lasted about thirty seconds, though. The apartment had ALREADY been rented to someone new before he took the first box out!

162

The emotion that followed was rather surprising. Something snapped inside of me. It wasn't until I realized that independence, freedom and solitude were taunting me from only ten feet away from my front door that I wanted to move SO badly. My eyes narrowed. My lips began to pull tight against my teeth. Savage mentality began to set in.

When Karm casually told me about the tenant, my wicked woman skills went into overdrive.

These were the facts I was presented:

Fact: Newbie is moving from Orange County to live closer to her boyfriend. He lives down the street.

Fact: Newbie works in Santa Monica.

That was all I needed to hear. After confirming with the manager that there was no way that she wasn't moving in, I started making plans on how to welcome our new neighbor right out of her lease.

1) Be overly friendly. Invite myself over often, bearing fresh-baked goods to establish rapport and trust.

2) Invite Newbie out for Sunday brunch to discuss the neighborhood. Share facts about mysterious recent death on around the corner on Ambrose, the auto theft problem, frequent vandalism inside the parking garage, schizophrenic neighbor and noisy neighbors...all with a warm, Joker's grin.

3) Invite her over to dinner. Make sure The 38 Year-old, Gay, Schizophrenic Male is there. Encourage him to share his thoughts on the world with her. (She will start repacking the moment she leaves the table.)

4) Discuss the terrible shame that it is that she isn't living WITH her boyfriend. Moving from Orange County ALL the way to Los Feliz sure is far not to live together. Constantly remind Newbie of how LONG and FAR her commute to work is each day. Two-and-a-half hours (at least) of driving a day without traffic must be just HORRID! (Heavy drama. Lots of concern for her well being.)

5) Go to next door neighbor and plant seed of uncertainty about Newbie. Show concern for her guests' safety.

6) Leave nasty anonymous "don't park in my spot" note on her vehicle.

7) Awkwardly and nervously ask her if she got any mysterious unmarked packages left on her door by mistake. When she says no, freak out on her, telling her little, yet pretend to be under control. (Being pale and sweaty would add to the farce.)

8) Complain to the manager that Newbie has been seen stealing detergent in the laundry room and has been leaving the main gate propped open.

9) Place a dirty personals ad in the LA weekly with her address and apartment number in it to call for "a special evening of massage."

10) Ring her doorbell at all hours of the night and run away.

11) Seduce Newbie's boyfriend. Duh. That should have been #2.

Beat.

Beat.

Beat.

Ok. Fine. Anyone who knows me knows I wouldn't do any of this. I will probably (and hopefully) wind up liking the Newbie. If you have lived like I do, you would probably be plotting much worse! But a fire was sure lit under my ass when I realized that right now I could be lounging in my very own apartment in MY building! I did spend a great portion of the weekend enduring a mental train wreck of ideas on how to get out of this apartment.

The 38 Year-old, Gay, Schizophrenic Male is so sweet, despite all of his uniqueness. I just don't want to live with anyone anymore. A weekend alone in the apartment made that quite clear.

*I actually do think it's pretty odd that Newbie is moving all the way from Orange County and not moving in with her boyfriend only to endure a LOOONG commute to Santa Monica everyday. That's fishy. Perhaps #3, #4, #5, and #8 might reach actuality. Hmm...#11 in reverse might be cool if he's hot...

Anyhow, I promise I'll behave and attempt #1; only nothing will be freshly baked. I barely bake for people I want to keep around!

As you were.

Friday November 10, 2006
Set On Agitate

In order to live in LA there are many things that you must adapt to. One of these is learning to deal with the fact that this city is like a washing machine-not just any washing machine, but one of those huge, industrial ones that can hold an entire months worth of laundry in one wash. Loads and loads of people think it's a good idea to throw themselves blindly into the agitate cycle without pre-soaking in LA. Before they are half-acclimated to the water temperature and still trying to take in enough soap they realize that they are in the same load as some pretty heavy towels and jeans that they are no match for. Barely rinsed out and completely out of control, they are sent straight into the spin cycle where a draining force pulls more than just soap and water out of them-it leaves behind limp and lifeless articles that need to dry out. Many, if still in one piece, are quite ready to move after that. Then again, some seem to learn how to use the proper settings and stick around.

That was probably a terrible metaphor to introduce thoughts regarding my week and how transient this fucking town can be. Everyone is constantly moving in and out and back again. The 38 Year-old, Gay, Schizophrenic Male, much too my amazement and glee, called me while I was at work on Wednesday and left a voicemail telling me that he was moving! I was so excited, yet instantly tossed into a decision-making mode. I had to start looking for a new roommate or figure out how I was going to pay for a one bedroom or a studio on my own…It was the best kind of uncertainty I had felt in a long time! I started calling people, talking to the apartment managers, posting ads and really jumping into action. Early into my frenzy, I was presented with lots of folks talking about moving as well, or stating that they just moved into new places. One of my sixth month goals of drastically improving my living situation was happening quite quickly. Two days into the process, he came to me and said that his plans fell through. I tried to hide my complete disappointment in his news. Just when I thought the spin cycle was going to throw him out of my wash once and for good, he somehow managed to work his way back in.

He does use a lot of bleach and has a sick love for cleaning products…maybe he's got an "in" with the machine that I don't know about. Hmmm…

Ugh, all I know is that I really thought I could just toss myself in as well almost two years ago when I arrived. But, I've had to take a step back and spend some time in the permanent press cycle. Trust me, I'm not a delicate girl, yet I need to take some time to take care of me and make sure I'm sturdy enough for the heavy duty loads around here. Perhaps living with this delicate guy is actually helping me toughen up.

Maybe I'm just looking at all this laundry I know I need to do, and that's why I thought about this instead of just stomping my feet and screaming like a bratty bitch, that until further notice, I'm stuck living with The 38 Year-old, Gay, Schizophrenic Male.

Oh, the roller coaster…wait…LA is like a roller coaster…yeah, a roller coaster…

Ok…I'll give up on metaphors for the now…

As you were.

Saturday November 11, 2006
Trailer Tragedy

While watching "Grey's Anatomy" on Thursday at Jason's place, I experienced the amazing way Hollywood can use you and lose you as if you never existed.

As I mentioned reviously, back in April, I got a call from Central Casting (an extras casting agency that I registered with for shits and giggles) telling me that I had been photo-selected to be in a scene for Nancy Meyer's new film, *The Holiday,* starring Kate Winslet, Cameron Diaz, etc...

I spent five very long and very fun days at an old bank building in downtown LA with about two-hundred other extras shooting this scene that was supposed to be set in a London News Room. This is where The Jewish Cowboy and I became friends as we kinda' got paired together for all of the different shots. The final scene we shot had both him and me standing with Kate Winslet in a pretty tight shot. After I was fiddled with, (wardrobe change, make-up change) I was pulled from the scene. All I heard was, "Pull the girl who's prettier than Kate." That was horrifyingly flattering. Kate Winslet is gorgeous.

Skip ahead to last Thursday in Jason's apartment. Commercials were running and suddenly on the screen were Kate Winslet and The Jewish Cowboy! And there I WASN'T! Holy shit. It was *The Holiday* trailer! There was just a hole where I once stood. What a weird feeling to be able to recall all of the sensory memories of that moment, standing in that shot, but to have no trace of ever being there.

Now let's get serious...I could have been in a nationally broadcast movie trailer. For someone who has no desire to ever be a lead in films, that's HUGE! My family would have had a field day with that! How frickin' cool would that have been?

Well, I guess you will just have to ask The Jewish Cowboy...

Hmph.

As you were.

Saturday November 11, 2006
Now Serving Fantasy Fulfillment At The Friar's Club

Midweek, my friend Kim called and asked if I would like to go to a party with her in Beverly Hills on Friday. "What's the occasion?" I inquired. "Some schmoozefest for industry people. I'll get more details later," she replied. "Cool. I'm game," I finalized.

It turned out that we (Kim, her roommate Rachel and I) were headed to The Friar's Club on (Little) Santa Monica. Cool, huh? It's the revamped version of the old private club started by Milton Berle back in 1961, which is famous for it "Roasts." Rad. Just being inside made me think about all the Hollywood glitz that had paraded through those "members only" rooms. If I shut my eyes, I could hear Frank Sinatra singin' away at the urinal in the john before heading back to a hand of poker...

Those days are long gone, and the crowd I was a part of was pretty plastic, I'd have to say. Even after spending the entire evening there, being interviewed by some online news crew, seeing a fashion show, and hearing different stories, I still have NO IDEA what function I was a part of. First it was a launch party for a website, then it was a fashion show and then there was talk of raising money for Africa...What? I don't know.

Despite not knowing what in the hell I was attending, my purpose in being there surfaced toward the end of the evening...I was going to make someone's night.

While watching the fashion show (Barely; it was lame...The group of people I was standing with labeled ourselves "The Haters" as all we did was dance and talk shit about the event.) I noticed a TDH (tall, dark and handsome) becoming a part of our group. I made my way near to him and began to do chit-chat about the stupid clothing, the camel toe, and visible cellulite of the volunteer models. He had nice hair, good bone structure, good teeth, excellent shoulder width...seemed to be able to keep up with my wit, yet there was this unassuming sweetness about him. And then I looked down toward the next important feature that I adore...nice hands...and they were strong looking, nice finger shape...with big black "X's" on the back of them.

Oh my God, NO! The "X" that marks the under twenty-one...NOOOOOO!

I turned to Kim, who had been giving me the "go get 'em" face and said, "He's not even twenty-one." She looked as shocked as I did. When the words, "I'm only nineteen," came out of his mouth, I nearly fainted.

166

He then said, "But that's ok, Tommy said you're only twenty-three." (God Bless, Tommy! ...boyfriend of friend of a friend...) "That's right, I'm only twenty-three," I girlishly fibbed with a wicked grin on my face and a sparkle in my eye.

Enter more lame people, stupid dancing to defeat lame people and a few more cocktails here...and the night began to wind down...

I headed to the bar to close my tab. Along the way I bumped into 19. (Imagine one of those romantic, chemistry-filled scenes in an old classic movie, but throw in the twist that I suddenly was channeling the character of Samantha Jones from "Sex and the City".)

Me: Hey. (Bite lower lip; make eye contact; tilt head to the side casually; raise eyebrows and smile.)

19: Where have you been?

Me: Around. I've got a question. Are you really only nineteen?

19: Yeah.

Me: Where are you from? (Lean in and tilt head forward to show interest.)

19: Georgia.

Me: Mmmmm. A Southern Boy. (We started moving closer to each other.)

19: Well, I grew up in New York for a while before moving to Georgia.

Me: When did you move out here? (I put one hand on his arm.)

19: Two months ago.

Me: You've only been in LA for two months??? Wow. You have so much to take in. How has it been so far for you? (Now both hands were on his arms, and his breathing was getting a little shallow.)

19: It's been pretty good.

Me: Well, it's about to get a whole lot better. (And with that I seductively pressed myself up against him like a minx, wrapped my arms around him and began to kiss him like an older woman kisses a younger man-something I had never, ever done.)

It was a hot little moment, there...Sugar, open a window because I wasn't done yet.

Me: (After the exchange, and with my arms still around him as he so cutely trembled a bit, I broke eye contact and grazed my lips on his cheek near his ear and whispered): I have a secret to tell you. I'm not twenty-three. Let's just say I'm closer to thirty. Now you can go tell all of your friends that a hot, thirty year-old woman couldn't resist you at a trendy Beverly Hills event and made out with you in the middle of two-hundred people. Welcome to Hollywood, sugar. It keeps getting better.

And with that, I kissed his cheek once more and walked away.

First of all, what in the hell came over me??? I don't make out with random people in public (anymore). And certainly not nineteen year olds! The oldest child I used to nanny is nineteen, and he is a freshman in college!!! Oh my God! Secondly, Hollywood doesn't get better; it gets only more insane! I mean, OBVIOUSLY! I realized in part how every significantly older guy I've ever dated has felt about me. There was this small sense of duty and honor to give him a rise and teach him a little something about the power of an older counterpart, boost his confidence and have a little fun for myself.

As I drove the girls home, giggling about what I had done, Dean Martin's "Memories Are Made of This" played in my mind. I thought back to earlier in the week and wondered if Kim might have actually said "Smoochfest" and not "Schmoozefest." At least she didn't say "Schmuckfest" if I was going to misunderstand her...::shrug::

::sigh::

Just another typical Friday night in my world. Compliance Administrator by day, Steamy Seductress by night. What are you gonna' do, you know?

I seriously never cease to amaze myself.

As you were.

Sunday November 12, 2006
Take That, Bush!

Following my temptress episode with 19 at The Friar's Club, I continued with activities of such an out-of-character nature on the drive home...

It was certain. There was no waiting until I got home to pee.

With a bladder full of gin screaming to be released, I flew into a gas station and hopped out, car still running. I scampered in my heels to the door of the snack shop only to find it locked. Fuck! Clip. Clip. Clip...I scurried around the corner of the store to the window, where I basically pushed a guy out of the way to beg to be let in to use the facilities. While the attendant ignored me and the other patron laughed at me, I saw the most painful words posted on the ladies room door only ten feet behind the glass: "Out of Service"...

"Oh for Christ's sake...Fuck it," I said as I took off in my heels around the back of the building. I was about to do something I have a lot of trouble doing and have only done once as an adult and maybe once as a child...I was going to pee outside. ::ugh::

Around the back of the building was a man...probably strung out on drugs, perhaps homeless...He was kinda' talkin' to himself and walking around in circles. I knew I could handle him. (Remember my roommate...)

As I clippity-clopped closer to him, seeing my bathroom of bushes dead ahead, I said to him, "Excuse me, Hun. Do you mind going around to the front of the store? I need to pee, and I want some privacy. A lady needs her privacy. Go on, please. I'll only be a minute."

"No problem, lady," he said and wandered off.

I managed my way into the little manicured bushes, worked my very cute pencil skirt up over my hips, squatted down and let the flood gates open. I actually didn't think I was ever going to stop peeing. I was laughing so hard. Just thirty minutes prior I was at some ridiculous "to be seen" Beverly Hills event, playing with barely legals, and now I was trying to keep from leaking on my shoes somewhere just North of Koreatown.

When I finally emptied the tank, I put myself back together, hopped out of the bushes and scurried back around to the building from the other direction. Kim and Rachel were looking at me like, "Where the hell did you go?" Before I made it to the car, I saw the transient fellow from behind the building. In the light, it was now obvious from the scabs on his face, his thinning hair and bad teeth that he was a meth-head. Yet, full of my natural, radiant charm I thanked him and told him he was free to resume his place behind the building. He then asked for some change. I normally don't give money to such causes, but this time I said, "Since you let me pee in peace, here..." I dug out my coin purse and gave him a wad of my laundry money. "Now, promise me you will use this for food and not drugs. No meth. It's a night of doing things that are out-of-character." He smiled and said, "I promise."

And with that, I hopped back into the car thinking, "I've got to get home before I do something REALLY stupid!"

Once again, I never cease to amaze myself. I attribute these open forms of expression to the Democrats finally being in congressional power. Conservatism is dead! Thank you, America, for your recent stand at the polls. I can now officially, freely, piss on the Bushes! ::shrug::

As you were.

Monday November 13, 2006
Doin' It the Dark

Remember your high school counselor and the kind of questions they would ask you like, "If money was no object, what would you do all day?" in efforts to motivate you to brainstorm potential career ideas? I thought that was a really dumb question to ask a teenager. How many teenagers can fathom a world where money really is no object? Unless they are C.O.P's, (children of privilege) they probably don't have a clue.

I think they should refocus the question away from money and into time constraints. If my high school counselor asked me, "Robin, if you knew that your alarm clock was going to go off at 4:00 am every morning, what would you hope to be getting up to do? What would motivate you to get up at 4:00 am?" I would have probably given a better answer. I know I can now.

Being an employee within the brokerage industry on the West Coast, I have learned that there are people who get to our office before 5:00 am to work along with the New York Stock Exchange. Ugh. I can't imagine it. I already get there pretty early, but damn. I can't imagine getting to work that early to watch trades and stock prices dance around. You couldn't pay me to process someone else's money at 4:00 am while juggling several departments' requests and regulating a section of that industry.

However, if I get a call for a make-up gig where I have to be on location by 5:00 am and it is fifty miles away, I nearly spring out of bed when the alarm sounds. Twice now

I've had jobs that put me either in the desert with no running water, or in a random parking lot without a generator from which to run lights and power.

Last year I got to assist on a music video for the metal band, Bleeding Through. It was shot way the hell out in the desert in Palmdale, and typical of the industry, the video was shot out of sequence. The lead singer was supposed to be really bloody and gross towards the end, yet the bloody gross stuff was shot first. When it was time for the guy to shoot the "clean scenes," I had to spend an hour making small talk with him as I washed fake, coagulated blood out of his hair and skin with bottled water!! Did I mention that it was thirty-two degrees??? That guy was a good sport, but then again, I'm sure they are used to it. If you name your band anything with the word blood in the title, you're sure to get painted up often. (Good thing the word "shit" isn't in their band name...)

If you've ever gotten dressed in the dark and accidentally put on two different colored socks, then you get an idea of what it's like to try to match foundation to someone's skin tone without a light. What's even worse is trying to do it in really bad lighting. Nothing is more unflattering than the glow of a security light on the side of a building! And that was just my experience recently as I worked on a spec commercial. I had to pat myself on the back after the sun came up. Somehow I had actually managed to base match in the dark. Now don't get me wrong, I certainly had touch-ups to do, but no one was the wrong race or anything!

I'd love to see some of these brokerage guys have to do their job in a building with no heat or air conditioning, no toilet and be expected to be there for over eight hours. Over eight hours? ::gasp:: Yep. Sometimes on set work takes you well into the night.

Nothing like putting in a twelve to eighteen hour day, simply to create something that might entertain one of those brokerage guys as they sit in front of their plasma screen televisions…Ironic, huh?

It's true…When you like what you do, you never actually work. Too bad I have to do both right now.

Grrr…Not forever. But at least I'm on the right track. A girl can hope.

As you were.

Wednesday November 22, 2006
The Girl Who Cried Roommate

One day I will look back on my current roommate situation and laugh. The 38 Year-old, Gay, Schizophrenic Male has finally pushed me to the point where I will not speak to him. Yep. He has been so completely irrational that I have had to resort to ignoring him so he will go away.

There have now been FIVE different letters drafted and delivered to the management about his departure. We started out with the surprise announcement, then moved to the changed-my-mind letter. This led to the letter in which he stated that he was going to prorate his rent as he wanted to move out on December 8th, then the 17th and now it's the 22nd. Oh my fucking God. I have never had to deal with such utter lack of consideration when it comes to money. Each new letter has been spawned by some sort of unsettling experience for him which actually translates to: If he sees anyone else in the apartment with me, he freaks and runs to his computer to type up another letter. At this moment, I would pay people to camp out in the living room and the hallway if I thought it would make him run away.

He revealed to me that I am the main reason he stays sober. Oh for the love, screw that. I'm no one's crutch for sobriety. That's the saddest thing I've ever heard. I'm pleased that I have brought…whatever it is that I have brought into his world that makes him not want to do drugs, but I'm not the cure! If that's the case, I'd be living with him for life! Uhhhhh NO!

Not only have I decided not to talk to him, but he has posted a "Do Not Enter" sign on his bedroom door. The last time I had a sign like that on my door, I was ten. Is it possible that my roommate's mentality is that young in some regard?

What is most stunning about this whole situation is that I have had to explain all of this to potential roommates! Do you know what a loon I look like showing a dark, oddly-decorated apartment with heavy shrouds and a "Do Not Enter" sign on a bedroom door??? And with all of these date changes, etc., do you know how ridiculous I sound trying to give potential roommates a move-in date? I only wish they could see him at his finest. You know, when he's wearing his ear-plugs, a plastic shower cap, a mint-julep mask and a wife beater, dancing for his fish in the living room. Totally harmless, rather entertaining, yet it's the reality that I'm currently living with. One of the roommate interviewees asked me, "Why did you move in with him, knowing he had such problems?" Saying, "Yeah, like, it was either that or move in with my ex-con boyfriend," just doesn't help the situation at all, now does it?

The management has given up. They aren't going to talk to him about his erratic letter-writing campaign until his final move out date. They treat him like Texas weather; wait a minute, and he'll change.

God help me if that man comes to me and tries to say that he's not moving out... ::enter heavy cheesy organ music, big Tammy Faye Baker make-up and hair and a spotlight on me as I tearfully beg with a twangy Southern accent to the sky above:: "I'm witnessing to you Lord. Lord grant me strength. Hold me up so that I will not fall against your will, Oh Heavenly God, I'm in need of patience and understanding. Lord, keep me from turning against my 38 Year-old, Gay, Schizophrenic Male Brother." ::insert big cry scene and then flash the Send Money sign::

Is it wrong to put a man with mental illness on my Fucktard List?

Fuck. Fuck. Fuck.

Oh wait. Did I mention that he's sleeping IN his closet these days? Yeah, that's right; in his closet. ::sigh::

As you were.

Thursday November 24, 2006
The Pilgrims Would Be Proud

It's Thanksgiving morning, 2006. I'm just waking up and thinking about what Thanksgiving means to me. What comes to mind most is that this holiday keeps getting better and better every year. I like to travel, meet new people and learn how others feel about Thanksgiving.

A few years ago, I spent this day with my eighty-something year old nudist great uncle and his family in the Northern California town of Paradise. I had never met him or any of those family members before. That portion of my family consists of artists, scientists, a lawyer and a poker chip manufacturer. We enjoyed one of our big meals at The Sierra Nevada Pale Ale Brewery. These are my kind of people! What a blast! Go ahead…Imagine me driving around with an eighty year-old nude man. Please...*Ok… He wasn't nude. But I still made you think about a nude eighty year-old man.

Last Thanksgiving was pretty amazing. I had the pleasure of working out of The Chiodo Brothers Production Lab (The guys who brought the world *Critters, Killer Klowns From Outer Space,* and *Team America…*) and we had just wrapped production on *Trail of the Screaming Forehead*, for which I was the special effects make-up assistant. I followed the lead actor around making sure his giant prosthetic forehead didn't lift from the heat of the sun for several days. I had also just finished being a part of the team of people who decorated Three Time Oscar Award Winning Make-up Artist, Ve Neill's house, for her annual Christmas Party. Seeing those golden statues sitting on top of the entertainment center in her house was rather surreal. (Of course I held them…and made a secret acceptance speech to The Academy when no one was looking.) I was feeling pretty on top of the world.

So naturally, I headed straight to Vegas to see my best friend, Alba, for Thanksgiving. I spent eight straight days in Vegas. I'm not sure that's healthy for a person who doesn't live there. (Then again, I'm not sure that anyone who lives there is healthy.) I'm inclined to believe that pretty unique characters spend a "family holiday" in Vegas. I say this because Alba and I found ourselves stumbling out of The Spearmint Rhino, a gentleman's club, at 7:00 am on Thanksgiving morning after we somehow managed to pick up a group of married men at The Rainbow Bar and Grill. What? How can an entire group of married men get away from their families for a Vegas getaway like that? Good God. And no, gutter brains, neither one of us did anything with any of the married men. One of them told me that he knew we were safe. When I asked how he knew, he said, "You're in a Vegas nudie bar, and you're wearing a huge turtleneck sweater." ::shrug::

Our actual Thanksgiving meal was had at the steakhouse inside Circus Circus with Alba's dear friend and business partner at the time, Ray, and his parents. I don't know what was more entertaining that night, Ray telling funny stories about us or Ray's very sweet sixty-something year-old stepmother talking about her Jell-O shot recipe. By the end of that adventure it got to the point where I could close my eyes and see the lights of The Strip flicker on the inside of my eyelids. Before I had a full on seizure, I decided it was time to go. Fan-fucking-tastic time.

So, Thanksgiving 2006…It's off to a pretty fun start. Last night I spent part of the evening interviewing roommate candidates and then headed to Compton to meet-up with Sol for a turkey fry and to play dominos. Yes. I said Compton. Sadly, I got there quite late, and most of the turkey was gone. The crowd was pretty boozed up...and kinda' lookin' at me like I was lost. Dominos didn't happen. I had forgotten the rules of the game, and all I got while trying to learn again was that you're trying to build the dominos out on the table in multiples of five, and when you're not winning, spill your drink on the table so you have to clean up and start over. Later I found out that some of the guys there thought I looked like Punky Brewster. Wow. That's silly. My Chucks were the same color! **Hello people, Punky wore two different-colored shoes...And shall we remember that real life Punky had a BREAST REDUCTION? I'll never have that problem! What were they thinking?

I guess you could say that I'm a Pilgrim in my own right on Thanksgiving. I seek out and conquer new places, cultures and people. We share food and fellowship. But I DON'T STEAL, RAPE, OR GIVE OUT STD's! Remember I have the paperwork to prove that...

Bring on the FOOD!!! Who am I kidding? Bring on the wine!!!

As you were.

Sunday November 26, 2006
It's Not A Confession If You Know You Will Do It Again

I started it. Yep. It was me.

Brace yourselves. Here comes the part where I become my utmost human. Are you ready to gasp and groan with disapproval? Awesome.

I...I...Slept with Cholo last night.

Ok...Go ahead...Say what you will...Now, shut the fuck up, and let me explain.

Cholo's birthday was two weeks ago, and I woke up thinking about whether or not I should send him a little message for his birthday. I know most people would think that would be the last thing on my mind, but if you know me, this is the mysterious part of me that emerges when most would rather set someone on fire. I just have this gift or flaw that allows me to put myself in the other person's place and let things go. After mentally stomping around his shoes while getting ready for work I sent the message:

"Hey there. Happy Birthday. I hope you are doing well. - Robin"

And then I began to breathe like I was about to have a small panic attack. All of those stupid girl things took over the rational part of me, and I began to wonder what he might be thinking, seeing a message from me.

Shortly thereafter I heard my phone vibrate across my desk at the office...He responded:

"You are so sweet. I truly appreciate you thinking of me today. My b-day wish is that I can undo any hurt/harm I have caused."

I sat there looking at those words thinking, "What in the hell does that mean?" My response:

173

"You are so welcome. Careful now, saying that you want to UNDO something implies that you are willing to put forth effort and action to make it different. Since it's a birthday wish I guess I should grant you the opportunity to try."

His response came through in an instant:

"Thank you!!!"

I sat there at my desk, staring out the window at the mountains with my phone clutched in my hands thinking, "Oh dear God, what have I started?"

The weekend arrived, and I worked on a spec commercial all day Sunday. While standing in the parking lot at 5:00 am eating my breakfast in the cold, a big truck blaring music came driving up, nearly taking off a chunk of my ass. The driver rolled down the window and with a huge attitude he leaned out and asked me, "Where's the rest of the crew? Where do we set up? You doin' make-up?" I was instantly taken back to the day I met Cholo on the beach and how he acted when he rolled up on the set. Without even asking, I knew this guy was the grip.

Sure enough, the grip took to me like a bee to honey. It was creepy how much this man reminded me of Cholo...similar style of dress, vehicle, set attitude...so much so that I once again fueled the fire of communication with him by sending him, oh yes, you guessed it...a text message. Fucking T-mobile and their cheap unlimited text messaging. I couldn't help it. Being around this tool, reminded me of the things I truly miss about Cholo. Sure enough, a text message conversation ensued.

I sent:

"Does the Local 80 send out a memo to grips instructing them to drive big pick-up trucks, wear camo cargo shorts, New Balance sneakers and to instantly hit on me? I think I have met the Caucasian version of you."

He responded:

"Are you trying to make me jealous? Damn it!"

The textsation went back and forth and back and forth. It got a little serious in that I admitted that he had been on my mind and our relationship was such a whirlwind and I missed the idea of his friendship. He then killed that by asking if we could be friends with benefits. Ugh. How in the fuck would he think that I would want to sleep with him after he showed an utter lack of respect and cheated on me? Grrr...

The following week was Thanksgiving week, and in the spirit of the day I sent out a warm and fuzzy early blanket text to all my friends, wishing them all the happiness and bullshit of the day. Cholo responded:

"Wanna' come over tonight and cuddle?"

Frozen. I was frozen in utter shock and disbelief. "He must be out of his fucking mind. Has he forgotten how we last saw each other? What the hell is wrong with him? He's really brave. He's...like me! Wait. Could that be possible? Could it be possible that he really is sorry and wants to try to get passed what happened? Well, once again, he's not taking the time to do things right. He's not going to get what he wants that quickly."

174

Last night I was out with a friend at The Lucky Bar in Los Feliz. Something took over me again, and more textsation with Cholo began. I have no recollection of what I said to start the evening's banter, but before I knew it, it was several hours later and I was tipsy at home, having a live conversation with Cholo. I had forgotten how much I loved his voice. He tried to say that he just wanted to have sex with me, and that was his only reason for any communication. I'm not stupid. Dudes don't take this kind of time to get laid. And if he just wanted to get laid, why would he choose me? Up until then, there had been no real conversation about anything, just pleasantries. He at least knows that I'm not that easy. This was his way of trying to undo what he'd done.

We talked for about an hour. It was one of those stream-of-conscious-style chats where important things were said, but, you know, they weren't said logically. Truths bubbled up and things made sense even though the exact dialogue didn't. The main points about our relationship were stated: He tried to move too fast. I was so unhappy with the way things were going in my life that I couldn't make anyone else happy. The more I tried; the worse it got. We never really got to know each other. He made the biggest mistake by cheating on me. I was crazy for showing up at his house like that at 2:00 am. He was just mad because he got caught. We both missed each other for our own reasons and wanted to be with the other.

Before I knew what I had done, there I was standing at his front door again at 2:00 am. Only this time, I was invited in.

I can't lie. I was really uncomfortable standing in his apartment. I had to use a bull-dozer to push all of the horrific images of him with a bunch of dumb girls in there out of my mind. Technically, at that moment, I could be seen as one, so the only logical thing to do while feeling uncomfortable standing was to lie down. ::sigh:: I crawled into bed next to him, and as if in a game of Twister, we slowly began to intertwine. It was nice to feel his familiar warmth and smell his familiar scent. Again things were said. Truths bubbled up. There was laughter and sweetness. (Ok...cover your eyes...This is the part that you aren't allowed to see...Insert bau-chicka-bau-bau music...You didn't think I was going to get graphic did you? Come on...You know me...It wasn't about the sex for ME!) And as we drifted off to sleep, this once horrible beast held me close to him and repeatedly kissed my neck in such a manner-that if kisses could be translated into words-each one would have said, "I'm sorry."

The morning came and it was like any other morning I had ever woken up with Cholo, only this time during our conversation I was struck by something he said. The Former Object Of My Affection casually worked it into the conversation that he didn't like being called "Cholo." He said something to the effect of: "it's like that whole Cholo image you came up with; it's not me," almost in passing. I realized aside from wanting to clear the air in being together, we both also wanted to show that we weren't how the other previously saw each other. I was thrilled to let him know that I was on my feet and forging ahead with all of the things I had intended. And a part of me felt guilty for possibly belittling him in any way. He and I share a huge personality trait, bullheaded-ness coupled with the most surprisingly overly sensitive hearts.

After we got up for the day and decided to go to lunch (Yes, we went to lunch...He was trying to treat me like a lady), the weirdness started to set in. He still had some of my things, which he put with my bag. (Yes, I had a bag...This wasn't my first rodeo...)

175

Lunch was pleasant. Pie n' Burger is one of our old haunts. It was crowded; we were starting to get grumpy from hunger. Our conversation was sparse, and I could tell neither one of us knew whether to be affectionate or not to the other. Damn, that was a good burger. When we got back to his apartment, I gathered my things and proceeded to leave. He walked me to my car. We chided each other a bit. He gave me a huge hug and kissed me twice. Suddenly, a heavy feeling sank in that made tears well up in my eyes. "This might be it. This could be all he can do. This was him making me see that he didn't want to hurt me and that he isn't a bad guy. This is him getting closure on what he feels unsettled about." I wanted to say something, but I was truly afraid of hearing him say something to reject me or ruin the nice image that had been created, so I just said goodbye and drove away.

When I got home I looked at the few things of mine that he had returned. Among them were two jars of Smucker's Red Plum Jam. While shopping together one afternoon, we accidentally found my jam at a Ralph's in his neighborhood in Pasadena. He saw how ridiculously excited I was, and he bought all of the jars that the store had, telling me he would do anything to keep me here in LA.

So…I did the most logical thing I could think of…I sent him a text message:

"I have mixed feelings about what happened in that I am left to wonder if you ever want to speak to me again. I propose that we take things slowly, and truly get to know each other like we should have before. Think about it."

I haven't heard from him. ::shrug:: I guess he's thinking really hard. Ha ha ha ha.

For what it's worth, his name isn't Cholo. It's Joe. He's a man with a rugged past and higher hopes and dreams for his future. We came into each other's lives for a reason. I can't tell why I came into his life or if he really learned anything from me. Yet I do know that if I hadn't met him, it is likely that I'd be in Chicago right now, freezing my ass off, trying to figure out how to deal with snow and wondering why in the world I ever left Los Angeles. There are many things I adore about Joe. I wouldn't have dated him if there weren't. He's got a great laugh and when he smiles his eyes sparkle. The touches of silver in his hair are sexy and certainly earned. He's incredibly hard-working and passionate about his job. I'll never forget the way he looked at me the moment we met, how he would hug me from behind and kiss my neck while I loaded the dishwasher or how he held me all night when I got the news that my grandmother had passed away.

I forgive him for his shortcomings, and I hope he understands mine.

Yeah…There's a heart TWO times the size of Texas under this bathrobe…Fuck.

As you were.

Monday November 27, 2006
Heard In Silence

In an effort to be incredibly forward thinking and to take charge of my future and my destiny and all of that crap, I lost sight of some of my compassion. I am putting myself on my own Fucktard List. Yes, it's true…::sigh::

My roommate situation pushed me to a new level of irritation. I got to the point where frustration brought me to speechlessness. The only times I'm speechless are when dead to the world sick or…well, I think that's it…

In my speechlessness, I was able to brood, to stew and I actually wound up listening. What I heard today was the voice of a person I took for granted. The 38 Year-old, Gay, Schizophrenic Male opened up to me and said, "I'm sorry I've been waffling so much. I'm making decisions I've never had to make before, and it's really hard for me. I've never lived alone before. This is a huge step for me. I'm going through a lot."

That little factoid I had never known. To make this more clear, not only has he never lived alone, he's never had to make simple decisions like where to live, what company to call for certain services or how to handle tough financial situations on his own. I can't imagine what that must be like.

(In the words of Napoleon Dynamite: "Lucky.")

It's hard to tell any of this by looking at him. Sure, he's quirky as all hell, but for all practical things in life he's rather normal. He gets up, grooms and feeds himself, goes to work, exercises and has a little routine just like most Americans. He's well-traveled, reads books of interest, loves all living creatures and is super sweet to me.

From that angle, I'm a shitty person for being too critical. I actually have to say that I'm quite proud of him for finally making the decision to move out on his own. I'm sure my fireball ways are simply overwhelming for a quiet internalizer like him. Hell, they're too much for me sometimes.

I'm thankful to say that we are both speaking to each other again. We are enjoying old reruns of "Will & Grace" together in our pj's and our mint julep facial masks as we lounge on my gorgeous couch while he eats gluten products, and I sip red wine.

God, what am I going to do if the new roommate doesn't like "Will & Grace?" ::sigh:: I completely forgot to put that in my ad!

The roommate issues…When will they end???

As you were.

Thursday November 30, 2006
Stick Around Saturn

Ok…So I'm twenty-seven now. I've gotten a very unique response to the big 2, 7 on several occasions. It sounds a little something like this, "Twenty-seven? Oh, you're in for a lot of change. This is the beginning of Saturn's return."

I'm no astrology buff. Anything past my horoscope in "Harper's Bazaar" and the Mai's Fortune cookies in Houston and I'm pretty done. So, naturally, the first few times I heard this, I gave a confused look and said, "Do what?"

According to all of my sources, every seven years Saturn (the planet, not the car) makes its way back to "your house," and with it comes the opportunity for a lot of positive change, if you allow yourself to go with the change.

If you look at my current life and all that is going on, I can attest that I am in the process of going through a lot of change and many opportunities are around me. In October, I started the goal-setting conference calls. I'm brainstorming new ideas for business and my odd brokerage company job is going well. The roommate situation is working itself out. Blah, blah, blah...

Ummm...How will I know when Saturn has officially arrived? Will there be a candy-gram delivered? Will Her rings come busting through the walls of my apartment in the middle of the night while some small child stands in my living room staring at the television saying, "She's heeeeeeeeeeere?"

And how does one entertain Saturn? I've had some pretty demanding house guests be-fore, but they were children and boyfriends. Exactly how long is Saturn going to stick around? I'm happy to make room for prosperity and all, but how much can I handle? What does a planet need? I can only provide so much in the way of atmosphere...

But here's my serious question...What the fuck is going to happen to me when good ol' Saturn decides that the hoopla at my house is over and it's time for Her to shove off? Am I going to fall stricken with illness? Is everything I have worked for going to crumble before me?

Hmmm...If all goes really well, maybe I can bribe Her to stick around a little longer. What if I bargain for an extra year of her wonder love? What about a kidney? I've got two of those. Do planets need makeovers? What about a promise ring?

Will I at least get a warning that She's about to go? Or am I just going to wake up one morning in a dumpster wondering why I'm bald, toothless and wearing a colostomy bag?

A friend of mine answered all of my questions in one sentence: "Just as long as you have your head out of Uranus when Saturn arrives, you'll be fine."

I'll be damned; my friends can be funny and wise...

Well, here's to Saturn. I'm ready when you are!

*This bitch better not snore or use up all the hot water...

As you were.

Thursday December 7, 2006
Barfin' In Burbank

Good God. I was walking to my car after work and chatting away on my cell phone (I know, so hard to believe...) As I had just crossed the street, a car came around the corner, stopped, and the driver flung open the door and began to hurl his guts up on the street.

Aside from almost hurling myself, I was reminded that around this time last year, I actually had to deal with that uncertain experience of driving and having to vomit. I'm telling you right now that as a person who (until recently) can't pee outside, the idea of vomiting outside or while driving is torture. I'm surprised that I'm alive to recall it. This event pushed my personal growth limits to new heights in an all-time low way.

The weather was chilly, and I had spent the day in Castaic decorating Ve Neill's house for her annual holiday party. The make-up artist I was working with at the time, Frank, otherwise and often known as, Crankie Frankie, had driven us up there in his truck. We arrived early in the morning and spent the day testing strings of lights, hanging a million ornaments and blanketing her home in holiday cheery bullshit with a bunch of other make-up artists. I hadn't eaten anything for breakfast and wound up having an English muffin followed by two really gross tacos with some orange soda (which I loathe) later in the afternoon. I noticed that the cold weather was making my head hurt. Slowly, I started to feel like I was getting sick. My head started to hurt the kind of hurt that throbs with every inhale. I was fading fast. I was getting a migraine. I have only had a couple of those in my life, and let me tell you, I was fucked. I found myself unable to keep my eyes open and curled up on the couch under some pillows while some guy hangin' tinsel strand by strand on the main living room tree chatted away at me. Thankfully, Crankie Frankie could see that I was about to die right there, and we headed out. As I was waiting by his truck, it happened. Right there, I threw up in Ve Neill's front yard. I was only partially mortified as I kinda' felt better. Then again, I had just thrown up in an Oscar Award Winning Make-up Artist's front yard.

Gross; there were the tacos I ate earlier.

Into the truck I went, eyes still unable to handle light, praying that I was done puking. Crankie Frankie was driving as fast as his vehicle would let him. Every bump in the road was like an atomic bomb was being dropped on me. Fuck, just thinking about it makes me queasy again.

::Deep breathe:: Whew...

We were almost to Crankie's apartment where my car was parked. I must have looked like hell to him because just as he was handing me a McDonald's food bag and asking me if I was going to make it home, I began to retch into that paper bag with such force that my spew was coming out of the bottom of the bag! Lord, I have to say, Crankie was pretty good about it. He instantly grabbed another plastic bag from somewhere and actually helped me get the paper one into it. Now that's a friend and a person who really doesn't want puke in his vehicle!

By the time we got back to his place, I was feeling ok to drive. It was a Saturday around 7:00 pm, and surely there wouldn't be any traffic...I was going to be home and in my bed in no time, right? Oh Christ, of course not. I found myself sitting on the 5 South staring at a sea of taillights, hoping that I would make it home soon. The combination of the temperature, the lights and the migraine were too powerful. Fuck, fuck, fuck if I wasn't about to hurl again. I was in the center lane. There was NO WAY I was going to throw up on myself in my car. In retrospect, perhaps I should have just hung my head out the window, but I couldn't tell how sick I was going to be. With one hand over my mouth, I started honking at cars to let me over to the shoulder. At first they weren't budging as I'm sure they thought I was just trying to get into that lane to zoom down to my exit. Frankly, that was a part of the plan, but I really needed to get the fuck over. I suppose the look of a little chick in a big black sedan, holding her bulging cheeks with her eyes poppin' out of her head made them snap to the reality of the situation. Soon I was putting my car in park, throwin' on my hazards and fleeing my vehicle, only to find myself on my hands and knees on the side of the freeway, power-vomiting the paint off the highway.

And there was the English muffin...

The whole time I just kept thinking that if I could do something as awful as this and live through it, I could probably make it through anything. I had been throwing up so hard that I was gasping for air and tears were coming out of my eyes. When I caught my breath and felt like I could stand up, I turned around and there was this chain of cars just watching me lose all of my dignity on the side of the road. No one asked if I was ok. No one gave a sympathetic wave or smile. They just watched.

That day, I was that train wreck situation that you would rather not see, yet are insanely mesmerized by on the road!!!! Perhaps if I had been on fire, people would have offered to help me. What would they have done had I passed out and looked like a corpse? There was certainly a moment or two where I couldn't see or breathe and thought I was dying. I kept thinking that if I didn't hurry and get up, I was at risk of some dumbass with the bright idea of speeding down the shoulder, rear-ending my car and smearing my ass all over the pavement!

Dear God, that was a terrible experience, yet at the same time, it was a hell of a day. I had met an Oscar Award-Winning Make-up Artist, spent the day having fun decorating for the holidays and proved to myself (again) that I can handle most any situation with some sort of grace.

Typical me-got up from the ground, dusted myself off, smiled at the people staring at me and got back in my car and did just what they were hoping I wouldn't. I drove as fast as I could down the shoulder to my exit, honking the whole way. I was home within five minutes facedown in my bed with my head buried in the bedcovers.

The stupid shit I do when I'm drunk or shooting my mouth off is one thing, but how I manage to pull off such impression-making events like these, wow...I just can't wrap my brain around it.

And as for the poor schmuck who made me remember My Great Toss of 2005, I gave him a smile and a sympathetic wave as I expelled my horrified disbelief into the phone to my friend. It's the least I could do. When I was ass-end up, digging my nails into the freeway, I would have been so grateful for some acknowledgement. ::shrug::

Nothing like a good migraine story at the holidays, you know?

As you were.

Thursday December 7, 2006
What The Elf Did You Say?

On Thursdays I leave work and head to the temp agency where I am still drawing a paycheck until I become "permanent" at my new job.

It's a comically busy office with women who have worked together for almost twenty years! Their desks face each other and they work like bees on the phones, trying to place people in jobs so they can make commissions that will lead them to their goals. How do I know this? They have goal collages plastered everywhere, full of pictures of dream cars, houses, and destinations they would like to visit. The time I spend in there is less than the time it takes to blink, and I often have no conversation with anyone while I'm there.

Today was different.

As I was walking out the door, this desperate voice said to me, "Excuse me. You look like a size two. Are you working Saturday?"

I looked at her with the, "Ummm...Do you have me confused with someone else" face.

She continued, "We're looking for someone to dress up as an elf for a Christmas party, and you look small enough to fit into the costume."

What the fuck? What kind of professional temporary agency am I listed with??? An elf? Do I really look like the kind of woman who would be able to pull off the pointed ears and shoes gag? Ok...yeah. I know I do. But still, what a random question to be asked at 4:30 pm on a Thursday, you know?

I took a second and did a mental scan of my current life situation. Do I really NEED to dress up like an elf at a party for money? Will I have fun doing this or feel stupid? Is the pay even worth it?

Nope. For the first time in a very long time, I didn't feel like I had to perform a task just to get by. And it felt pretty good. I'm no way out of the woods financially. But who really is?

I walked to the car with my little head held as high as a five-foot-tall girl could.

*On the way to the car, I passed by some mirrored glass and caught a glimpse of my-self. I was wearing this light green super cute jacket...And the elf image really came together...uggg...I came home and painted small toys for children around world for an hour-and-a-half.

As you were.

Monday December 11, 2006
Virginity On Hold

My job often requires a substantial amount of time on the phone. Part of my job is to facilitate third party payment to vendors for our clients. What does that mean? Instead of our clients having to sit on hold for thirty minutes to figure out why a bill is still listed as a debit and not a credit, I do it.

181

Grrr…Compare this to taking on the responsibility of calling Visa anytime one of your neighbors has a problem. Oh, the joys…

Today, however, I had an experience that took me back to being eighteen and a freshman in college. How did I get there you ask? Hold music…What was playing? Celine Dion's, "My Heart Will Go On" - you remember it. It was the big song from the big film, *Titanic*.

As I sat there with the phone cradled between my shoulder and ear, flipping through paperwork and reading emails, I was reminded of the last time I was preoccupied with that song droning on and on and on in the background…The night I lost my virginity.

Yeah…::sigh::…here goes…I'm sure you are on the edge of your seat.

The date: Labor Day weekend, 1998

The person: A very handsome young man who was twenty. His name was David. I met him at the bank in downtown Houston where he worked. He was this well-built Mexican man who had served in US Army, loved Ford Mustangs, rock music, Keeblers Fudge Stripe cookies, women and alcohol. He had piercings and tattoos. Mmm… Yeah…My lovst (love/lust) for the inked-up Latino man started long ago…

The place: His room in his parent's house.

The story: I had just moved into my college dormitory and had enjoyed an evening of dancing at Rich's with friends. As Rich's was predominately known for being a gay club, David had declined to join me, but invited me to come to his place when I left the club. And that's just what I did, feeling that the college life was just primo. It was 2:00 am, and I was driving around, doing what I wanted, not having to be home at a certain time…Yeah, baby! I'm an adult now! Who-hoo!

After I got to his house, we curled up and started watching *Titanic*. One thing let to another, a condom appeared, Celine, Kate and Leonardo were cheering me on and poof, I was no longer a virgin. Nothing scary, nothing painful; it was actually rather nice. Not bad for a first run at things, if I do say so myself.

And just when you thought I was telling a boring story, here comes the fun part. Afterward, we were lying there in silence. Then I started an unforgettable, life-shaping conversation that went like this:

Me: So I guess this changes our relationship, huh? (Keep in mind we had been dating for a month and were barely legal.)

David: What do you mean?

Me: Well, it makes it more serious. (Naïve and delusional)

David: Sure, I guess. (Hesitant to respond)

Me: David, I probably should have asked you about this before, but how many people have you had sex with? (Trying to be responsible)

David: What does it matter? We used a condom. (Trying to avoid the question)

Me: It's important.

David: I was really hoping you wouldn't ask about this.

Me: (Suddenly feeling like my magic moment was over) You're twenty. How many people could you have had time to sleep with? Five?

David: Higher.

Me: Ten?

David: Higher.

Me: Fifteen? (My faith in true love and romance fading…)

David: You have to remember I was in the military…(Hmmm…I didn't know that sex with multiple partners was a part of basic training…)

Me: David, just tell me!

David: (After a few beats) I think you make, like, thirty-two.

And that's where I nearly fell off the bed. At that time in my life I hadn't met thirty-two people I would consider dating, much less sleeping with, and come to think of it, I still haven't. Needless to say, that was an eye opening experience during my first month of college, followed by another eye-opening conversation with David three months later when he broke up with me by saying flat-out, "I just don't think you're the one."

Two years later he tried to come back. I reminded him how we ended things, pumping up his ego by letting him know that he was right.

A fucktard, before fucktards were fucktards…Hello adulthood.

I also learned another memorable sentence in dating him: "Young, dumb and full of cum."

When Celine's "You're here…There's NOTHING I fear…" was abruptly and appropriately cut off by the sound of a monotone operator, ready to assist me with my account concerns, I was more than ready to delve into someone else's problems! *Oh who am I kidding; I really wanted to tell the person on the other end my hilarious story.

Damn, desk jobs leave a lot of time for personal reflection.

If you learn anything from me, let it be: KNOW YOUR SEXUAL PARTNERS. IT WILL SAVE YOU TIME, MONEY and HEARTACHE.

As you were.

Tuesday December 12, 2006
Paper for Pondering

It is often said that a fragrance can take you back, right? Well, today I realized that a piece of paper can do the same thing.

One index-card-sized piece of paper made me stop dead in my tracks, revisit some serious memories and unlocked an unfortunate amount of situational comparison and analysis. I held it in my hands, felt its weight and let my mind wonder and wander.

I took a journey through some very fond and sour memories. I remembered all the times I was the bigger person, the voice of reason and even the times I showed vulnerability…The times I was the companion, the lover and the secret. Oh! The secrets. I felt a rain shower of emotions over moments so far away, and stood amazed at the ones that were so amazingly close. Until that fucking piece of paper was in my hands, I really thought I had let it all go. I was surprised at how I was reacting. Good thing I was alone. No one likes to look that engrossed in uncomfortable introspection in front of people. It was not flattering…even worse than tapered-legged jeans on women with wide hips and thighs. (And why are leggings popular again? Ugh!)

Anyway, after chewing and digesting my thoughts, I shit out the reality: Timing really is just a bitch.

It was never the right time then.
It's certainly not the right time now. (Although, it would make for a great movie of the week on that Pantyshield Channel.)
And I have 99% doubt that it ever will be.

What causes me the most internal friction is knowing that I have to swallow all of the details of this situation even now to keep from causing ripples in other places outside of myself. That is unfortunately what real love for someone else dictates that you do. That dictation is so fantastic that it actually causes real pain. It truly hurts to feel that others would see my feelings as bitterness or jealousy. They are not. It truly hurts each time I realize that I'm the one left holding that piece of fucking paper.

But don't worry about me; I always work through things. I thought about the old joke where a man goes to the doctor and says, "Doctor it hurts when I go like this," and the Doctor tells him, "Well then, don't go like that." I realized that if it hurts to hold that fucking piece of paper, I should put it down. And so I did. And then I promptly put my wine glass on it. That little fucker makes a great coaster.

You all know I'm a "lemonade out of lemons" gal…

Ain't nothin' gonna break my stride, ain't nothing gonna slow me down…Oh, not no, but HELL no.

As you were.

Friday December 15, 2006
Rockstar Roommate, Almost (The brettfarkas Story)

::sigh::

::ugh::

Los Angeles…Why do you hate me???

I'm numb.

After finally breaking down and posting an ad on craigslist.com for a roommate, I spent two weeks reviewing responses. After reading some of the most bizarre responses and sifting through the ones I deemed "normal," I narrowed my list of candidates down to about five based on written response alone. I spoke to them and then, based on their conversations, met with three of them. I figured if they could handle seeing the way I lived now and could envision a brighter place free of The 38 Year-old, Gay, Schizophrenic Male's belongings, they might just work out.

After the meet-n-greets and showings, I found a guy named Brett Farkas to be a great fit. What a nice guy...Laid back, non-threatening, pleasant to be around, fun to talk to...turned out he was a musician who grew up in Michigan and moved to LA to give music a real shot. (And he's not doing too badly, either. His band, Population Game, is working on an album and playing regular gigs and touring...Hot. Hot. Hot...) I loved the fact that he's a skinny white dude who teaches little black kids in Inglewood about blues music on the side. I can't lie, I was diggin' the images of waking up to go to work to find his band members sprawled out in the living room after a late night of rockin' out (or whatever it is that bands do). Brett was so simple and smooth that his name just seemed to run together, and he will forever be brettfarkas to me. And get this: He passed his credit check. Shit, I was in roommate love when I heard that. (Too bad his jeans are skinnier than mine, otherwise I mighta' tried sop him up with a biscuit...) *Let's get real...at this point ANYONE who didn't strike me as insane was looking good.

Sadly, just like all the boys I fall for, I got a call today from brettfarkas that left me at a loss and having to once again make more decisions about the coming doomsday: The 1st of the month...

brettfarkas: Hey Robin, it's Brett. I need to talk to you. I kinda' found a place closer to my studio space that's cheaper.

Me: (not all that shocked, but still disappointed) Oh, wow. Well...

brettfarkas: I'm really sorry to have to do this to you. I feel really badly, but this is a really good deal.

Me: I actually understand. We've got to do what we've got to do in this town. (I just got quiet.)

brettfarkas: Seriously? You're taking this really well. I didn't even think this was going to pan out. (He started to babble a bit) I was just walking down the street in Studio City. I saw this sign and filled out an application. I hadn't heard from your apartment manager and was getting a little worried. Studio City is where I wanted to live all along...This is hard because you are really cool, and I was really liking getting to know you...You gotta' understand it's me, not you.

Me: (I felt like I had let him grovel enough and cut him off, laughing): brettfarkas are you breaking up with me?

brettfarkas: (Relieved to hear my humor) Oh God, it sounds like it doesn't it?? I have felt bad all day. If there is anything I can do to help you find someone else, I will. Is there anything I can do?

Me: (Biting my tongue on asking him to pay the first months rent regardless) Oh brettfarkas, don't worry about me. I've got another person in mind who might need to stay here in LA for at least six months. She's a fashion designer who just got a job out here and is having to relocate from Colorado. This is by far the least difficult situation I've had to deal with in LA. (Then I said the most common line during a break-up that follows the ol' "it's not you; it's me" line) Let's just be friends.

I repeat. I am numb. I'm not sure how much of this I can take. The roommate roulette is starting to wear on me. But I wasn't lying; in this town you have to do what you have to do. As long as people are honest and up front with me, I'm cool as a cucumber about it. So much for my working-girl fantasy of wearing my "Fuck y'all; I LIVE with brettfarkas" t-shirt to his shows... ::sniff sniff::

Can't keep a boyfriend, can't keep a thirty-eight year-old gay schizo male and even random craigslist.com roommate dudes dump me. Christ! What the hell is wrong with me?

*I really do have a person in mind. My new friend Chelan Gabor could be the perfect fit. Chelan is a fashion designer married to a rocket scientist who lives out in the country in Colorado in one of those geo-something-or-other dome homes. Her husband wants her to follow her dream and pursue fashion design for a while to see if she really likes it. If she does, he will work with his company to be transferred out here. How cool is that? (I think on detail alone I need her for my repertoire of roommates.) Once again, no hopes up...but I do have a good feeling about her. My intuition is always stronger than my hopes.

**Damn, life sure is a pill sometimes. Fuck-fuck-fuckity-fuck-fuck-fuck...Whew. That's better.

As you were.

Friday December 15, 2006
What Remains...

Wow. He's gone.

The 38 Year-old, Gay Schizophrenic Male is gone. I walked into a completely empty apartment after work. The almost creepy part about it is that if someone who had never been here before saw the place, they would probably not be able to tell that there was ever another person here. In one afternoon he managed to get EVERYHING out. Toilet paper, faucet water filter, my measuring cups, switch plates, the doorstop and so many other little things aside from his massive furniture. Amazing.

I swear I saw the apartment this morning! It took me a second to realize that it was still the same Friday!

I kinda' walked around for a bit, studying each room. I felt like had just woken from a ten year coma and was learning about my surroundings again. I half expected some child to come running out of the bedroom calling out, "Mommy, you're home!" (to which I would have screamed, "Get away from me!")

As quickly as I could, I did what anyone else in my position would do, I got naked. Fuck yeah, I did. Then I proceeded to enjoy the sound of my own voice echoing about in the empty rooms. I was no longer going to live trapped in my room!!! I was a twenty-seven year old version of the teenager whose parents went out of town for the weekend. I didn't know what to do first, jump around on the furniture, get loud and test out the liquor cabinet, dial sex chat lines, or announce a party. So I did the next best thing; I threw on my pink bathrobe and started surveying the apartment.

All of my exhilaration began to lessen as I realized what a gross state the apartment is in. I never could tell because his crap covered every inch of space. As I focused in, I saw four years worth of his funk on the walls and in the carpet. White boxes where pictures once hung, now shown through like false windows on what I thought were beige painted walls...Nope. Cigarette stains...Gross. The carpet?...Looked like crop formations in the bedroom. *That would explain A LOT!

He left behind three items that I'm pleased about:

1) toaster oven: He didn't have room for it, and I use it all the time.
2) microwave: Not sure why he did that...Said he was leaving the drapes, but he didn't and left the microwave instead. Gay man...go figure. ::shrug::

And the best thing he left behind...

ME!!!! I am so thrilled to be in this apartment. When I said I wasn't moving out of this building in June, I meant it. Despite a few very tempting pieces of forbidden fruit, I stuck to it and HERE I AM!!!

Back to running around naked!

It feels so good to be home!

*This totally lets me forget about brettfarkas breaking up with me this afternoon...What a fucking day, I swear.

As you were.

Saturday December 16, 2006
The Social Disorder

Oh Lawd, if you haven't laughed at me yet, you will right now!

My friend Ryry, (aka, Poodle) and I met in Houston several years ago while working for The Firm atop the Wells Fargo Plaza. Long story short, I figured out he was gay. He figured out I truly am Julia Sugarbaker, the Texas Edition. The thickness of thieves ensued and years later we somehow managed to flee Houston for LA around the same time. Naturally, we now take turns going to functions together.

Last night it was my turn to accompany him to his law firm's Holiday Party. (He went with me to mine the week prior.) It was held at The Social on Sunset...cocktail attire, sit-down dinner and dancing. La-ti-dah...

I threw on a cute, short black dress and a fantastic jacket and heels. Just as we were walking out the door I thought about how short the dress was and how Britney Spears had just made her "downtown waterpark" famous after pictures of her stepping out of a car were plastered all over the Internet, leaving nothing in her hoo-doo zone to the imagination. Trying to salvage myself from an embarrassing moment, I threw on a black thong, and we were out the door. *I hate underwear and see them as tools for foreplay. Rarely wear the bitches.

The Social was nice. The crowd was very corporate. Attorneys in Hollywood are a different breed. Nothing like the good ol' boy, Texas tornados I was used to. Realizing it was going to be a long night after the first conversation with the first set of lame lawyers, drinking began. Mmmmm...Lemon drop martinis!

Dinner...Mmmm...Salmon AND filet mignon after lobster bisque! Yiippeee! Oh, yea! The infinite wine pour with dinner!!!! I learned at dinner that Ryry hadn't told anyone he's gay, and they assumed that we were a couple. What??? Good God. Warn a girl when she has to turn her beard on! More wine!!! Sometime between the salad and the lobster bisque, I was beginning to remember why I don't wear undergarments. That stupid thing was getting on my nerves. Somewhere between the green beans and the salmon, I got the wicked idea to try to gracefully take off my thong at the table, under the tablecloth...Just to see if anyone would notice me doing it. (It wasn't my party...) Sadly, I wasn't slick enough to pull it off. More wine!

After more wine and Ryry holding my hand explaining why we don't live together, I had had it with the ass flossing for the evening and headed to the ladies room to cut ties with that string. The bathroom stalls have (what I recall) fifteen foot floor to ceiling smoked glass doors that you can see out of once inside. The walls and floor are a shiny black finish and of course the tirlet is black. The only light in the john was coming from a dim sconce reflected in the mirror hanging over the tirlet. I got in there and ripped that damn thing off and momentarily drifted into the dark euphoria as a feeling of great relief came over me.

Suddenly I was back in the moment and my hands were empty. Where did it go? In a wine haze, I tried looking on the floor and in the commode, but they were both as black as my thong. I looked up and down. I checked my pockets and my purse. What in the hell had I done with that thing? I looked into the mirror and thought, "If this thing is on my head, so help me, I'm checking myself into The Betty..." Nope. And then in the mirror, I saw it.

It was hanging around my elbow! When I took the time to pull my arm through it, I cannot recall. Thongs are so sneaky...They just creep all over the place!

I started laughing at myself, remembering how my Grandma Sue once lost her slip. She came to me and said, "Robin A, I cannot find my slip. I've looked all over the place. If you can find it, I will give you a dollar." Pushing my glasses back on my nine-year-old nose, and looking at her smugly I said, "You're wearing it." "Oh good golly Moses, I'll get my purse," she expressed, looking down at her lower half. I thought about how hilarious it would have been to walk back to the table and tell Ryry, or perhaps his co-workers, the same thing with my thong danglin' from my arm! Behaving the best I could, I instead wadded that little torture device up, put it in my purse and went back to the table after taking commemorative photographs of myself in the stall.

Almost out of breath from laughing so hard, I shared the story with Ryry, who cringed knowing that my drawers were in my handbag. More wine!!! An insane amount of dancing took place after dinner. We actually danced our way right out the door and into the car and were given bottles of MORE WINE to take with us. Still laughing and deciding to "punish" him for putting me on the beard spot, I pulled out my thong and hung it on his rearview mirror. "Didn't you know that's what straight boys do with their girlfriend's underwear???!!" Ryry recoiled and drove with his face practically pressed up against the driver's door window to be as far away from anything vagina related. And I did the same, only I was super tipsy and needed to lean on the window for support…

Tried to keep from pulling a Britney, wound up being a beard and then decided to bare it all anyway. I'm just an underwear amateur. How lame! I think the whole day of brettfarkas breaking up with me and The 38 Year-old, Gay, Schizophrenic Male leaving finally got to me…Anyhow, no one saw a thing. I'm Julia Sugarbaker, the Texas Edition for heaven's sake. Always a lady on the outside…

*I wonder if Ryry has removed the undergarment from his rearview mirror yet? I'm sure some WeHo street queen would take it if he tossed 'em out the window…

Watch out for creepy thongs; they'll get you when you least expect it!

Hey! Look! MORE WINE!

As you were.

Friday December 22, 2006
Gliding Through Puberty

While visiting with a woman at work today about what her children want for Christmas, the age of her daughters came up. One of her daughters is eleven years old and is in the fifth grade.

Think back…Do you remember what happened in the fifth grade? You remember. There was a day in the fifth grade that changed how you looked at members of the opposite sex and changed your life FOREVER! It's all flooding back to you now, isn't it? It was the day that they separated the boys from the girls and explained in the most vague terms how babies are made and how horrific and awkward your hormones were going to make life starting at any moment! Then you were thrown back into class together, left to stare at each other all day wondering if anyone was having a period, an erection or had somehow made a baby in math class. And you remember that the only way to get through it was to giggle like a fool, right? Oh, what fun!

I asked the woman how her daughter handled the big talk. Like most parents she grimaced, and began to recount the conversation that took place during the car ride home. It went a little something like this:

Daughter: Mom, I understand what's going to happen to me. I will release an egg. And I understand that boys make sperm. I know the sperm has to go inside the egg. But how does IT GET IN THERE?

189

Mother: (Gripping the steering wheel, realizing just how vague the talk really was) Well, the sperm comes out of the boys penis, right? And your egg has to stay inside your body because that's where a baby grows, right? Well, the boy has to put his penis inside your vagina to release the sperm so that it gets to the egg.

Daughter: (Perplexed and once again horrified): Oh my God! How long does IT have to stay in there???

*Later in life our young friend will find the joys of continuous birth control and learn that you want him to stay in there as long as possible…

I enjoyed a hearty chuckle with my co-worker, amused at how long ago those awkward days seemed.

Oh wait. Puberty isn't the end of the awkwardness of sexuality. Oh my, no! I was promptly reminded of that fun factoid when I got home at 6:00 pm to find the carpet cleaners at my apartment door ready to steam clean. What? Who does this at 6:00 pm?

One of my Eastern European neighbors was standing outside and offered to help me move some furniture around so that they could get in and out as fast as possible. How kind. She came into my room and tried to pick up my vanity table (Of course I have a vanity table). When she tipped it forward one of the drawers slid open, and something flew out onto the floor. Just as I realized what it was, she was already swooping down to pick it up. Oops.

Yikes. It was a bottle of Astroglide that I haven't seen since…well…since sometime last year. As if having a random neighbor pick up my bottle of personal lubricant wasn't awkward enough, it turns out that the bottle had been on its side and HAD LEAKED! Oh yes. That woman was standing there in my bedroom with her hand all slick and slimy! And just like the label on the back of the label warns, I scurried to get a towel to clean up this spill. Wouldn't want anyone to slip! Her response was pretty great. She just handed me the bottle and wiped her hands, saying in her accent, "Oh-oh, I got a little something on my hands here. I think the bottle is leaking; you might want to throw that out."

I couldn't help but feel like a fifth grader for a bit. Staring into the face of a middle-aged woman in my own bedroom reminded that the awkwardness of sexuality never really goes away.

And just like a fifth grader, I began to giggle…uncontrollably…for like, ten minutes. My belly ached, my face was red and I was just shy of gasping for air. Being twenty-seven and in the fifth grade again was great, and I was amazed to see that the same remedy of giggling like a fool was still the best at alleviating common awkwardness.

Call me immature, but laughter really is the best medicine. Oh, I deserve detention!

*I bet my neighbor never offers to help me move anything again. Perhaps I should make her a cake or buy her a dozen jelly filled donuts as a "thank you." That would be funny. Tee hee.

As you were.

Tuesday December 26, 2006
Have Yourself A Jewish Little Christmas Now...

This is the first year ever in which I will not be with my immediate family for any of the winter holidays. Long story omitted, it's just not going to happen. Christmas Eve was rather odd because I have never spent it completely alone before. Usually I spend it with my little brother. (He's my half-brother by my biological father's second failed marriage and is thirteen years younger than me.) Even though it was a mix of choice and no choice to stay in Los Angeles this year, I started to get a little stir crazy on Christmas Eve. This town was a frickin' ghost town, and I just wanted to hang-out with someone. The only plans I had were to have dinner at my neighbor's place Christmas night.

Just in the nick of time, my solitude savior popped up, out-of-the-blue, with a text message that said, "Do you want to go skiing tomorrow?" It was The Jewish Cowboy. My semi-glum mood jumped to immediate glee! I had no interest in learning to ski, but learning to snowboard is on my "100 Things To Do Before I Die List!" We chatted, and it was determined that we would embark on our journey up to Big Bear around noonish. Why so late? "Only Jews are going to be out on the slopes," said The JC. Hmmm...Everyone I called about snow gear seemed to think he was wrong about that. (And he was)

I woke up on Christmas morning excited like a child, waiting to see what gifts were going to be under the tree. While I dressed, I listened to the "Charlie Brown Christmas Special" music. I had come to the realization that I wasn't going to be able to actually participate in any snow activity as I couldn't find anyone in town that could loan me the appropriate apparel. I was fine with that and was actually just excited to see some mountains, snow and to experience a holiday excursion that kids like me growing up in Texas only saw in movies. So naturally, I began to drink wine. What else was I going to do but sit in the lodge, drink wine and look at boys? Might as well start early and enjoy my day! I prepared a to-go cup and bounded out the door when The JC arrived.

"You ready to be Jewish for the day?" he asked. Believing that we were going to be at our destination in just two hours, we sped away, heading to the mountains.

As The JC's car slowly crept around Rim of the World Way well into our third hour on the road, I had to laugh. He was pretty naïve to think that only Jews were going to be heading to snowy scenery on Christmas Day. This is Los Angeles! We all know the demographics of this city. The views were breathtaking. The higher we drove, the more winter wonderlandly it became. Yes, a winter wonderland of boneheads with jalopy cars loaded with children and families in shorts and t-shirts, stopping on incredibly dangerous cliff-sides to sled, have snow ball fights and possibly fall right off the side of the mountain, causing awful traffic...(Go fucking figure...) Frustrated, The JC looked at me and said, "You would think there was one of those Maria Guadalupe Santa Maria Don Pedro Our Mother of Fajita Maria Mecca Churches up here or something..."

Finally, after a ton of satellite radio, hip-hop and country music and wine in the car, we got to a snowboarding shop so that The JC could pick up some gloves. I went in just to see what the inside of one looks like, and the most amazing Jewish-For-A-Day Miracle happened. I found out that not only could I rent a snowboard and boots, but I could also rent the clothing!!! Holy Shit! Much of the clothing was 50% off!!! A true Jewish-For-A-Day Miracle!!!

191

Too tipsy to know what was good for me, I had purchased my gear, rented a board, boots, a lift ticket (in case you don't know, that's what puts you on a ski lift...news to me) and was standing at the bottom of a snow-covered mountain, asking The JC how to put on the snowboard.

"Where do I practice?" I asked.

"Over here," he pointed as he scooted toward the line of people getting on the ski lift. (The act of walking with a snowboard partially on is quite awkward. Imagine walking with one foot completely pigeon-toed inward while it's strapped to a fifteen pound piece of wood that is over one hundred and thirty inches long while the other foot has to guide you along in a straight line through the snow...Fuck. Left to my own devices, I would have gone in a circle around the fucking world!)

Instantly I realized my fate.

Smartly, The JC asked, "How does a momma bird teach her babies how to fly?"

My only response was, "You do realize that I've never been on a ski lift before, much less been in snow like this, right?"

Swoosh! We were on the ski lift!

Aside from wondering if I was going to suddenly fall off due to the weight of the board on my left leg and fearing the dismount that was quickly approaching, I felt like I was in heaven. The air was crisp, the slope was so pretty, the sky was clear and I could see lots and lots of people on the slope just zipping along having the time of their lives. I couldn't wait for that to be me.

Much to The JC's surprise, I didn't fall when I got off the lift! I was off to a great start. He showed me how to strap my feet into the bindings and helped me stand up. I slowly began to slide away from him, and (very casually and rather gracefully) hit a fucking tree.

And as the saying goes, it was all downhill from there.

I never imagined something that looks like so much fun would be so incredibly painful. The first few falls were no big deal. Though I was like a turtle on my back trying to get up each time, I was feeling pretty good. The JC was great in telling me what to do, too bad I'd never heard terms like "carve" before. Hearing, "it's kinda' like riding a skateboard," was the same as rattling off some differential equations. Fuck if I know...

As I began to head down the mountain, I took some falls that knocked the fucking wind out of me, left me seeing stars, made loud thuds on snow and had The JC asking me, "Are you going to be OK?" There came a point when my answer was, "I'm not really sure." I started making sure I could wiggle my toes and fingers after every fall.

One thing was sure though, a cute girl struggling to get up is a guy magnet on a mountain. I met so many sweet boys who were more than willing to help me up and teach me things. Too bad I was so horrible at learning that I quickly became a burden and was taking up their riding time. "No worries," I told them, "I'll be right here the next time you come around!"

Finally, The JC lost all hope and took off to utilize as much of his lift ticket as possible and left me to fend for myself. My time alone on the mountain consisted of:

Fight to stand up.

Balance.

Slide.

Imagine being Shawn "The Flying Tomato" White.

Fall down.

There was a myriad of versions of "Fall down" that included, "Destroy wrists," "Bust ass," and "Full on face plant."

I had fallen so many times that I honestly couldn't push myself up off the ground any-more. I was drenched with sweat, still kinda' drunk and couldn't see the bottom of the hill. If one more nine year-old came whizzing past me on a cell phone singing Jingle Bells to his grandma in Michigan like he was bored out of his mind again, I had decided I was going to trip him and eat him.

Those medical snowmobiles kept driving by me, not even pausing. Fuckers.

Deciding that I was tired of staring at the stars on my back for the last time, I was done. I'm not going to lie. I walked the rest of the way down the hill. I carried that board down the hill and even rode it a little ways like a sled. I was so happy to see The JC. *I think he was happy to see that I was in one piece as well. I was even happier to see the woman selling cocoa with liquor in it. I felt like an alien in a waterproof space suit trudging through invisible sand. Every movement was labored. I couldn't lift my arms over my head. Parts of my body were numb from the cold. I had just had the most amazing work-out I've had in a LONG time.

Over dinner I looked at The JC and said, "I had no idea being Jewish in 2006 still involved so much suffering. How do you do it day after day? Oy vey."

*I did it. I went snowboarding. I SUCKED. It hurts to move, breathe, stand, sit and it honestly even hurts to type. I'm twenty-seven years old and non-athletic. Taking serious blows to the body like I did is truly foreign. But like a crackhead looking for the next fix, I can't wait to go again!!! Only next time, I'm going to go early, possibly sober and have a lesson, probably with a bunch of three year-olds. And I will wear impact pants. Maybe two pairs...

Get out and live, people. No pain. No gain.

As you were.

Monday January 1, 2007
Resolution Launch

::Robin pokes head out from under blanket, looking at the world with one eye open wondering if it's safe to come out::

Slowly I got up this fine morning and looked at my cell phone. "1/1/2007"…New Year's Day! No more 2006!

In true LA fashion, the original plan for New Year's Eve changed. We were going to camp out at The Rose Bowl Parade in Pasadena. Kim, Tracy, Tracy's out of town friend, Stephanie and I spent a Saturday decorating floats, and though that was a very unique experience, somewhere throughout the day we realized that we would have a lot of fun "camping out" up until about 4:00 am. By that time, any buzz we would have earned while bar hopping would have worn off, and we would just be waiting outside in the cold for another four hours for the parade to begin. Yeah…not good.

I was determined to do something fun and unique for my favorite holiday. The common consensus fell in the realm of "I don't want to pay a cover charge," and "I don't want to fight stupid crowds." Amen!

Fearing that I might be bored on New Year's Eve, I decided to throw an impromptu party. Somewhere between writing a few emails, a hot shower and a trip to Target, I decided that we should have a Resolution Launch Party. With a few waves of my magic wand, I had about twelve people coming, a dozen helium balloons being picked up, a pan of lasagna and a cake in the oven. Much to my delight, my new roommate, Chelan, was on the way!

All according to my thirty-second plan, after food, drink and much gabbing and laughing, the crowd grew serious and wrote their resolutions on index cards. I was surprised at how contemplative everyone looked. Some people read their's allowed and others folded their's up, so no one could see. All of us stapled our index cards to the strings of the helium balloons and prepared to let them go into the sky at the stroke of midnight. Sounds pretty dreamy, huh?

Well, let me throw this twist in for you. I decided that it wasn't just enough to go outside and let them go…Oh, no. We needed to hike up into Griffith Park a ways, and let them go from a place with a really great view of the city. In my party planning frenzy I kinda' forgot to think about the fact that not everyone likes to hike like I do, and certainly wouldn't be thrilled to do it drunk!

Alas, my Napoleon side came out, and I convinced everyone to hoof it up the hill. Like a band of merry men, all decked out in stupid paper hats with noise makers, we bounded through the neighborhood and up into the hills, catching a wave and a honk from people here and there, trying to make it to wherever they were headed by midnight. Sadly, we didn't quite make it to the point I was hoping we would by midnight so some people had already let their balloons go. When we got to the ridge where the cityscape was in view, the rest of us launched our intentions into the air! And then we stood there staring at our balloons as most of them sank or just politely hung a few feet off the ground.

"What the fuck? Are you kidding me? I've got a party of twelve people out-of-breath and sweating up here looking for hope, prosperity, love and a whole lot of other shit for 2007, and you're just going to hang there and mock me???" I screamed at the balloons. *Cuz you know yelling at rubber and helium on a string does the trick.

Unfortunately, the LA air was so heavy and rather humid that the helium had…well, whatever happens to helium molecules when the air is like that, and they weren't going anywhere.

I looked at my balloon and thought, "Ain't no such thing as a free lunch." I can put my resolutions out into the universe, but it's up to ME to make them float. Damn it. And here I wanted a fairytale ending...

We all caught our breaths, hugged and laughed, shared a bottle of champagne and listened to LA's melodic version of Auld Lang Syne played out with sounds of the big sparkling city: cheering groups of people, crackling fireworks, gunshots and sirens.

The actual ending came in the next few hours when the living room of my apartment became completely covered in confetti. This was followed by Tracy getting up and entertaining us with a fantastic story about seeing an old man at the airport stirring sugar into his cup of coffee at a snack shop while seeming completely oblivious to the fact that he had his own shit soaking through the entire side of one of his pant legs. Yeah. Uh-huh.

People were ready to jet after that shitty little story.

After everyone was gone, I spent some time doing an initial clean-up and talking to Alba on the phone. I hadn't felt this happy in a while. Warm, content and truly calm for the first time in about a year, I went to sleep.

Oh? You want to know my resolutions? Ok...

> 1) Get car registered in the state of California; been here quite a while now...
> 2) Continue exercising regularly.
> 3) Make money doing make-up jobs part-time.
> 4) Reduce debt substantially.
> 5) Do some volunteer work.
> 6) Enjoy having health insurance again.
> 7) If I'm going to sleep with someone, make sure he's healthy and weathly.
> *Oh, what? Would you rather I say, "only have one night stands with poor wretches? Besides, how many men really fall into that category anyhow? Let's get real here, people. You know what they say, "Aim for the moon, if you miss, you still land among the stars!"

Overall, they aren't that exciting, huh? I'm thinking that's ok. I didn't want to stress myself out! Hell, I should have added, "Be boring every now and then." That might help boost the results on #4 and #7... ::shrug:: ...These are all very vague ways of saying: Get your shit together, keep out of trouble and stay away from fucktards!

Thank God 2006 is OVER!

*I don't think I'm ever going to completely rid my apartment of this confetti. I have found it in my armpit, my bed, my closet and in the fridge so far. My hair dresser is going to have to cut it out of my hair. That foil shit mutates. Something strange: While cleaning up the confetti, I noticed that there were pieces of it that had words on it. Static electricity made a piece cling to my hand. Trying to shake it off, I realized it said something, just one word, "Sorry." Hmmm...Wow. What company puts out apologetic/sympathetic confetti? Alone in the living room, I stood there wondering if I was being sent a message from someone. Is someone saying that they are sorry for something that happened or is ABOUT to happen?

Christ, it's New Year's Day...Better not test it...

I'm going back to bed where it's safe. Wake me when it's time for work. Work... Good, steady, corporate work. I hate Excel...but I do love some me some normalcy... For a minute at least.

Go eat some black-eyed peas and floss or something.

As you were.

That's A Wrap

Tah-dah. There you have it. A solid year of a whole lot of everything and nothing stated as I saw fit in a raw, real, candid and honest way. As I revisit each blog, I feel like I need to take a nap! Had I not had the time to document these experiences, I'm not sure I would have been able to recount it all.

This act of self-expression is probably what kept me from losing my mind during one of the most unique years of my life so far. There were days that I truly felt upside down. I made good choices and bad choices. Few were dull; all were learning experiences for sure. Money came and went and will come again. I certainly played in my bed, made it and am still lying in it. There is nothing more powerful and amazing than owning your truth.

With the passion for writing and utilizing blogging via Myspace.com, I had an outlet through which I could clear my head, air my thoughts and gain feedback from people I cared about. Had it not been for my ability to trudge through a tough time, find the humor in it and share it with people, I might have either tucked tail and moved back to Houston or found a stripper pole between my legs and a heroin needle hanging out of my arm. Ok, probably not that latter, but I know that I would have started to lose myself into a never before known level of personal darkness.

I must admit that since Steve Morrissey questioning my knowledge of blogging was the catalyst for my big adventure, I have to wonder what would have happened had the circumstances been slightly altered. Seeing as I spent a year blogging my ass off, what if we were working on a case of different nature and his question was something like, "What do you mean you don't know how to make five million dollars a year?" The year might have been even more insane, but perhaps I might have enough money for all the therapy I would need to get over it! Damn it!

At the end of the day I can honestly say that I'm not one bit sorry or regretful for choosing to leave a good job that I found very unfulfilling and travel an uncertain path in this very unforgiving city of Los Angeles. Along the way I reconnected with a really good person: myself. I had been away from her for far too long. She's a pretty cool chick.

Now that I am out of full-on Survival Mode, I can once again pay better attention to the rest of the world around me. There is a part of me that takes my writing for what it is, raw expression, and then there is a part of me that takes a step back and says, "Wow-you were a bit self-centered there, kiddo." It was difficult to put current events in true perspective while making sense of the reality I was living in during 2006. Our country is at odds with itself over a war. There are 90,000 homeless people in Los Angeles. New Orleans is still suffering after Hurricane Katrina. Bees are confused. Global warming is no joke. Healthcare issues in America are constantly baffling to me. The list goes on and on. Oh, it feels good to be back! And just in time. An election year is just around the corner.

What I find a little sad is that since my life has been a little more "normal" and organized, I haven't wanted to write as much. The routine and (rather) mundane daily events don't quite fuel that creative energy that in times of uncertainty seems to course through my veins. I'm sure it's just a phase, a quiet before the next storm. [insert wicked grin and side glance.]

Before you get back to living your life, I'd like to leave you with some thoughts that are scribbled on the chalkboard of my mind and have kept and do keep me moving forward as 2007 is warming up:

1) Sure. Shit rolls down hill, but you have to be strong enough to catch it and throw it right back.

2) Some days you ride the bus, and some days you have to hold onto the bumper.

3) If you wear your dirt with pride, no one can dig through it behind your back.

4) Fall hard a few times. Learn how to get back up. The every day stumbles won't phase you as much.

5) Take care of ya' twat; it's the only one ya' got.

6) Allowing yourself to be human is not a crime, but being a fucktard should be.

7) Floss. Stretch. Call your mother.

Read. Memorize. Recite. Recycle.

As you were.

All proceeds from the purchase of this book go toward the reduction of my credit card and make-up school student loan debt. Seriously. *I thought about marrying for money to get rid of my debt, but writing a book was a whole lot more fun and a lot less work. Oh yeah, and I don't know anyone with money that would give me a look, not even if I was stuck under a bus or dangling from a burning building. Besides, I write about finding things in my pubic hair. What guy in their right mind wants THAT girl?

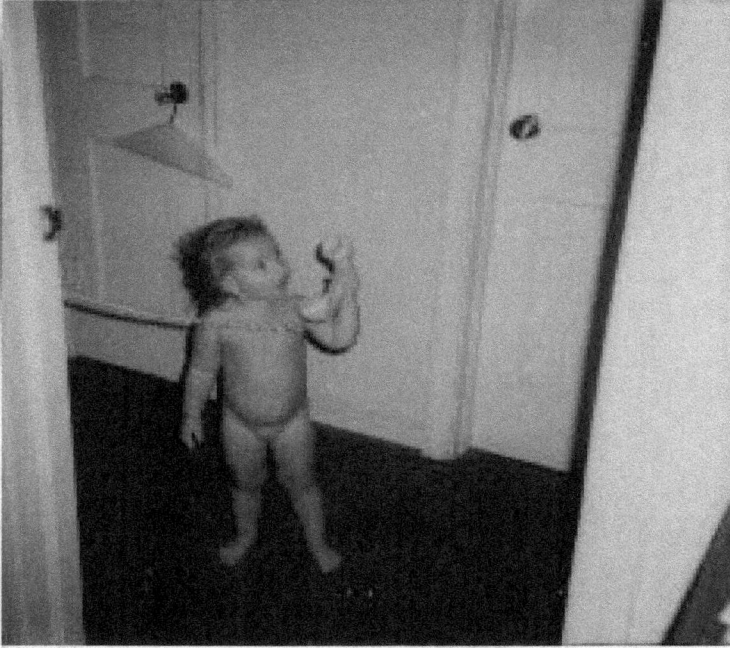

Giving people a hot piece of my mind since way back when.

You Made Me Look So Good!

I may not know any rich men who want to let me marry them just for their money, but I do have some very talented friends who love a good project and like to dream big. My book wouldn't be a book without them. My gratitude for their contributions is infinite. I am so pleased that they took on key roles throughout this process, donating their precious time and glimpses of their crafts. I look forward to working with them in the future as the projects keep getting bigger and better for all of us.

Cover Photography
Sarah Prikryl - Incito Photography (www.incitophotography.com)
I have always loved your brilliant photography and finally found an excuse to get in front of your camera. I hope there are more excuses to come. *I told you, only ten shots! (Having Miss Simmonds give me some bounce surely helped as well.)

Cover Design
Kimberly Graczyk
With your wonderfully creative eye for graphic design, I felt like you dragged your mouse across the images in my mind while creating my cover and transforming my document into a book. You're right. Mac's are pretty nifty.

Editing
Stephen Matzke
When I received your edits, wine-stained and "bloody," I fully realized how crucial you were to this whirlwind project idea of mine. With your attention to syntax, diction and your lust for the hyphen, you let me keep my voice while helping me sound like I might have paid attention in school.

And I think they call this the epilogue...

It's Already Storming Again…

"An unfortunate, yet potentially powerful afterthought and tribute," is how I would like to envision this unforeseen section to my first attempt at writing a book. What you have just finished reading was supposed to be a fun, outrageous, raw, heart-warming look at how I, a twenty-six year-old girl, handled a year of life in the midst of personal choices and challenges. I had no idea when I was writing my conclusion to *In Her Bathrobe She Blogged…* that I would so quickly refocus on serious issues. Just when I thought that last chapter was done and copyrights were complete, a reality check was delivered to me in the form of the death of my college boyfriend. Sgt. Charles B. "Trey" Kitowski III (also lovingly known as Jackass to our circle of friends) was killed by an enemy roadside bomb while serving in the Army in Afghanistan on August 12, 2007.

Initially, flowing streams of words were my comfort, my coping mechanism and my natural way to relate to others that were mourning the loss together. As the words pooled together in front of me in the forms of blogs, I realized that I had to include them in this book despite the fact that they were outside of the scope of the year I had established as my boundary. My old friend deserves to be remembered and memorialized. There have been many beautiful acts performed to do such already-a military funeral with over five hundred attendees, medals of honor awarded, several flags presented to his family, a chapel paver and tree planted in his name on the campus of our university, a star named for him and countless hours of reminiscing about his life with reunited groups of friends. Including my recorded thoughts is the best way I know how to keep him alive for as many years as a copy of my book can exist in time.

Along with fumbling through dealing with grief, I was given all-that-too-close-to-home reminder that there are serious wars raging on with thousands and thousands of people being injured and killed to return home forever disabled or honorably resting in flag wrapped boxes. After Charles' passing, my awareness and attention to media heightened effortlessly and my paradigm began to shift. I felt my soapbox begin to rise under my feet as I angrily absorbed more and more disappointing news coverage. All I was hearing was George W. Bush asking for more money for the efforts in Iraq and less money for domestic issues while seemingly ignoring Afghanistan. I met a woman named Jaque Line at a film festival in Hollywood. Through polite conversation, she lit a fire in me to make my position on politics known. It turns out that Ms. Line had moved to Washington, DC during the Veitnam War to be a constant peaceful protester outside The White House. She told me that my generation is too selfish to make such a sacrifice for democracy and that supporting the troops is knowing when it's best to take them out of harms way. Her comment stuck with me, and I thought about her for weeks after the film festival. I was inspired and filled with fire.

I had originally included my thoughts on my future intentions here, but then I realized that was taking away from Charles. I won't lie and say that I was excited about Charles joining the military. It was quite the opposite. And I made the mistake of not sharing that with him when I had the chance. Though I'm sure some are disap-pointed that I am including a political challenge along with memorialzing his passing, as he died doing what he felt strongly about, I assure you that Charles wouldn't mind. I speak confidently about this because Charles was highly against one of the biggest decisions I made while in college. I decided to join the Catholic Church. Charles, a cradle Catholic, was completely opposed to the idea. He kept asking me, "Are you sure you want to put yourself through this? Have you learned nothing from me?" On the day of my Baptism and Confirmation he gave me a card, which read, "Well, you did it. We all know that I am not the most devout Catholic, and I know I haven't been your biggest supporter, but I know this is important to you and that's enough for me. I'm proud of your resolve. I believe that people like you can make a better community of believers. Welcome to the club, and Happy Easter. Love, Charles." Had I had reached out and taken the opportunity to talk to Charles before he enlisted, I'm sure my thoughts about his joining the military would have been quite similar. He and I knew how to debate issues. We would agree to disagree, always being very proud of the other for taking a stand. I am very proud of my old friend for sticking his neck out, refusing to be an Armchair American, but I don't have to be proud of the reasons that lead him to have to make that choice. However, I'm (surely shockingly) putting the expression of my feelings on the world on the back burner for now and leaving the rest of the pages of my book to Charles.

The following are the blogs I wrote before and after his funeral.

I have started to write this several times since I heard the news that Charles Kitowski, my college sweetheart, was killed serving in the military in Afghanistan. It began as just a story, but my thoughts were all over the place. Sitting on the floor, wedged between my bed and my bookshelf with my laptop in my lap, I decided to write directly to him, one last time, to help me focus. I wrote this imagining that I was standing in front of his casket.

Hiya handsome-

I can't believe I'm standing before you, and I know you won't be able to respond. I'm having trouble breathing as there is a knot building in my throat, but I'm feeling stronger now that I'm actually here. This week has been a whirlwind.

I was downtown at the Bikram yoga studio Monday where I work one night a week in exchange for a free membership when I saw that Robyn Pennington (Riley) had called my cell phone several times. I called her back and by the tone of her voice, I knew something was wrong. She said, "What do you know? Have you talked to anyone?" A stiffness and a cold chill came over me, and I asked her to tell me what was going on. "Charles died in Afghanistan," she responded. I asked what happened and when. She said that she thought an IUD had exploded near your truck. We agreed that an IUD was a birth control device and that we needed more information. Later she forwarded me an article that said it was an IED, which made more unfortunate sense.

Before I got the article, the phone began to ring off the hook. I talked to our old roommate Michelle Micheli, Michelle Atkins, Danny Elustondo, and my mother within about fifteen minutes. My initial reaction was rather stoic. I cried a little because news of this nature has a gut wrenching affect on a person. When I opened the article Robyn forwarded me and I saw your face pictured in military gear, I felt so removed from the situation. I don't know you as a soldier. It's been quite a long time since we've seen each other. I can't even remember our last conversation. Frankly, when we finally really stopped dating, I tucked you away. We both began living truly parallel lives. You wound up moving to Dallas to work for Southwest Airlines and I wound up in Los Angeles.

I talked to Denise Bailey on the car ride home, and by then MySpace was buzzing with emails and comments about you. People were asking me if I was ok. At first my response was pretty standard. I was greatly saddened, but why should I not be ok? You and I are old news, right? I finally remembered that the last time I saw you was in 2005 at a group dinner at the Macaroni Grill, where we waved at each other from opposite ends of the table. But then when it was dark and I was alone at the computer reading emails and letting this new fact sink in, I started wondering why I felt so separated from heavy emotion in regard to you. We did date for two years while I was in college. I realized how significant that really is, and I let myself start to dig through old memories. I pulled out a photo album and started looking at great shots from birthday parties, our couple's trip to San Antonio, Halloween, fun nights out, etc. I forgot how good lookin' we were together. I even found the first picture we ever took together. It was at a clubhouse party at the old apartment by The Ritz. You had invited me after giving me your pager number (yeah remember pager numbers?) at the Timber Wolf Pub where I was a waitress. Man we look like children. And how did I have all that poofy curl in my hair??? Brandt Schneider and I started exchanging emails. Through the course of the exchange Brandt said that he never understood why we broke up even though he thought we made better friends than significant others. I think I told him it was a combination of timing and young people's bullshit. I think that's essentially true, but I started letting myself go backward and revisit what really happened. I have dated people and remained friendly with them afterwards. Why didn't we stay in touch? After really thinking about it--you and I know the real answer and there's no need to get into all of the details and growing pains. It was a rough, dark time for both of us, and we were both dealing with heavy matters. I think we were getting a little toxic for each other. We never hated each other, but we had to get away from each other. You know how UST is. Everybody is so close and on top of each other that in order to change and get things straight for yourself you have to step away from The Circle a bit.

The more the reality of your death started hitting me, the more I started feeling like I stepped too far away. Charles, I knew that you were going into the service. I was already out in LA when you left. Plenty of time had passed for us to be able to have conversation on the phone. I know I should have picked up that phone or at least sent you an email. Babe, I'm so sorry. Anger and heavy guilt pinned me down. I started telling people, "I'm almost twenty-eight years old, and I have finally found something I regret." Tuesday was a dark day. Everyone I talked to seemed to kinda ramble and cry a lot or not know what to say. I did nothing at work. I had cried so much and so hard and gotten so little sleep that my eyes were dehydrated and my nose was flooded. I sat and obsessively checked my email and had conversations with people like Brian Lowe and Aaron Stryk. By the way, I'm really ticked at you for getting arrested for DUI in Alabama after Brian's graduation. I used to hate it when you would say, "I actually drive better drunk because I have to be more alert to pay more attention." Anyhow, I guess I'll let that slide.

When I got home, I started going through old cards, letters and my journals. (I have to say that my journaling is pretty funny. It certainly shows that I was a college girl with few grown-up priorities. Oh, how that has changed. To tell you the truth, Babe, I was a real uptight bitch at times back then. I'm sure it was young girl insecurity masked by the belief that I knew exactly what I was doing. I'm not sure we ever really do, but I think we get better at making it look like we do.) I pulled out the cards you had given me. Seeing something with your handwriting on it was like finding treasure. I found one that you gave me around Christmas of 2000. You said some really sweet things about me and our relationship, but what stood out the most was the last few lines, "I don't know what the future holds for us, but promise me that there will be no regrets. Love you always, Charles." Those words danced in my head. It was like you knew I was hurting and feeling guilty. That was exactly what I would have wanted to hear from you. Thank you. Thank you. Thank you.

Feeling less like shit and a little more at ease, I began thinking of how awesome you were to me. I'll never forget that you bought me a computer for my birthday one year. That was crazy and amazing. You looked so proud when you wheeled that dolly into the dorms. I'll never forget how you took Michelle Atkins and me to a Tori Amos concert at The Woodlands and fell asleep standing on your feet because you were both bored and exhausted from working at Vastar. God, you hated that job. Remember the time you helped color my hair for Halloween with Manic Panic? I went as The Goddess of Fire and you went as the well...an Army soldier. I guess we should have seen the decision of you going into the service coming. You love to blow shit up, you are incredibly intelligent and meticulously organized and clean. Blowing stuff up...I will never forget the days out at Dan and Joe's during the 4th of July. Didn't the whole yard catch on fire one year after Brian Lowe got a hold of the matches? Remember when you guys tried to launch Vickie and her husband's stuffed monkey, Mojo, into space with fireworks? It wasn't party unless someone was almost on fire, everyone doing shots that were on fire or someone was picking on Erika Kimble making her say, "Oh noooo...Wait a minute, wait a minute, wait a minute!!! Ok. You are acting a little special now. You need to behave." (You always did the best impersonation of her.)

You and I took really good care of each other. You sat at my place for hours while I was knocked out after I had my wisdom teeth extracted. When you had your laser eye surgery I took you to the doctor and when I came down with the worst flu of my life to date, you hauled me to the doctor and had me stay at your place a great deal of the time.

Your place...with Michelle. It became your place with Michelle, Aaron and me for a long time, huh? The four of us actually made it to two apartments together. I still have the keys the last apartment in one of my journals with a note from you that says, "Hold on to these just in case." Don't worry, I still will! Oh god, remember how when we first started dating we slept in your old twin bed? That was hysterical. Good thing we weren't the same size! Before the big bed arrived we started sleeping on the floor in the living room on an air mattress. Watching you use a bicycle pump to manually inflate that thing up every night was a riot. No matter how much air we put in it, we always woke up with out butts on the floor the next morning. Mornings...You would try to be so quiet when you got up for work trying not to wake me. I would always wake up so you wouldn't leave without kissing me goodbye. Sunday mornings. I can't count how many Sunday mornings I woke up to the answering machine going off and hearing, "Trey Boy, it's Mom. I was just calling to see what time you were coming out..." I'm thinking a lot about your folks. I get ill when I think about how they are going to present your mother with the flag that's on your casket. I keep playing the scene over and over in my head. I'm sharing whatever strength I have with your parents these days. I wish I could have seen you arrive. They don't allow that footage to be played on the news. It's such an honorable moment when the soldier finally comes home and is brought to the arms of the people who love him.

Speaking of love, I asked a couple of people if you were ever able to find true love. A few people said you were seeing someone, and it made me really happy. While trying to look up information about your situation online I ran across The Southwest Airlines blog that mentioned you and your girlfriend, Berri Gentry. The Internet is amazing, isn't it? (By the way, you are a total rock star. If you type your name into Google, over 34,000 entries pop-up right now.) I then went to the next best place online for finding people, MySpace.com and there not only was Berri, but you as well with her in a fantastic photograph on a boat, drink in hand, smiling the smile that makes my grandmother still ask about you. I then sent her a message. I was so scared to send it. I didn't want to freak her out or upset her that an ex-girlfriend of yours was contacting her on such an emotional day. I just didn't want her to think that we didn't think about her. I wasn't sure if she was close to some of the group, and I wanted to make sure she was included with all of our festivities if she wanted to be. Dan told me that your mom said you were thinking about proposing to her. Charles Bernard Kitowski III, I am so impressed. That says so much about where you were in your life. I can't imagine what she's going through right now. I know how I strange and surreal everything has been for me knowing that a man I have shared so much personal and intimate time and space with is now physically gone forever. I'm sharing strength with her as well.

I'm having a lot of trouble with the things I can't control. I want to know exactly how you died. I want to know that the medics did everything they could to save you, not once, not twice, but fifty times. The news article that is going around uses the word "suffered," and I am haunted by it. I have horrible visions that you were conscious until the end. I couldn't sleep the other night because I kept wondering if your body was being treated ok. Your body used to sleep next to mine quite often. The thought of your body looking any other way at rest than you did in your boxer briefs under soft sheets in a safe bed, is just about where I lose it. I can still smell your fresh scent after you showered and feel the silkiness of your hair. I can still feel the scar on your hand from your surgery and hear the sound of you clearing your throat. And what I really wish I could hear right now is the sound of your high-pitched, "Heh-heh" expression after you come around that corner and tell us all this is just a little joke from Chuckles. I'd beat your ass, but I'd be elated to do it.

I'm really elated to be here, and I actually have Southwest Airlines to thank for it. Last minute plane tickets were through the roof in price. I am seriously not in a position to throw another $900 on a credit card. I called the airline and told them I knew you and a really nice woman named Van Nguyen was able to discount my ticket. Once again…You're a rock star. All I had to do was drop your name and poof, direct flights both ways! It gets better. Michelle was able to get on the same flight. You brought us together as friends and we came home to honor you together.

I had to be here for you. You were always there for me. Remember when my dad had his heart attack? You were there at the hospital in no time, providing love and support for my mother and me. She still tells the story of how after we left the hospital, we went back to the house with my step brother and his wife and all stayed up drinking together. When she was ready to go to sleep, you and I went upstairs and crawled in bed with her to tuck her in. She laughed and told us that she had to sleep between us as we were not allowed to sleep together in her house. My dad sent me a really nice email about you today. He said that he liked being around you and always thought you were a neat guy. For him to do that says a lot.

Remember my big trip to Argentina for study abroad after New Year's in 2000? That was one of the first great adventures I ever took where I was a part of a collective group representing UST and in a way, America, as a student. You called me so much while I was there. That phone bill must have been insane. When I came home, you were there with my parents to greet me. Charles, I really look at your military experience as your great adventure, learning about other cultures and not only representing, but protecting and defending America. I know you were having the time of your life doing what you felt is right and just. There's no comparison in our adventures, yet I am here today to welcome you home and to add as much wholeness as possible to a group that will always have emptiness without you.

And don't worry, we're not going to forget you. That's impossible. You have obvious-ly left a mark on all of us in a profound way. And you know where the crew is headed, right? Grif's, of course! What other bar would the let the guys do a Twenty-one Head-butt Patron Shot Salute in your honor? And just so you know, I lobbied for all of us to actually ride up here in the Grif's Party Bus blaring your favorite music because I know you always wanted to rent it. However, I think it is best that we did not. We are slowly going to share your wild side with your family. In fact, I have a few pictures that your mom might blush over when she sees them-like the one of you wearing nothing but my old sparkly pink bathing suit wrap! You thought you were going to shock me, but I shocked you by having the camera handy! I laughed out loud when I found that one.

We may not have been able to keep in touch for life, but you have left me with a life-time of memories.

This is where I start to feel that knot in my throat again as I see that my time with you is up. So, per your request-no regrets and love always.
Hearts and stars-
Robin

Oh by the way, do you remember our talks about BS? Wink, wink...nudge, nudge.

The Army Soldier and The Goddess of Fire...
Halloween costumes say a lot about a person.

Friday August 31, 2007
Stretching Out Grief

Emotional roller coaster.

Blurry whirlwind.

Physically exhausting.

These are several ways I have described the days after we lost Charles. Each of us deals with grief in our own way. I have had several conversations with people in which I have admitted that I didn't know how much grief was acceptable for me to have or that I was afraid of offending Berri by recounting my retired emotions for the love of her life. I am dealing with guilt and overwhelmed by how fast Charles outgrew the scope of the man I knew him to be. In two years time he became a war hero. A war hero? War? Where has my mind been?

If you know me, during any type of crisis, I go into a mode of information hog. I read, research and absorb anything that I can to rationalize my emotions.

At the beginning of the week I realized that I had already been home an entire week since the funeral. I hadn't done anything around the house. My suitcase was on the floor still. I only did laundry because I wanted to have clothing to wear to work. I had slept for almost two solid days only getting out of bed to go to the bathroom and to turn on the fan. I started to wake up in my own reality and realized that the adrenaline rush that had carried me wide awake for almost one and half weeks had now gone away, and my system was crashing. I had felt like I had done the things I was supposed to do by going home, being with friends, having my moment with Charles, etc., yet I felt awful. My body hurt from crying, flying, not sleeping or eating correctly.

I Googled the stages of grief. Some say there are five, some say there are four. Either way, you basically get denial, anger, bargaining, depression and acceptance. Grief is different for all people-the stages aren't set in a perfect order-you sometimes never get past grief-blah blah blah. Nothing made me happy. I couldn't put my emotion into any of the categories.

My emotion? Plainly stated, I pushed Charles away once upon a time when a different time and place dictated that I do such. Right or wrong, I put all of our good times and our bad in a box and in journals and essentially forgot them. I had to physically dig into my past and unlock my memories of one of the nicest people I've ever known. Frankly, that's just fucked up. I am really ashamed that I let that person like him slip out of my life completely. As horrible as I was physically feeling and how much I wanted to feel normal and function as I should, I was really afraid to stop feeling that way. Stopping the pain is like letting him go again.

When I showed up for my one shift at the front desk at the yoga studio, Ana, one of the instructors completely called me out for not being class for nearly two weeks. She said she could tell something was wrong by looking at me. "I can tell you're holding something in by the way your breathing. It's too shallow." *I love people like her. And like I was talking to my own mother, I explained the emotional position I was in. She basically marched me into the yoga room. She told me that I had to get past the part that gave my physical pain because I would wind up getting sick if I didn't. She also reminded me that doing the yoga series would help me work through my emotions. I admitted that I didn't want to go to yoga because I was afraid to cry in the room. She laughed and said, "You know you will, so accept it and do it. We all understand what yoga does to the body. Do it." And I did.

At the beginning of class, I took a moment sitting in the hundred'n five degree heat and humidity and said to myself in the mirror, "This is for you, Charles. I dedicate the next ninety minutes of meditation, sweating, stretching and emotion to you." It was a really full class. We had new students who had never tried Bikram yoga before. That's always exciting. There was a lot of energy in the room. All thirty-five of us were moving beautifully together. I could feel my muscles relaxing and my mind wandering. Visions from the past week kept flowing over me and then I would snap back into class.

Suddenly my meditation was interrupted when a first timer wanted to leave the room. "It's too hot. I can't do this. I feel like I'm going to pass out," she said. The teacher, Jill, joyfully told her, "We all feel like we are going to pass out. Raise your hand if you want to leave but you are determined to stay." Every other hand in the room went up as we panted like dogs, dripping with sweat. "Just stay in the room. Lie down. You don't have to do everything. Just learn to enjoy the heat," Jill told her. Breaking my concentration, I turned around to face the direction of the girl. She was standing in the middle of the room with her mat and water under her arm ready to go. Out of no where, I said rather sternly, "You can do it." I softly started to clap, as did the teacher and then the rest of the class. As she turned to return to her spot in the room, I lost it. Floodgates opened and tears just exploded out of my eyes. I felt so much release. I was so proud of that girl. I had so much pent up emotion, and it all just came out when she decided to finish what she started. ::shrug::

It was time for Camel Pose-a posture where you are on your knees and you push your hips and stomach forward, squeezing your glutes together as you gracefully lean over backward as if you are on a giant beach ball to grab your feet and thrust your body forward without actually flinging yourself into the mirror. This opens up your heart, lungs and chest. Anything you have been holding onto comes out once you come out of the posture. Sure enough. I was blubbering again, but this time it was because I had a revelation. It seems so simple now, but at the moment, I realized that I don't have to lose Charles again. I can keep all of the memories active without feeling guilty for shunning them once before. Simple clarity that I just couldn't get to because my physical being was all knotted up.

And just like that, I was a little further down the road to healing. I realize that the only way to keep Charles alive is to live and to be proud of who he became and what his intentions in this world were. In order to show the world how happy he was, I must show the world his happiness through my own. To show the world what a good friend he was, I must be a good friend to others. To show the world what a giving and caring person he was, I must reach out to others in a caring way as well.

I tell people all the time that yoga will help them. I'm so thankful there was someone there to help give me a dose of my own medicine.

Stretch it out, people. (Seriously-physical exercise will help)

As you were.

Tuesday September 4, 2007
The Final Peace?

Due to the summer heat wave and rolling blackouts that have been zapping my Los Angeles neighborhood, I have been without power and Internet service off and on since Friday. I have wanted so badly to sit and share an amazing dream I had early Saturday morning.

After enjoying a really fun evening out with friends during the beginning of what I like to call a series "West Coast Snow Days," I got home around 2:15 am on Saturday morning, took a shower and headed to bed. I was fast asleep and began having very vivid dreams (as I tend to do). Some scenes of an unimportant nature zipped past, and then I was in a bar. I recall telling myself that it was silly for me to be in a bar in my dream as I had just left one in real life. I felt very happy to be there. Though I didn't know the specific name of the bar and can't recall the song on the jukebox, I felt comfortable and knew I was certainly in a familiar place.

I was around people I knew and liked, yet the only person I can recall by name is the first person I hugged, Kevin Loper. As I hugged him, it hit me in my dream that I was giving him the exact same hug I had given him as I did the day I saw him at Charles' funeral. He was the first UST person I crossed paths with that day in the foyer of St. Bart's.

Then I looked up, and Charles was walking toward me. My emotion was just pure joy. He was smiling and laughing as per usual, wearing light jeans, a white t-shirt with some logo on it, tennis shoes and that brown leather jacket of his that I always hated. (Thank God, he wasn't wearing any of those vests he used to wear. I thought I threw all of those out!) He and I sat down at a table, and he reached out and put his hands in mine. I swear to you that I could feel his hands. They were soft, yet slightly dry, as I always remember them being (from a face wash he used to use) and as we sat hand in hand, I could feel the scar on his hand as my thumb rubbed back and forth across it.

I do not recall specific dialogue at this time. I recall having images and representations of things that were on my mind kinda flash by like "War," "Family," and "Future." There was a constant sense of contentment and peace. I then verbally asked him if he was OK. He verbally responded to me, "Don't worry about me. I'm fine," in an aww shucks, proud kind of way. He then stood up, walked around the table and put his arms around me in a solid hug and then put his hand on my head in a comforting way, and said, "I just came to check on you, Sweet Pea, and let you know that everything is going to be alright, but I have to go now." The embrace ended. He turned and I watched him walk out the door.

I then woke up on my right side with my left arm over a pillow in this ethereal type of state where I know I had a bit of a grin on my face...almost like one might feel waking up from a nap in a hammock on a tropical island with the breeze dancing on their face. My whole body was cool to the touch and I was incredibly relaxed. My thoughts were calm. I recall softly thinking, "I'm so glad he's ok," and just as the thought came to my mind, I snapped into the reality of where I really was. I started breathing kind of hard, and I felt that the temperature of the room was high and that I was starting to get clammy from the heat. It hit me full on that I had just had this dream, and I kinda' laid in bed trying to get back to that exact dreamy pleasant state, but it was gone. I was back in real time, yet I felt confident in the actuality of the events surrounding Charles for the first time since the whirlwind started. Up until that moment, everything had been surreal.

Now, me being the rational/practical being that I am most of the time, I started to analyze this as soon as I could get my morning started. I was so gleeful that I had the dream, yet was curious as to how real I should accept it as being. I asked a few friends what they thought and after the goosebumps left their arms or the lump left their throat, I got varied answers. Chelan said, "Awww. You had the goodbye dream. You're starting to get over this." Elene said, "I think that's wonderful, and I've had similar experiences." Sarah C. said, "Maybe you were dreaming about this because you can't have it on Earth." Diella said, "Don't kid yourself. You know your spirits were meeting. You know you are one of those people who is open to the spiritual realm. Rejoice in this." As I explained this to my mother, she was the one who said what I could be most sure of and agree with, "Oh Robin Amber, I don't know how to explain the unexplainable. Just be so thankful for having this dream instead of having nightmares about how he died." I thought this was remarkable because she struck a cord in me. I haven't had a dream with Charles in it for as long as I can remember. Through all of the recent events, not one single bad dream...Not one single dream about Charles at all...

I have never had a dream with that much texture, sound and detailed visual content. I will never forget the content and comfortable look on his face, the feeling of his hands in mine during our friendly banter, his hand on my head as he hugged me or the sound of his voice as he told me that he had to go. I watched him walk away. It was beautiful-normal-peaceful.

I am at peace with all of this. I believe he is at peace. I hope this brings many of you some sense of peace. And if anyone has had similar experiences, please share.

Now, perhaps I can get back to my off-color, zany, tacky, saucy, bold, fun, and wild writing that is what I tend to be known for and that our ol' Jackass appreciated.

Let this be an end to the mushy and sappy, yet let the legend of our friend live on.

As you were.

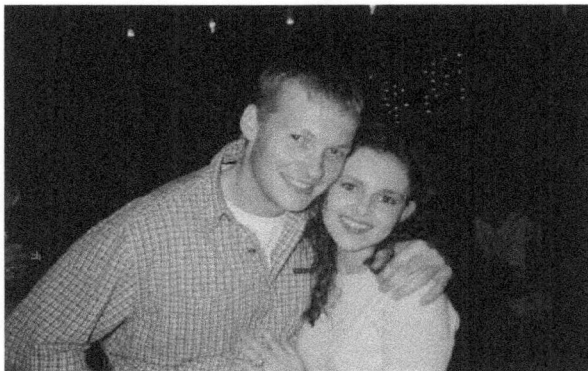

Sgt. Charles B. "Trey" Kitowski III August 10, 1976 - August 12, 2007

www.ingramcontent.com/pod-product-compliance
Lightning Source LLC
Chambersburg PA
CBHW030923090426
42737CB00007B/298